Grammar and Meaning

Learning About Language

General Editors: Geoffrey Leech and Mick Short, Lancaster University

Already published:

Analysing Sentences
Noel Burton-Roberts

Patterns of Spoken English
Gerald Knowles

Words and Their Meaning
Howard Jackson

An Introduction to Phonology
Francis Katamba

Grammar and Meaning
Howard Jackson

Grammar and Meaning

A Semantic Approach to English Grammar

Howard Jackson

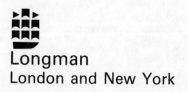

Longman
London and New York

Longman Group UK Limited,
Longman House, Burnt Mill, Harlow,
Essex CM20 2JE, England
and Associated Companies throughout the world.

Published in the United States of America
by Longman Inc., New York

First published 1990
Third impression 1992

British Library Cataloguing in Publication Data
Jackson, Howard, *1945–*
    Grammar and meaning : a semantic approach to English
    grammar. – (Learning about language).
    1. English language. Semantics
    I. Title   II. Series
    422

    ISBN 0–582–02875–2

Library of Congress Cataloging in Publication Data
Jackson, Howard, 1945–
    Grammar and meaning : a semantic approach to English grammar /
    Howard Jackson.
        p.   cm. — (Learning about language)
    Includes bibliographical references (p.
    ISBN 0–582–02875–2 (pbk.)
    1. English language—Grammar—1950–   2. English language–
    –Semantics.   I. Title.   II. Series.
    PE1106.J29   1991
    425—dc20   90–6016
                                                                CIP

Set in Linotron 202 11/12pt Bembo
by Columns Design & Production Services Ltd, Reading

Produced by Longman Group (FE) Limited
Printed in Hong Kong

Contents

List of Key Diagrams
and Tables

Acknowledgements

I am very grateful to Jürgen Esser for his helpful comments on many of the chapters, which have no doubt saved the book from more blemishes than it would otherwise have had. I would also like to thank Geoffrey Leech and Mick Short, as editors of the *Learning about Language* series in which this book appears, for their suggestions for improving the text before it became public, and the publishers Longman for their encouragement and for piloting the book through to publication.

The publishers are grateful to the author, Ralph Whitlock, for permission to reproduce an extract from his article 'Dew-Pond Myth' from *The Guardian Weekly*, May 1989.

For HILARY and LYDIA

Introduction

Human beings communicate messages to each other in a variety of ways. In our culture it is customary to shake hands with a person whom you meet for the first time. If you refuse to do so it would convey the message that you did not accept, or that you were holding something against, the other person. Similarly, in an appropriate context, a nod or a wink, the wrinkling of the brows or the raising of a finger may serve as a means of communicating some message or other. Such means of communication may, for example, serve to indicate bids at an auction.

When we communicate messages by using gesture or other forms of bodily movement, we call it 'non-verbal' communication; that is, communication without words. The implication of that term is that we regard 'verbal communication', i.e. communication using words (or language), as somehow primary or more usual. And this is indeed the case. Non-verbal communication is extremely limited in the range of messages it can convey, and it often serves to reinforce rather than replace verbal communication. Language, on the other hand, is an explicit, versatile and extendable means of communicating messages, from the simple 'I'm fed up' to the most complex theory of nuclear physics or the most profound philosophical reasoning.

Meaning

Messages are meaningful. It may be argued that rituals like the 'How do you do?' of a polite introduction are meaningless because they are predictable and are not chosen from among a set of alternative messages. But even in such contexts, a message of polite greeting is communicated, however conventionalised the language may be, and such greetings have an important social function in enabling human beings to interact. What is clear is that messages do not all have the same kind of meaning or function; nor does a particular message have only one function. We probably think that the primary function of language is to convey propositional or representational meaning, e.g. making a statement about some event: 'The telephone's ringing.' But the utterance, 'The telephone's ringing', in its most likely context of use, is less a statement of fact than a hint or instruction to someone to go and answer it. In other words, this utterance has simultaneously a propositional meaning ('something is happening') and an interactional meaning ('you do something').

Language messages have diverse functions; they are also stylistically diverse, and there may often be a relationship between the function of a message and its style. We can make an initial stylistic distinction between spoken language and written language, but within both these styles there are many varieties, from playground rhymes and advertising jingles to sermons and formal speeches in the spoken style, and from jottings or personal letters to legal documents or scientific reports in the written style. Not every individual uses a language in all its functions, and no language user has occasion to exploit all the diverse styles. But all language users can construct messages with a variety of functions and in a variety of styles.

Structure

An important word here is 'construct'; because for communication to be successful, messages need to be structured
according to the conventions of the language being used.
Messages, then, have organisation and structure; and so
does language. We refer to the structural or organising
principles of language as **grammar**. Consider the following
message:

> The telephone's ringing. Stay where you are. I'll answer it.
> Are you expecting a call from someone today?

This 'message' is constructed from a number of 'propositions' (e.g. 'The telephone's ringing'). The propositions in
turn are constructed from: an event (or action or state), e.g.
'ring'; the participants involved in the event, e.g. 'the
telephone', 'you', 'a call'; and the circumstances connected
with the event, e.g. 'today'. The labels 'message', 'proposition', 'participant', etc. describe the construction of this act
of verbal communication in generalised semantic terms. If
we wish to describe its construction in grammatical terms,
we shall use labels like 'text', 'sentence' and 'word'.

Verbal communication (language) may therefore be
analysed and described in at least two ways: from the
perspective of its meaning and the meaning of its constituent parts, and from the perspective of its grammatical
structure and the grammar of its constituent parts. In this
book we shall combine the two perspectives by beginning
with meaning and then proceeding to grammatical description. We shall begin with questions such as 'What kinds of
things do we talk about?', and then go on to examine how
these meanings are organised grammatically.

Why both semantic and grammatical analysis?

There are two main reasons which justify this dual analysis and description. The first one is the simple observation that there are linguistically interesting things to say about meaning and grammar separately, and about the ways in which they interrelate, which justify assuming two levels of organisation in the construction of language. The second reason has to do with the observation that meaning and grammar are not in a one-to-one relationship in linguistic structure. For example, the meaning of elements in related structures may remain constant while the grammar changes. Compare the following structures:

[1] Nathan washed up the dishes
[2] The dishes were washed up by Nathan

In both examples, *Nathan* has the semantic role of 'ACTOR' (the one doing the washing-up) and *the dishes* have the semantic role of 'AFFECTED' (the things affected by the action of washing-up). The meaning of these elements is constant while their grammatical function changes. The change in grammar can be seen merely from the order of elements: *Nathan* is first in [1] and last in [2], reversing positions with *the dishes*. Put more technically, *Nathan* has 'Subject' function in [1], whereas in [2] *the dishes* has Subject function.

This discussion illustrates the point that there are two systems of construction operating in language: a semantic system, concerned with the meaning relations between elements of constructions, and a grammatical system, concerned with the grammatical relations between elements of a construction. We are therefore justified in analysing and describing linguistic constructions from both a semantic and a grammatical perspective and in seeking to relate the two analyses.

Structure of this book

Each chapter begins with a discussion of the aspects of meaning relevant to the topic of the chapter. Then the discussion moves on to relate the meanings to the grammatical aspects of the topic and to describe the relevant grammatical systems and structures.

The first three chapters treat the essential elements of propositions or sentences: in Chapter 1, the central element, which refers to the states, events and actions that we want to talk about and which is represented grammatically by verbs; in Chapter 2, the participants in these states, events and actions, which are represented grammatically by nouns; and in Chapter 3, the circumstances (e.g. of place or time) attendant on the state, event or action and which are represented grammatically by adverbs and prepositions.

The next two chapters consider the ways in which semantic and grammatical elaboration or 'specification' occurs: of states, events and actions (i.e. verbs) in Chapter 4 by notions such as 'time' and its corresponding grammatical category 'tense'; and of participants (i.e. nouns) in Chapter 5 by means of items which identify, classify and describe them.

Chapter 6 brings together the topics of the preceding chapters and examines how these elements combine together to form semantic constructions (propositions) and grammatical constructions (sentences).

The next two chapters continue the discussion of propositions (sentences), but show how one proposition may 'embed' in and be a constituent of another proposition, either as a participant or specifier (Chapter 7) or as a circumstance (Chapter 8).

The final two chapters take the discussion beyond the construction of propositions to the ways in which propositions combine. Chapter 9 looks at the means of co-ordination and conjunction which combine propositions. The last chapter considers the structure of messages (or texts), which are propositions in combination for the purpose of meaningful human communication.

A glossary of key terms used in the discussion is provided at the end of the book.

Examples

We shall illustrate the points being made with copious examples from naturally occurring language. Most of the examples are taken from the *Lancaster-Oslo/Bergen Corpus of British English, for use with digital computers* (S. Johansson, G. N. Leech & H. Goodluck 1978). The *LOB Corpus* is a computer corpus of printed British English published in the year 1961. It contains extracts from a wide variety of types of text, organised under fifteen categories, as follows:

A   Press: reportage
B   Press: editorial
C   Press: reviews
D   Religion
E   Skills, trades and hobbies
F   Popular lore
G   Belles lettres, biography, essays
H   Miscellaneous (government documents, foundation reports, industry reports, college catalogue, industry house organ)
J   Learned and scientific writings
K   General fiction
L   Mystery and detective fiction
M   Science fiction
N   Adventure and western fiction
P   Romance and love story
R   Humour

The categories have different numbers of texts in each, but there are 500 text extracts in all, of approximately 2000 words each, amounting to a corpus of over one million words. When sentences from the *LOB Corpus* are used as examples in this book, they are given a reference which corresponds with the category, extract number and line number in the corpus: for example, 'K06: 145' means 'line number 145 from text extract 6 in category K'.

The examples were obtained from the *LOB Corpus* using the *Oxford Concordance Program* (S. Hockey & I. Marriott, Oxford University Computing Service 1980).

In the final chapter, though, a complete text is used to illustrate the discussion of messages and texts. It is an article taken from *The Guardian Weekly* newspaper, written by one of the newspaper's regular columnists, Ralph Whitlock.

Terminology

The linguistic terminology I have used in this book derives in large part from the most up-to-date descriptive grammar of English: *A Comprehensive Grammar of the English Language* by R. Quirk, S. Greenbaum, G. Leech and J. Svartvik (Longman 1985). This grammar is frequently referred to by the acronym of its title, *CGEL*, and that is how we will refer to it when we need to. You will find that a small number of terms are used which do not derive from *CGEL*, mostly relating to semantic description. The difference between *CGEL* and this book is that *CGEL* is a reference grammar that aims to be 'comprehensive' (or as comprehensive as one can be in the present state of linguistic knowledge), while this book is a textbook or coursebook which aims to present and expound a scheme of description of contemporary English, building up the description gradually through the book. It cannot therefore expect to be as comprehensive as the 1779-page *CGEL*. You will not find every aspect of English grammar dealt with here, but you will be given a sufficient grounding to enable you to look up a point of grammar in *CGEL* and understand what it says with relative ease.

Exercises

Each chapter, apart from the final one, contains a small number of exercises at the end, and a note within the chapter indicates the appropriate point at which to attempt the exercise. The aim of the exercises is to provide further illustration of the scheme of description being expounded in the book, and to encourage you – the reader – to develop your analytical skills on language data. A key to the exercises is given at the end of the book.

CHAPTER 1

States, Events, Actions: Verbs

What do we talk about?

Imagine a typical conversation that you might have with a member of your family or a friend, or think of the reconstructions of conversations in the dialogue of novels or plays, such as the following (from: Angus Wilson, *Anglo-Saxon Attitudes*, p. 52). What do we talk about?

> [1] 'Mrs Salad sent you her love,' said Gerald to his son.
>
> 'How the wicked prosper!' said John. 'You ought to meet her, Elvira; she's the living example of that Marxist myth, the lumpen/proletariat.'
>
> 'She sent you a message,' said Gerald.

We talk about things that happen: 'the wicked prosper'. We talk about what people do: 'She sent you a message.' We talk about the way people or things are: 'She's the living example of that Marxist myth. . .' We will label these meanings: **event** (*prosper*), **action** (*send*) and **state** (*be* – the *'s* in *she's* is a contraction of *is*, which is a form of *be*). And we will also refer to events, actions and states by the general term **situation types**.

Situation types

We have identified three situation types, which represent the general content of the messages that we communicate by means of language: STATES, EVENTS and ACTIONS (we will use capitals for semantic labels). Although the whole utterance (e.g. 'She sent you a message') may be regarded as reporting a situation, we have identified one item (*send*) in particular as representative of the situation (in this case an action). This item, together with the others that we identified (*prosper, be*), belong to a class of words called **verbs**.

Words in a language are grouped into a number of word classes (about eight in English) and subclasses, to enable us to make grammatical descriptions. Where grammar is concerned with words, it is in terms of classes and subclasses of word that the description is made, not in terms of individual words. The word-class to which a word belongs is shown traditionally in dictionaries: noun, verb, adjective, adverb, preposition, conjunction, pronoun, etc. We will discuss all of them in the course of our investigation of English grammar. In this chapter, though, we are concerned only with verbs, as the class of words whose meanings refer to situation types.

[*Exercise 1*]

States

We start our detailed examination of situation types by considering states. States refer to the way people or things are, what they are like, the condition they are in, where they are, the position they have taken up, and the like. Look at the examples in [2] to [8] below, which illustrate states. Do the verbs in these sentences all have the same kind of meaning?

   [2] It *was* a quiet place   [L07: 29]
   [3] She *was* silent again   [L06: 90]
   [4] He *had* security, comfort, for a little at least
                                                        [L06: 182]
   [5] Andrea *knew* that it was purposeless to stay
                                                        [L08: 21]
   [6] I don't *like* the risk   [L16: 122]
   [7] She could *hear* faint voices the other side   [L06: 10]
   [8] It *hurt* most when she tried to twist the foot
       outwards   [F31: 25]

Clearly, a rather wide range of meaning is expressed by the verbs in [2] to [8], though they may all be classed as state verbs. Let us now distinguish the types of state to which these verbs refer. The verb *be* occurs in both [2] and [3]: in [2] *be* predicates a **quality**, whereas in [3] *be* predicates a (temporary) **state**. A 'quality' is a more-or-less permanent characteristic of someone or something, while a 'state' is a less permanent type of situation. The use of *have* in [4], with its meaning of 'possess', refers, like *be* in [3], to a temporary state. *Have* may also be used to refer to a quality, e.g.

[9] Spiders *have* eight legs

The remaining examples, [5] to [8], contain verbs which refer to what are called **private states**. We can distinguish four types of private state: **intellectual** states, illustrated by *know* in [5]; states of **emotion** or **attitude**, illustrated by *like* in [6]; states of **perception**, illustrated by *hear* in [7], and accompanied by *can/could*; and states of **bodily sensation**, illustrated by *hurt* in [8]. These verbs refer to subjective states of mind and feeling.

Consider now the perception verb *taste* as it is used in the examples at [10] to [12] below:

[10] This soup *tastes* of garlic
[11] I can *taste* the garlic in the soup
[12] Would you kindly *taste* the soup?

In [10] *taste* is used in the same way as *be* in [2], to refer to a quality. In [11] *taste* is used like *hear* in [7], to refer to a state of perception. In [12], however, *taste* refers to an action. The action of tasting – deliberately and intentionally taking something into the mouth – may lead to a report on the state of perception which ensues from the action, as in [11], or on the quality of the food or drink, as in [10]. A similar triple use of a verb to refer to a quality, a state of perception, and an action, occurs with *smell* and *feel*. With hearing and seeing, though, different verbs are used. For the quality situation type, the verbs *sound* and *look* are used, e.g.

[13] It *sounds* a good idea   [L11: 193]
[14] They don't *look* very exciting   [L05: 78]

For the state of perception situation type, the verbs *hear* and *see* are used, e.g.

[15] She *could hear* his steps   [L21: 142]
[16] I *could see* its clean baked concrete   [L09: 173]

For the action situation type, the verbs *listen to* and *look at* are used, e.g.

[17] Tom would not even *listen to* me   [L15: 102]
[18] *Look at* the names she called your mother
                                                                      [L22: 208]

One further type of state remains to be identified. It is illustrated by [19] and [20] below:

[19] She *was standing* right in front of him   [L04: 7]
[20] The couple *were sitting* on a low couch against one
      wall   [L11: 44]

The verbs *stand* and *sit* in these examples refer to **stance**, the position that someone or something is in. In [19] and [20] these verbs clearly refer to a state. Look at [21] and [22] below, however:

[21] *Stand* on the sidelines and cheer on anyone. . .
                                                                      [L14:132]
[22] Shall we *sit* down?   [L11: 106]

In these examples, *stand* and *sit* seem to be referring to actions rather than to states. Like so many verbs (e.g. the perception verbs discussed above), they refer to different situation types according to context of use; or they may be said to belong to more than one semantic class of verbs.

Let us now summarise the distinctions we have drawn among different types of state in the following diagram:

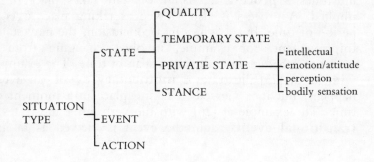

Reading this diagram from left to right, you move from more general labels to more particular ones. An intellectual state is a (more particular) type of private state, which is a (more particular) type of state.

[*Exercise 2*]

Events

Events refer to things that happen. There is no stated human or other animate instigator or agent for an event: they simply occur. In essence this is the feature which distinguishes events from actions. Actions are set in train by a (usually) human agent; events occur without a human instigator being involved. Look at the examples in [23] to [26] below, which illustrate four different types of event.

> [23] In this modern age very few of those reminders of man's early attempts at mechanisation on a fairly large scale are still *working*   [E10: 9]
> [24] The general condition and appetite *improved*
> [J17: 133]
> [25] The steering wheel *hit* his chest   [N29: 134]
> [26] I *arrived* at the Oldham Empire with the gang
> [A39: 218]

The example with *work* at [23] illustrates a type of event termed **goings-on**: an event takes place involving an inanimate force or object. The event is viewed as being in progress (going on), and there is no indication of an end to the goings-on. The example at [24] with the verb *improve* illustrates a **process**: a change of state takes place or is implied. A process is also viewed as taking place over a period of time, but it issues in a conclusion, the new state. Improvement, for example, involves changing from a worse to a better state, during a span of time. The example with *hit* at [25] illustrates a **momentary event**: an event happens, but it is viewed as taking place in a moment of time. The example at [26] with the verb *arrive* illustrates a **transitional event**: again the event is viewed as taking place in a moment of time, but the event also entails a change of state. In the case of *arrive*, the change is from not being in a place to being there.

You may have noticed from this discussion that two features in particular serve to draw distinctions among the four types of event. One is the feature 'change of state', which distinguishes processes and transitional events, involving a change of state, from goings-on and momentary events, which do not. The other feature is the view of the event as lasting through a period of time, contrasted with the view of it as taking place in a moment of time. This feature distinguishes goings-on and processes, lasting through time, from momentary and transitional events, which are momentary. For the first feature the terms **conclusive** (involving a change of state) and **non-conclusive** (no change of state) are used. For the second feature the terms are **durative** (lasting through time) and **punctual** (taking place in a moment of time). We may express the distinctions between the types of event in the following matrix:

	DURATIVE	PUNCTUAL
NON-CONCLUSIVE	goings-on	momentary event
CONCLUSIVE	process	transitional event

Actions

Actions do not just happen. Actions are usually performed by human, or at least animate, agents or instigators. They are normally the result of the exercise of a will or intention on the part of the agent. Actions are done by somebody. We can identify four types of action, corresponding to the four types of event which we discussed in the previous section. They are illustrated by the examples at [27] to [30] below.

[27] She *sang* in clubs and in concerts [A39: 114]
[28] In 1901 Landsteiner *discovered* the ABO blood group system [J13: 139]
[29] He *kicked* the razor clear [L03: 43]
[30] He *began* his search [L08: 153]

The example with the verb *sing* at [27] illustrates a type of action called **activity**: a person or other animate agent is involved in doing something. The action is viewed as durative (lasting over a period of time), but no result or achievement is implied (i.e. it is non-conclusive). The example at [28] with *discover* illustrates an **accomplishment**: a person undertakes an action with a result or achievement, i.e. it is conclusive. Like activities, though, accomplishments are viewed as taking place over a period: they are durative. The example with the verb *kick* at [29] illustrates a **momentary act**: an agent performs an action which is viewed as punctual (taking place in a moment of time), but the action has no end-result (i.e. it is non-conclusive). The example at [30] with *begin* illustrates a **transitional act**: again the action is viewed as punctual, but it is also conclusive. It involves a change of state, in the case of *begin* from not happening to being under way.

The same features are used to distinguish the four types of action as we used to make the distinctions among types of event: durative vs punctual, and conclusive vs non-conclusive. They distinguish types of action in the following way:

	DURATIVE	PUNCTUAL
NON-CONCLUSIVE	activity	momentary act
CONCLUSIVE	accomplishment	transitional act

There is therefore a match between types of event and types of action. The feature which distinguishes events from actions is termed **agentive**: actions are 'agentive', events are 'non-agentive'. Agentive means that a human (or other animate) decision or intention is involved, so that verbs expressing actions are usually accompanied by a word referring to a doer or agent. Non-agentive means that an event occurs without a human decision or intention being involved. Events and actions, though, as we have seen, do share common features, which mark them off from states.

We may summarise our discussion of situation types by relating the different types of situation in the following diagram:

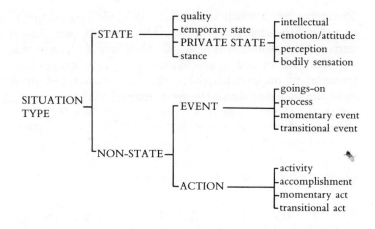

Semantic classes of verb

The terms in the lower case letters (quality, process, etc.) represent the most specific situation types. We may regard these terms as representing fifteen semantic subclasses of verb, since we have identified the word-class of verbs especially with situation types. We should note that a verb word may belong to more than one of the semantic subclasses. We have seen this already in [10] to [12] for *taste*, which belongs to the 'quality', 'perception' and 'activity' subclasses. There are many verbs which belong both to the 'goings-on' subclass and to the 'activity' subclass, e.g. *work*:

[31] Every new machine would not *work*   [G19: 153]
[32] He *worked* for me for two years   [G10: 38]

Other verbs belong to the 'transitional event' subclass and to the 'transitional act' subclass, e.g. *stop*:

[33] The tractor *stopped*   [G19:28]
[34] He *stopped* working   [G26:163]

As a final example, we may cite the verb *write*, which belongs to both the 'activity' subclass and the 'accomplishment' subclass:

[35] I *write* very little and very quickly   [G25: 4]
[36] I *wrote* letters for some of the illiterates
     [G25: 56]

These are but a small sample of the kinds of multiple class memberships that may occur. The semantic subclass of a verb, or the situation type to which it refers, determines, as we shall see in the next chapter, the participants that are required to occur with the verb. Before that, we need to examine in more detail the grammar of verbs.

[*Exercise 3*]

Verbs

STATES, EVENTS and ACTIONS are represented grammatically by the word-class of verbs. Verbs referring to states include: *be, seem, have, believe, like, hear, ache.* Verbs referring to events (in at least some of their uses) include: *breathe, fall, become, arrive, float, shine, die.* Verbs referring to actions (in at least some of their uses) include: *sing, laugh, throw, decide, encourage, push, clean.* Each of our examples earlier in the chapter has contained a verb word, e.g. *have, like, hear, stand, stop, work.* You may have noticed that they do not always occur in exactly the form in which they are written here: *have* appears as *had* in [4], *stand* as *standing* in [19], and *work* as *worked* in [32]. A verb word takes on different forms according to its grammatical context and the grammatical meanings or categories associated with it, while preserving its meaning as a state, event or action. Our discussion of the grammar of verbs will relate the grammatical categories associated with verbs to the different forms of the verb word.

Finite verb forms

We note first a grammatical category of **tense** (see further Chapter 4). Briefly, tense is the representation in grammar of the distinction that we make between past, present and future in our view of time. In English we encode the distinction between **present** and **past** tense in different forms of verbs:

[37] This machine *works* well
[38] He *worked* until 8 o'clock

In [37] the verb *work* is in the present tense form, and in [38] in the past tense form. For almost every verb, there are two present tense forms (e.g. *work, works*) and one past tense form (*worked*). The present tense forms are distinguished from each other by invoking the grammatical categories of **person** and **number**. 'Person' relates to the person or thing doing an action (e.g. working) or undergoing an event or being in a state. If it is the speaker or includes the speaker, we refer to it as **1st** person, which is associated with the pronouns *I* and *we*. If it is the one being addressed, we refer to it as **2nd** person, which is associated with the pronoun *you*. If it is the one being talked about, we refer to it as **3rd** person, which is associated with the pronouns *he, she, it, they*.

The category of 'number' relates to the distinction made in several areas of grammar between reference to one person or thing (**singular**) and reference to more than one person or thing (**plural**). In respect of the pronouns, *I, he, she* and *it* have singular reference, *we* and *they* have plural reference, and *you* may have singular or plural reference according to context. It may refer to one addressee or to more than one. We may summarise the intersection of person and number in respect of the pronouns by means of the following table:

NUMBER

		singular	plural
	1st	I	we
PERSON	2nd	you	you
	3rd	he, she, it	they

Returning to the present tense forms of verbs, we can now say that the form *works* is associated with a '3rd person singular' pronoun, while *work* is associated with the other persons/numbers. The present tense form *work* is in fact the same as the form known as the **base** or **citation** form: when we talk about a verb we use this form, and it is the one used as the headword in a dictionary entry. The others (*works, worked*) are formed by adding an **inflectional suffix**: *–s* for the '3rd person singular present tense', and *–ed* for the 'past tense'. The '3rd singular present' is always formed with the –s inflection in writing, and the regular way of forming the 'past' in writing is with –ed or –d (e.g. gaze–d). In speech, however, there is some variation, depending on the quality of the final sound of the base form; compare the following (pronunciation is given in the symbols of the International Phonetic Alphabet):

[39] work–s   /s/   work–ed   /t/
     load–s   /z/   load–ed   /ɪd/
     gaze–s   /ɪz/   gaze–d   /d/

A number of verbs (250 or so) form their past tense in an irregular way; that is, other than by adding the –ed inflection. The past tense inflection of some of these 'irregular' verbs is an internal change in the spelling and pronunciation of the word, instead of an inflectional suffix, e.g.

[40] choose   /tʃuːz/   chose   /tʃəʊz/
     run   /rʌn/   ran   /ræn/
     sing   /sɪŋ/   sang   /sæŋ/
     speak   /spiːk/   spoke   /spəʊk/
     write   /raɪt/   wrote   /rəʊt/

For other irregular verbs the past tense is formed by both an internal change of vowel and the addition of a suffix, e.g.

[41] feel   /fiːl/   fel–t   /fɛlt/
     keep   /kiːp/   kep–t   /kɛpt/
     lose   /luːz/   los–t   /lɒst/

Other irregular verbs inflect for past tense by changing the final consonant from a voiced /d/ to an unvoiced /t/, e.g.

[42] bend   bent
     lend   lent
     send   sent

A further group of verbs forms the past tense by retaining the initial consonant letter or sound of the base form and changing the remainder to ought or aught /ɔːt/, e.g.

[43] bring   /brɪŋ/   brought   /brɔːt/
     buy   /baɪ/   bought   /bɔːt/
     catch   /kætʃ/   caught   /kɔːt/
     seek   /siːk/   sought   /sɔːt/

One group of verbs keeps the same form for past tense as for present, namely the base form, e.g.

[44] cut, hit, put

In these cases you can only know that a past tense is meant from the context in which the verb and its sentence occurs; except for 3rd person singular contexts, where there is a contrast of form:

[45] he/she/it cuts   (present)
     he/she/it cut   (past)

Finally we must mention one verb whose past tense bears no relationship at all to the base form:

[46] go /gəʊ/   went /wɛnt/

This substitution by a completely different form is called **suppletion**.

The term 'suppletion' applies also to another verb, which is unique in the number of different forms in which it may occur. The verb is *be*. It has three present tense forms, which are unrelated to the base:

[47] am   (1st person singular – *I*)
     is   (3rd person singular – *he/she/it*)
     are   (other persons/numbers – *you, we, they*)

Be is also considered exceptional in having two past tense forms, which again are unrelated either to the base or to the present tense forms:

[48] was   (singular – *I, he/she/it*)
     were   (plural – *we, you, they*)

Non-finite verb forms

We have so far identified three forms of a verb:

[49] present tense   take
     3rd person singular present tense   takes
     past tense   took

We referred to these as the **finite** forms of the verb. Verbs in English also have three **non-finite** forms:

[50] infinitive   (to) take
     present participle   taking
     past participle   taken

The infinitive form usually occurs as a *to*-infinitive (*to take*); but it may occur as a 'bare'-infinitive (*take*), when it is identical with the present tense form. This is also the form that we have called the 'base' form. The present participle form is recognisable from its –*ing* suffix, which is the same for all verbs.

There is considerable variety, however, in the form of the past participle. For regular verbs, the past participle has the same form as the past tense:

[51] work–ed   load–ed   gaze–d   (compare [39])

Some irregular verbs also have identical forms for the past tense and past participle, e.g.

[52] bought   built   cost   fed   had   heard
     kept   shone

For a couple of irregular verbs the past participle is identical in form with the present tense:

[53] come   run   (and derivations, e.g. *overcome,*
                         outrun)

For the remainder, the past participle differs from the past tense and is formed either by an internal change or the addition of a suffix (usually –*n* or –*en*), or by some combination of these, e.g.

[54] begun   bitten   broken   done   drunk   flown
     seen   sunk   stolen   written

We may note that, by contrast with its finite forms, the non-finite forms of *be* are not particularly unusual:

[66] to be   being   been

However, the bare-infinitive form *be* is not identical with the present tense form, as is the case with other verbs.

The non-finite forms of the verb are used in certain syntactic constructions, which we will be encountering in the course of our investigations into English grammar. All verbs have non-finite as well as finite forms, except for a small group of 'modal' verbs (see Chapter 4, p. 103), which includes *can, may, will, shall, must*. So, for example, there is no infinitive 'to can' or present participle 'shalling'. These verbs in fact do not have 3rd singular present forms either: there is no 'mays', etc. One of them, *must*, does not even have a past tense form; and the others have the irregular past tense forms *could, might, would* and *should*.

[*Exercise 4*]

Exercises

Exercise 1

Identify the verb word in each of the following sentences. Say whether it refers to a STATE, an EVENT or an ACTION.

1. Our budgerigar disappeared yesterday
2. Lydia sings all day long
3. Mr Brown is rather pompous
4. The key is in the lock
5. Kehl lies on the east bank of the Rhine
6. We reported the incident to the police
7. The leaves fall from the trees in autumn
8. Not everyone empties the teapot down the sink
9. The passengers reached for their safety belts
10. She likes classical music

Exercise 2

To which type of STATE is the verb in each of the following sentences referring? Be as specific as you can.

1. Our neighbours have three cars
2. Many of our friends live in small country towns
3. Can you smell burning?
4. I believe that you have a set reserved for me
5. Children are charming sometimes
6. They fear that he was drowned
7. Going to the theatre sounds a marvellous idea
8. I ache all over

9. The tomato is technically a fruit
10. I really think I would like to

Exercise 3

To which situation type or semantic subclass does the verb in each of the following sentences belong?

1. Jane and Christopher are skating in Geneva tonight
2. I assume that you'll be late
3. The days are getting shorter at this time of year
4. She tapped him on the shoulder
5. Interest rates have fallen again
6. They are rather annoyed with the manager
7. We're just making the lunch
8. Your chimney is smoking rather badly
9. I can feel something crawling over my hand
10. Have you finished your work?

Exercise 4

Give the three finite and the three non-finite forms for the following verbs, in the order: 3rd singular present, present, past; infinitive, present participle, past participle.

1. shrink
2. mow
3. forget
4. drive
5. feed
6. talk
7. shut
8. do
9. wear
10. burn

CHAPTER 2

Participants: Nouns

What's in a situation?

In Chapter 1 we identified the situation type (STATE, EVENT, ACTION), especially with the verb word in a sentence; though, in a sense, a situation is expressed by a sentence as a whole. However, the verb may be regarded as the central element of a sentence, determining the character of the situation that is being talked about. The verb may also be regarded as determining what other elements may or must accompany it in the sentence. A verb (or a particular meaning or sense of a verb) is not only representative of a situation type, it creates a situation or 'scene' which contains persons who do things, persons or things that have something done to them, and so on.

Let us take an example: the action verb *send*. This verb creates a scene which includes a sender, a thing (or person) sent, and a destination (either a person or place) to which the thing is sent, e.g.

[1] Anne Archer stopped sending you money
[L22: 146]
[2] She sent me to London   [L22: 173]

The sender (*Anne Archer*, *she*), the thing sent (*money*, *me*) and the recipient (*you*) are **participants** in the situation which is created by *send*. They are the persons, other animate beings, and the things (both concrete and abstract) that are involved in the STATE, EVENT or ACTION. In general, these are the essential elements of a situation; they are what the scene is about. We could add to the sentences in [1] and [2] further elements, which would represent non-essential or gratuitous information about the scene, such as when it happened (*yesterday*, *last week*), how it happened (*by post*, *intentionally*), why it happened (*because of your behaviour*), and so on. We may refer to this information as the **circumstances** of a situation: we will discuss circumstances in detail in Chapter 3.

Semantic roles

Participants take on different semantic roles in a situation. In the case of *send*, we have referred to the participants by terms like 'sender', 'thing sent' and 'destination'. Clearly, these terms are rather specific to the situation of sending. We therefore need a set of semantic role labels which are generalisable to all types of situation. A number of lists have been proposed by different linguists, with some measure of congruence; but there is no generally agreed set of labels, as there is, for example, for word-classes in grammar. We will use the semantic role labels proposed in *A Comprehensive Grammar of the English Language* (paragraphs 10.18–10.33). Grammatically, participants are realised especially by members of the word-class of **noun**; and we will conclude this chapter with a discussion of some aspects of the grammar of nouns.

Participant roles in states and events

In Chapter 1 we identified a common semantic feature of STATES and EVENTS, which we termed 'non-agentive': neither STATES nor EVENTS have a participant which has the role of instigator. The primary participant role associated with many STATES and EVENTS is that of **AFFECTED**, e.g. in the situation types of quality and temporary state:

[3]   *The idea* seemed too ridiculous   [L02: 59]
[4]   *Abby* didn't seem discouraged   [L06: 92]

A participant takes on the AFFECTED role when it refers to some person or thing that is directly involved in a state or event but does not play an active part in it: *the idea* in [3], and *Abby* in [4]. The AFFECTED participant is in some state or undergoes some event. Besides being associated with qualities and temporary states, the AFFECTED role is found in the situation types of bodily sensation (see [5] below) and of many events ([6] to [8]):

[5] *His head* was aching with strain   [P09: 119]
[6] *The train* started on its way   [P23: 90]
[7] *It* must've fallen between the bed and the wall
                                                          [L12: 91]
[8] *Malone* had died from lack of oxygen   [L03: 67]

In these examples, the AFFECTED participants are, respectively, 'his head', 'the train', 'it' and 'Malone'.

The other regularly occurring or essential participant in situation types of quality and temporary state has the semantic role of **ATTRIBUTE**. The Attributes in [3] and [4] are, respectively, 'too ridiculous' and 'discouraged'; they relate directly to the AFFECTED participant and have the effect of being either an **identification** or a **characterisation** of the Affected participant. Identification Attributes provide an elaboration or specification of the Affected participant, which serves to identify it (see [9] and [10] below). Characterisation Attributes refer to some permanent or temporary characteristic of the AFFECTED participant (see [11] and [12] below).

[9]   The tune was *the same as that published by Lucy Broadwood*   [F37: 7]
[10] The leading spirit in this enterprise was *Dr Marius Barbeau*   [F37: 168]
[11] Every individual is *different*   [F01: 59]
[12] It is *short and familiar*   [F01: 81]

Another type of state in which an ATTRIBUTE typically occurs is the private state of emotion/attitude, with a verb like *consider* or *regard*, e.g.

[13] The Department of Public Prosecutions regards the evidence against him as *insufficient*   [L24: 9]

Here the ATTRIBUTE is 'insufficient'; 'the evidence against him' represents an AFFECTED participant, and we discuss the role of 'The Department of Public Prosecutions' below. ATTRIBUTES also occur in the EVENT situation type of process, with a verb like *become*, e.g.

[14] The pale blue eyes became *narrowed and bitter*
[L17: 100]

The ATTRIBUTE in a process is sometimes referred to by the term **RESULTING** ATTRIBUTE, because it refers to the state of the AFFECTED participant which results from the process denoted by the verb. ATTRIBUTES in STATE situation types (e.g. in [9] to [12]) are then known as **CURRENT** ATTRIBUTE.

We will now continue by considering the remaining participant roles associated with STATE situation types. In [13] above we gave an example of a private state of emotion/attitude. The semantic role of the first participant in that example ('The Department of Public Prosecutions') is that of **RECIPIENT**: the person concerned is said to be the one who receives a certain emotion or attitude. The role of RECIPIENT is also typically associated with the other private states of perception (e.g. *hear*) and cognition (intellectual, e.g. *know*), as in:

[15] *I* could hear the ticking of a clock   [L12: 177]
[16] *Madam* would know the word that unlocked the safe   [L08: 160]

In each case it is the first participant which has the role of RECIPIENT: 'I' in [15] and 'Madam' in [16].

The role of RECIPIENT is also typical of one of the participants in qualities and temporary states referring to possession, e.g.

[17] *He* has one of those dictaphone things   [L05: 155]
[18] Our world belonged *to Sonia and me*   [L12: 17]

In [17] the first participant ('He') has the role of RECIPIENT, and the second participant ('one of those dictaphone things') has the role of AFFECTED. In [18] the roles are reversed, with the AFFECTED participant first and the RECIPIENT second. The order of the participants reflects the difference in meaning between *have* and *belong*.

The RECIPIENT role label is then used in STATE situation types to designate both the possessor in qualities and temporary states, as well as the person or other animate being who is the locus of a private state (apart from bodily sensations). Some linguists would make a distinction

between these two kinds of role and use the label
EXPERIENCER to designate the recipient of a private
state. We will follow *CGEL* and not distinguish
RECIPIENT and EXPERIENCER. We shall find that the
RECIPIENT role occurs again in certain types of ACTION
situation.

There is one STATE situation type whose typical
participant roles have not yet been discussed, viz stance.
The person or other animate which has taken up a particular
stance has the role of **POSITIONER**, e.g. with the verbs
stand and *stay*:

[19] *Melville* stood by the window   [K03: 11]
[20] *He*'s staying at my flat just now   [K28: 159]

Here the POSITIONER role is taken by 'Melville' and 'He'
respectively.

Summarising, we have identified the following participant roles to be typically associated with situation types of
STATE:

AFFECTED   the person or thing being a quality, in a
        temporary state, or undergoing a bodily sensation;
        the knowledge, emotion, attitude or perception
        experienced by a RECIPIENT

RECIPIENT   the person possessing a quality or
        temporary characteristic, or experiencing a private
        state (intellectual, emotion/attitude, perception)

POSITIONER   a person or other animate having
        taken up a stance

ATTRIBUTE   the quality or temporary state which
        an AFFECTED participant is or which a
        RECIPIENT possesses

In situation types of EVENT we have identified the
participant roles of:

AFFECTED   the person or thing undergoing the
        event

ATTRIBUTE   more specifically the RESULTING
        ATTRIBUTE, which designates the state of the
        AFFECTED participant in a process resulting
        from the process

[*Exercise 1*]

Participant roles in ACTIONS

As we mentioned earlier, a semantic feature 'agentive' distinguishes ACTIONS from EVENTS and STATES. The same term, **AGENTIVE**, is used to designate the participant who instigates or causes an action. An AGENTIVE participant must be animate (human or non-human), since agentivity implies an exercise of the will and an intention to do some action. The first participant in each of the following examples has the participant role of AGENTIVE:

[21] *The chief in his white coat* was talking excitedly
with Father Felix   [K09: 181]
[22] *Janet* drank her tea   [K28: 10]
[23] *I* jumped up and ran from the room   [K25: 113]
[24] Then *she* suddenly stopped   [K11: 142]

These examples illustrate the ACTION situation types of activity, accomplishment, momentary act, and transitional act respectively.

Not all ACTIONS are instigated or caused by an animate AGENTIVE participant, however. Look at the following examples and consider what initiates the ACTION in these instances:

[25] *A sharper breath of wind* caught it   [P15: 147]
[26] *A computer* has prepared the bills
[27] *Mr Gilberto* held his hand over them   [M03: 115]

In [25] the ACTION is instigated by the participant 'A sharper breath of wind', which has the role of **EXTERNAL CAUSER**. An EXTERNAL CAUSER participant is usually inanimate and is therefore an unintentional instigator of an action. In [26], although no AGENTIVE participant is present in the sentence, one could be supplied and the sentence rephrased as:

[28] We have prepared the bills with a computer

However, as it stands, the action at [26] seems to imply that the action was performed by 'a computer', which in [28] is what the AGENTIVE participant uses to perform the action. The participant role of 'a computer' is termed **INSTRUMENT**, and it has this role in both [26] and [28].

This illustrates the important principle that semantic roles usually remain constant even though the grammatical structure used to express a particular situation may change. An INSTRUMENT participant is inanimate, like the EXTERNAL CAUSER. In [27] the first participant, 'Mr Gilberto', is animate, and it seems to have an AGENTIVE role: it has presumably instigated it or caused it. But this participant also has a role more akin to that of participants in the STATE situation type of stance, i.e. POSITIONER. 'Mr Gilberto' in [27] is in the role of AGENTIVE and POSITIONER in relation to the ACTION/STANCE of holding. A similar double particip-ant role may be recognised in respect of ACTIONS like *carry* and *wear*, e.g.

> [29] *Richie* shouldn't have been carrying a brief-case that morning [L12: 77]
> [30] *He* wore with pride a big collar inscribed: Peaslake [M05: 115]

Here the AGENTIVE/POSITIONER role is taken by 'Richie' and 'He', respectively.

In some ACTIONS, especially of the activity type, there is only one participant, usually with the AGENTIVE role ('Bill's working', 'You're laughing'). In most ACTIONS, though, there is usually at least one further participant, in addition to the AGENTIVE (or EXTERNAL CAUSER, etc.). In many cases the second participant has the role of **AFFECTED**, as in the following examples:

> [31] I drank *punch* in the wardroom [G12: 111]
> [32] She kicked *her nylons* towards the high, white sandals [P10: 61]

Here the AFFECTED participants are 'punch' in [31] and 'her nylons' in [32].

Some ACTIONS of the accomplishment type combine a process with that of an action: the activity referred to by the verb issues in a result, e.g.

> [33] In 1658 Robert Boyle invented *his improved air-pump* [J37: 180]
> [34] Taylor wrote *an encouraging report* [E22: 45]

The things (usually) which result from the ACTION, i.e.
'his improved air-pump' in [33] and 'an encouraging report'
in [34], have the participant role of **RESULTANT**. A
RESULTANT comes into being as a consequence of the
action carried out by the AGENTIVE participant. It should
be noted that the same verb may refer both to an activity
involving an AFFECTED participant and to an accomplishment involving a RESULTANT participant, e.g.

> [35] All cookers should cook *the same dish* at the same
>   setting   [E25: 80]
> [36] Our club chef cooked *Gefulter fish – a Jewish dish*
>   [G30: 176]

In [35] 'the same dish' has the role of AFFECTED
participant; the dish exists before the cookers cook it.
'Gefulter fish – a Jewish dish' in [36], however, has a
RESULTANT role; the dish comes into being as a result of
the chef's action. Not all accomplishments involve a
RESULTANT participant; in [37] the second participant has
the role of AFFECTED:

> [37] She discovered *the truth*   [P23: 123]

We turn now to consider the roles of participants which
typically occur as third elements in an action. Look at the
examples following, each of which has an AGENTIVE
participant, an AFFECTED participant, and the third
participant that we are considering:

> [38] Why did they send *you* nurses to this unhealthy
>   spot   [K23: 18]
> [39] Bart had found *them* grander ones at the Lord
>   Nelson   [G12: 140]

The third participant, 'you' in [38] and 'them' in [39], has
the role of **RECIPIENT**. We are dealing here with the
ACTION counterpart to the STATE possession situation
type, which we considered earlier (e.g. [17]). You will
notice that [38] and [39] have different kinds of
RECIPIENT: in [38] the RECIPIENT is the one who
receives the thing (AFFECTED) sent or given; while in [39]
the RECIPIENT represents the one who benefits from the
action undertaken. The latter is sometimes distinguished by
the term 'Beneficiary' or 'Benefactive'. We will follow

CGEL in not making this distinction. The RECIPIENT participant is always animate. In sentences like [40],

[40] He gave the door a kick

'the door' has the role of Affected participant, and the role of 'a kick' will be discussed later in this chapter under the heading 'Other participant roles'.

A further case of a third participant occurs in [41]. Again the first two participants have the roles of AGENTIVE and AFFECTED, respectively.

[41] She had appointed herself *my executioner*
[L12:137]

In this example, the third participant ('my executioner') has the role of **ATTRIBUTE**: it represents an ATTRIBUTE of the AFFECTED participant ('herself'). [41] is thus parallel in structure to the STATE situation of [13], where the AFFECTED is similarly the second participant in the situation. But the same relationship obtains in [3] and [4] and in [9] to [12], where an ATTRIBUTE likewise relates to an AFFECTED participant, though in these cases there are only two participants in the STATE situation.

Finally, we have already noted one ACTION situation with three participants, exemplified by [28]. Here the third participant has the role of INSTRUMENT, and the other two have the roles of AGENTIVE and AFFECTED, respectively. We give a further example of this ACTION situation at [42]:

[42] Joe Joe cut a piece of brown paper with the large wooden-handled all-purpose knife   [K21: 79]

Here the INSTRUMENT participant is 'the . . . knife', typically introduced by the word *with*.

Summarising, we have identified the following participant roles that are typically associated with ACTION situation types:

AGENTIVE   the animate instigator or cause of an action

EXTERNAL CAUSER   the inanimate and unintentional cause of an action

POSITIONER the person or other animate who takes up a stance

AFFECTED the person or thing directly affected or undergoing the action

RESULTANT the thing which comes into being as the result of an action

INSTRUMENT the inanimate means by which an action is undertaken

RECIPIENT the person or other animate who receives or benefits from the action

ATTRIBUTE the quality or state attributed to an Affected participant in an action

[*Exercise 2*]

Other participant roles

If you refer back to the example at [40] you will remember that we delayed discussing the semantic role of 'a kick' in that sentence. This participant has the semantic role of **EVENTIVE**. An EVENTIVE participant refers not to a person or thing involved in a situation, but to a happening (an event or action). A noun that has the semantic role of EVENTIVE (e.g. *kick*) is usually related to or derived from a verb that refers to an event or action. A noun with the EVENTIVE role may occur not only as the third participant in an ACTION, as in [40], but also as the first participant in a STATE, EVENT or ACTION, as in [43] to [45]:

[43] *External observation* is perfectly easy   [G38: 154]

[44] *A quarrel* would flare up   [G25: 119]

[45] *Their brief quarrel* had forged a bond between them
                                                  [L04:69]

An EVENTIVE participant occurs, additionally, as a second participant in ACTION situation types like the following:

[46] They were going to have *an open quarrel* any minute   [P03: 189]

[47] I'm going to make *a suggestion*

Here the EVENTIVE participant is almost an extension of the verb, which is usually from a fairly restricted set, including *give* (e.g. in [40]), *have, make, take*. Such sentences can often be rephrased so that there is a single participant (AGENTIVE) and the verb corresponds to the EVENTIVE noun. For example, [46] could be rephrased as [48], and [49] as [50]:

[48] They were going to quarrel openly any minute

[49] The boy is going to try to make a landing on the weather side of that pier   [N03: 144]

[50] The boy is going to try to land on the weather side of that pier

We will end this section with a problem of delimitation. We are considering a pair of semantic roles which more properly belong under the category of circumstance in the next chapter (where we will discuss them further) than among the participants in this. But in some contexts they act like participants rather than circumstances. The semantic roles are those of **LOCATIVE** and **TEMPORAL**, which refer to 'place' and 'time' respectively. We illustrate first of all first participants, in state situation types, which have the semantic role of LOCATIVE or TEMPORAL:

[51] *A path of bare, trodden soil* led to a gate in a high privet hedge   [L23: 162]

[52] *Tomorrow* will be a fine day

This is the most common position for LOCATIVES and TEMPORALS with a participant role. The LOCATIVE may also occur as a second participant with a number of ACTION verbs, as in the following examples:

[53] They have been walking *the streets* all night

[54] The girls have climbed *Ben Nevis*

Here, 'the streets' and 'Ben Nevis' are the LOCATIVE participants, with the verbs *walk* and *climb*, respectively.

We call the LOCATIVE and TEMPORAL items in [51] to [54] participants, because they have a clear participant role in each of the situations represented by those examples. They are essential and integral parts of the situation type and they could not be omitted without making the sentences nonsensical; they are referring not merely to background information about place and time: they are obligatory and central in these sentences. We may say the same for the LOCATIVE, which is the third participant in the following example:

[55] Mary put all her letters *into her purse* [L05: 86]

The Locative here ('into her purse') is obligatory: to leave it out would result in a nonsensical sentence. Consider now the following example:

[56] I pushed it back against the wall [L12: 87]

We might argue that the action of pushing involves not only an AGENTIVE and an AFFECTED participant (the pusher and the thing pushed), but also a place where the thing is pushed, i.e. a LOCATIVE participant. But the LOCATIVE in [56] ('back against the wall') is not as obligatory as the LOCATIVE in [55]: it could be omitted without making the sentence nonsensical, as in [57]:

[57] I pushed it

With [56] we are a further step along the way to sentences with purely circumstantial LOCATIVES, as in [58]:

[58] On April 23rd he died *in his cell* [L24: 69]

Here the LOCATIVE ('in his cell') could not be regarded as an essential element in the situation; it is entirely optional and merely adds some gratuitous information about the place of the event.

It will be clear that there is a problem of delimitation here. Some LOCATIVES, e.g. in [51] to [54], are clearly participants in the situation; others involve a shift in status from obligatory to optional and from being a central element of the situation [55] to being a peripheral element [58].

[*Exercise 3*]

Nouns

Participants are most often represented by members of the word-class of nouns. A noun is generally not restricted to a particular participant role, in the way that verbs are associated with particular STATES, EVENTS or

ACTIONS. For example, the noun *squirrel* could function as AGENTIVE, in a proposition such as 'The squirrel searched for the nuts', or as AFFECTED in 'The boy caught the squirrel', or as RECIPIENT in 'The boy gave the squirrel some nuts'. There are, however, certain correlations between the meaning of a noun and a participant role, e.g. the AGENTIVE role is associated with 'animate' nouns (see below). In considering the grammar of nouns, we will firstly discuss some semantic subclasses of noun and then, as with verbs, discuss the grammatical categories associated with the noun, concluding with a look at pronouns.

Semantic subclasses

Nouns constitute a very large class of words in English, and they represent a semantically diverse set of words. Some nouns refer to human beings, either by name, e.g. *Nathan, Kirsten, Lydia*, or by a general designation, e.g. *wife, son, child*. The former are sometimes called **proper nouns** and the latter **common nouns**. Proper nouns or names are not used exclusively of people (and their pets); they are used of places (*Birmingham, Germany, Asia, Aston Hall*) and other geographical features (*Derwent Water, The Solent, Ben Nevis*), of institutions (*Parliament, Bournville Junior School*), and as titles of organisations, publications, etc. (*Cadbury-Schweppes, The Guardian, Twelfth Night*). Proper nouns have a unique reference, whereas common nouns refer to a class of things or to an individual instance of a thing.

For common nouns a distinction is made between **concrete** and **abstract** nouns. Concrete nouns refer to 'things' which can be seen, have shape, and can be identified with the observation 'That is (a) . . . [table, cheese, hill]'. Abstract nouns, on the other hand, refer to unobservable 'things' like thoughts, ideas, emotions, attitudes; you cannot point to the referent of an abstract noun and say 'That is (a) . . . [decision, imagination, determination]'. The distinction between concrete and abstract is not crucial in determining the semantic function of a noun, nor is there a clear correlation between any particular participant role and either concrete or abstract nouns. There are perhaps one or two apparent tendencies: for instance, the second participant in a situation involving an EXPERIENCER as first participant, i.e. some private states, would tend to be an abstract noun, e.g.

[59] George knows *the reason for Bill's departure*

Here *reason*, the central word of the AFFECTED participant, is an abstract noun. But it is not difficult to construct examples which do not conform to the tendency, e.g.

[60] George knows *the castles you mean*

Here *castles* is a concrete noun.

A more pertinent semantic distinction is that between **animate** and **inanimate** nouns; that is, nouns which refer to animate beings and those which refer to inanimate 'things'. We have already noted that the AGENTIVE role is restricted to animate nouns, because the notion of agentivity implies intention, which can be imputed only to animate beings. Similarly, nouns with the participant role of INSTRUMENT or EXTERNAL CAUSER are always inanimate: EXTERNAL CAUSER is an 'unwitting' instigator and INSTRUMENT is by definition an inanimate tool with which an action is undertaken. The animate/inanimate distinction therefore has a direct correlation with particular participant roles. Further, the noun in the RECIPIENT role, both in possession situation types and in private states, must always be animate; and the nouns in the EVENTIVE role are always inanimate and usually abstract as well. Other participant roles, however, like AFFECTED, POSITIONER, ATTRIBUTE, may be filled by either animate or inanimate nouns.

Number

There is a further distinction which we must draw for nouns: between those which refer to 'things' which may be counted and those whose referents may not be counted. The former are termed **countable** nouns and the latter are termed **uncountable** or **mass** nouns. Examples of countable nouns are given at [61], and at [62] of uncountable nouns:

[61] box   star   tree   bicycle   proposal   decision
[62] china   information   flour   happiness   bread

Being countable means that for the nouns at [61] the system
of **number** operates. In English the number system has two
terms: **singular** and **plural**. This means that countable
nouns are either in the singular form, when they refer to
one individual 'thing'; or they are in the plural form, when
they refer to more than one 'thing'. The singular form is
'unmarked'; it is the base form of the noun as given in [61].
The plural form is 'marked', usually by an inflectional suffix
written –s or –es; e.g. for the nouns in [61] as follows:

[63] boxes   stars   trees   bicycles   proposals
decisions

For uncountable nouns, like those in [62], the system of
number does not operate. There is only one form, and the
noun refers to an undifferentiated mass. Uncountable nouns
cannot therefore be used with the indefinite article *a*: there is
no *a china* or *an information*, just as there is no *chinas* or
informations.

But let us return to the plural forms of countable
nouns. We have noted so far that the plural of nouns is
usually formed in writing by the addition of an –(e)s suffix.
The –es form of the suffix is required if the base form of the
noun ends in *s, z, x, ch* or *sh*:

[64] kisses   foxes   stitches   dishes

As far as pronunciation is concerned, this 'regular' plural
inflection has three variant forms. Compare the pronunciations of the following:

[65] buns   /bʌn–z/
bats   /bæt–s/
buses   /bʌs–ɪz/

The pronunciation of the plural inflection is conditioned by
the final sound of the base form to which it is added: /–ɪz/
occurs after sibilants /s z ʃ ʒ tʃ ʤ/, while /–s/ occurs after
other voiceless consonants, and /–z/ after other voiced
consonants and vowels.

There are additionally a number of 'irregular' forms of
the plural inflection, though the range of irregular plurals is

not as extensive as that of the irregular past tense forms. A small number of nouns has no marker of plural number; the same form is used for both singular and plural reference, e.g. *sheep*, *deer*, *horsepower*. Another small set of nouns forms the plural by changing the vowel of the base form, e.g.

[66] foot   /ʊ/   feet   /iː/
     mouse   /aʊ/   mice   /aɪ/
     goose   /uː/   geese   /iː/

For some nouns the irregularity is not in the plural inflection but in the base: some nouns ending in /θ/ or /f/ voice this final consonant in the plural form, e.g.

[67] paths   /pɑːθ/   /pɑːðz/
     calf   /kɑːf/   /kɑːvz/

The other major group of nouns with irregular plural inflections are those borrowed from foreign languages, especially Latin and Greek, which retain their original plurals, e.g.

[68] stimulus   stimuli   (Latin)
     formula   formulae   (Latin)
     referendum   referenda   (Latin)
     crisis   crises   (Greek)
     criterion   criteria   (Greek)
     libretto   libretti   (Italian)
     kibbutz   kibbutzim   (Hebrew)

Many of the foreign plurals appear to be falling out of use nowadays, and the regular plural forms are being substituted in their place, e.g. *formulas*, *referendums*, *librettos*. You may find it of interest to look out (and listen) for how English speakers form the plurals of such words. Two particularly interesting cases to observe are *data* and *media*: *data* (technically the plural form of *datum*) is frequently used as an uncountable (therefore singular) noun ('Your data is unconvincing'); and *media* (technically the plural of *medium*) is sometimes used as a singular countable noun (*a media*), to refer to one of the mass media.

Case

Another grammatical system which operates with nouns is that of **case**. Some highly inflecting languages (like Latin, Greek, or modern German) have a number of case forms of nouns, with names like 'nominative', 'accusative' and 'dative'. In modern English, there are only two terms in the case system: the **common** case and the **genitive** case. The common case is the 'unmarked' term in the system; nouns in the common case have the base form when singular in number, and the base + plural inflection when plural in number (*girl – girls, child – children*).

The genitive case is marked in a number of ways. In writing the genitive singular of nouns is marked by *'s* (*girl's, child's*). This form has the same pronunciation and variants of pronunciation as the common case plural form of regular nouns, e.g.

[69] girl's, girls   /gɜːlz/
     cat's, cats   /kæts/
     boss's, bosses /bɒsiz/

In the plural form of nouns, where the plural inflection is according to the regular –(*e*)*s* pattern, the genitive is marked in writing by an apostrophe added to the plural noun (*girls', cats', bosses'*). The pronunciation of these genitive plural nouns is identical to that noted at [69] for the genitive singular. This means that, while there is a written distinction between the genitive singular, common plural and genitive plural forms of regular nouns, there is no distinction between these forms in speech. Which form is meant must be determined from its context.

With nouns which form their plurals irregularly, the genitive is marked in the plural noun in the same way as it is in the singular: by the –*'s* suffix in writing (*children's*) and the appropriate *s*-variant in pronunciation (/tʃɪldrənz/). Consequently, for nouns with irregular plurals, the three forms (genitive singular, common plural, genitive plural) do have different pronunciations as well as different spellings, e.g.

[70]
man's   /mænz/   men   /mɛn/   men's   /mɛnz/
mouse's   /maʊsɪz/   mice /maɪs/   mice's /maɪsɪz/

The genitive case is more commonly used with certain types of noun (e.g. animates, especially humans) than with others (e.g. abstracts). Its use will be discussed further in Chapter 5 (p. 108).

Pronouns

In a number of our examples earlier in the chapter the participant roles being discussed were filled by pronouns rather than by nouns, e.g. *I* in [15], *he* in [17], *she* in [24]. Pronouns substitute for nouns (and their associated words – see Chapter 5): that is what the term 'pro-noun' means. They have an important textual function (see Chapter 10) and contribute to economy in language by reducing the repetition of nouns. We have already discussed the pronouns in Chapter 1, where we noted that the grammatical categories of **number** and **person** determined the forms of pronouns, as follows:

[71]   NUMBER

		singular	plural
	1st	I	we
PERSON	2nd	you	you
	3rd	he, she, it	they

The 3rd person pronouns are distinguished in the singular by the grammatical category of **gender**, which has the terms 'masculine' (*he*), 'feminine' (*she*) and 'neuter' (*it*).

These are not the only forms of the personal pronoun, however. The category of **case** applies, as it does for nouns, except that there are three terms for this category in the pronoun: 'subjective', 'objective' and 'genitive'/'possessive'. The forms at [71] are the subjective case forms of the personal pronoun. The complete set of forms is given below at [72]. You will note that the 2nd person pronoun has only two forms, *yours* (possessive) and *you* for the other two cases in both singular and plural number.

[72] NUMBER/PERSON		CASE	
	Subjective	Objective	Possessive
Singular 1st person	I	me	mine
2nd	you	you	yours
3rd masc	he	him	his
fem	she	her	hers
neut	it	it	its
Plural 1st person	we	us	ours
2nd	you	you	yours
3rd	they	them	theirs

The possessive pronoun substitutes for a genitive noun; compare [73] and [74], where *hers* replaces *Hilary's*:

[73] The shoes are Hilary's
[74] They are hers

There is another, related set of possessives – *my, your, his, her, its, our, their* – which are also sometimes called 'pronouns'. We treat them as 'identifiers', and they are discussed in Chapter 5 (see [31] and [32] there). The subjective and objective pronouns substitute for nouns in different syntactic contexts. For example, the subjective pronoun replaces nouns with the syntactic function of subject (see Chapter 6): *they* in [74] replaces *the shoes* of [73] with subject function. Similarly, the objective pronoun *them* in [76] below replaces *the shoes* in [75] which has the syntactic function of object (see Chapter 6):

[75] I have cleaned the shoes
[76] I have cleaned them

We have referred to the pronouns in [72] as the **personal** pronouns. There are a number of other subclasses of pronoun which we need to take note of at this point. Related to the personal pronouns is the set of **reflexive** pronouns:

[77] myself   yourself   himself   herself   itself
ourselves   yourselves   themselves

You will notice that the 2nd person has a different singular and plural form, because number is marked in the *self/selves* distinction. A reflexive pronoun is used instead of an objective personal pronoun if it refers to the same person or thing as the subject, as in [78]; or it is used as an emphatic pronoun, as in [79]:

[78] I've cut myself
[79] Sam opened the door himself

Also related to personal pronouns, though in meaning rather than in form, are the **relative** pronouns [80] and **interrogative** pronouns [81], whose uses will be discussed in Chapters 7 and 6 respectively.

[80] who   whom   whose   which   that
[81] who?   whom?   whose?   what?   which?

Again, these pronouns substitute for nouns in their appropriate contexts. *Which* and *what?* have non-personal reference, while the others refer generally to persons, except *that*, which may refer to both. A set that are called pronouns but do not replace specific nouns (and their accompanying words) are the **indefinite** pronouns [82] to [84], which are used where a noun is not appropriate because the person or thing referred to is unknown or indefinite.

[82] someone   everyone   no-one   anyone
[83] somebody   everybody   nobody   anybody
[84] something   everything   nothing   anything

The pronouns in [82] and [83] refer to persons, while those in [84] refer to non-personal animates and things.

The final major set of pronouns that we need to note are the **demonstrative** pronouns [85], which do have a substitutionary function.

[84] this   these   that   those

It will be clear that the grammatical category of number is operating here: *this* and *that* are singular forms, while *these* and *those* are the equivalent plural forms. A further grammatical category is also operating here, distinguishing *this/these* from *that/those*. We may call it a category of **proximity**, with the terms 'near' and 'distant'. We display the intersection of these categories in [86] and illustrate the replacement of a noun by a demonstrative pronoun in [87] by comparison with [88].

[86]   NUMBER

		singular	plural
PROXIMITY	near	this	these
	distant	that	those

[87] He hasn't addressed the envelopes here
[88] He hasn't addressed these

We have now looked at two major components in the structure of propositions which go to make up the messages of spoken and written communication. The two major components are the situation types, the topic of Chapter 1, and the participants in the situations, the topic of this chapter. We have also considered the grammatical word-classes that are associated with these two components: verbs for situation types and nouns/pronouns for participants. There remains a third component of propositions: circumstances. And we turn to this in Chapter 3.

[*Exercise 4*]

_____

Exercises

Exercise 1

Identify and label the semantic roles of the participants in the following sentences representing STATE and EVENT situation types:

1. Everybody could see the elephant
2. This cream has gone sour
3. My earrings have disappeared
4. Spiders have eight legs
5. My back is hurting
6. The bells are ringing
7. These are beech trees
8. Our friends don't like the sun
9. The children are sitting down
10. We think of him as a member of the family

Exercise 2

(a) Identify and label the semantic roles of the participants in the following sentences representing ACTION situation types:

1. Your parents are talking
2. My brother has written me a long letter
3. With these words he finished his speech
4. They made Stephen king
5. The floods damaged a lot of property
6. You must fill out this form

(b) Compose sentences with action situations using the verbs and participant roles specified:

1. invent [Agentive, Resultant]
2. shoot [Agentive, Affected, Instrument]
3. swim [Agentive]
4. wear [Positioner, Affected]
5. donate [Agentive, Affected, Recipient]

Exercise 3

Identify and label the semantic roles of the elements in the following situations. For any LOCATIVE or TEMPORAL elements, say whether they are participants or circumstances or indeterminate between the two.

1. We'll be watching that new video tomorrow
2. She's having a shower
3. Bob's in the kitchen
4. Did you hear the nightingale last night?
5. They accused him of theft
6. The artist showed me his pictures
7. Are you going to the concert?
8. The campaign was disastrous
9. The dentist removed the filling from the tooth
10. Paddington gave him a hard stare

Exercise 4

Identify the nouns and pronouns in the following sentences. Specify the formal features (e.g. number, person, case) of each of them.

1. The boys' boots need cleaning before they play football on Saturday
2. We have to make the beds and cook the meals ourselves
3. Alfred's theory baffles everyone with its complexity
4. This is the way that you should undo it
5. Does this dreadful noise alarm you?
6. She will probably not be able to survive any more serious crises
7. The man in the sweet shop gave Lucy five liquorice toffees as a birthday present
8. The technicians will repair your computer in a week's time
9. The company's accountant has discovered something wrong in the accounts
10. Who told you that?

CHAPTER 3

Circumstances: Adverbs and prepositions

A proposition, such as at [1] below, may be seen as representing a kind of drama:

[1] Bill offered Jane a chocolate on the bus last night

The drama has actors (or participants) who take on particular roles, and it takes place within a setting, which we may or may not choose to specify. In [1], the participants in the drama of 'offering' are *Bill*, *Jane* and *a chocolate*. The drama of 'offering' has the cast of 'offerer', 'offeree' and 'thing offered'; they have the semantic roles of AGENTIVE, RECIPIENT and AFFECTED respectively. The other two elements in [1] represent the setting (or **circumstances**) of the drama. They tell us where it took place – *on the bus* – and when it took place – *last night*. It is with the circumstantial elements of propositions that this chapter will be concerned.

How necessary are circumstances?

The participants are more or less obligatory elements in a proposition. A particular situation type, represented by a verb with a particular meaning, expects a certain cast of participants, represented by nouns with appropriate semantic roles. The situation of offering in [1] expects AGENTIVE, RECIPIENT and AFFECTED participants. The proposition is incomplete without the explicit or implicit presence of these participants. A participant may be implicit or 'latent' if it is implied from the context, e.g.

[2] What did Bill offer Jane?
   He offered a chocolate

In the reply, the RECIPIENT (*Jane*) is latent, but it can be supplied from the question; so that it can be regarded as being present by implication.

   Circumstances, on the other hand, cannot generally be said to be necessary for the completeness of a proposition. The circumstances of place and time, which are present in [1], have been omitted from [2], but [2] cannot be said to have been made incomplete as a result. Circumstances are usually additional, gratuitous information about a situation, which we may include in a proposition, or not, as a matter of choice. While this may be generally true of circumstances, subject to obvious constraints of semantic compatibility, there are some situation types for which a circumstantial element is more or less obligatory: compare [3] to [6] below.

   [3] They're singing Handel's Messiah *in the Town Hall*
   [4] I bought the vegetables *in the market*
   [5] The horses galloped *across the field*
   [6] I've put the sprouts *into the saucepan*

The proposition at [3] is like [1]: the circumstance *in the Town Hall* may be omitted without making the proposition incomplete; the situation of 'singing' does not require the expression of place. In the case of 'buying', however, represented by the example at [4], the situation has the expectation of a buyer, goods bought, and the source of the goods – either who from or where from. To omit the circumstance *in the market* makes the proposition incomplete, unless 'I bought the vegetables' is intended as a denial of 'I stole the vegetables' or 'I grew the vegetables'.

   With situation types involving movement, such as the example with *gallop* at [5], there is usually an expectation of a place from, to or within which the movement occurs, besides a person or thing instigating or undertaking the movement. If the circumstance *across the field* is omitted from [5] there is a slight change in the meaning of *gallop*, since it now implies a contrast with *canter*, *walk*, etc.. Neither here, though, nor perhaps in [4], is the circumstantial element absolutely necessary: if it is omitted, the proposition can still be construed as complete. In the case of [6], however, the circumstance *into the saucepan* is obligatory: the proposition which results if it is omitted cannot be construed in any way as complete ('I've put the sprouts'). Indeed, *into the saucepan* is almost like a participant in this situation type, along with *I* and *the sprouts* (see example [55] in Chapter 2 and discussion there). We might want to count *into the saucepan* as a circumstance because it refers to a place or as a participant because it is a central part of the ACTION of putting.

The distinction between participant and circumstance is not then clear-cut. Consider the propositions at [7] to [9] with the verb *send*, and compare [38] in Chapter 2.

[7] The manager has sent a letter to every employee
[8] The manager has sent his apologies to the meeting
[9] The manager has sent a substitute to the meeting

In [7] the situation with *send* has the participants AGENTIVE (*the manager*), AFFECTED (*a letter*) and RECIPIENT (*every employee*). In [9], however, the situation with *send* has the participants AGENTIVE (*the manager*) and AFFECTED (*a substitute*), and a circumstance of place (*to the meeting*) referring to where the AFFECTED participant was sent. Notice that [7] may have the paraphrase of [10], but [9] may not have a similar paraphrase.

[10] The manager has sent every employee a letter

The element *to the meeting* in [8] appears to be intermediate between these two interpretations. Does it answer the question at [11] or that at [12]?

[11] Who has the manager sent his apologies to?
[12] Where has the manager sent his apologies?

If [11] is the appropriate question then this would point to the analysis of *to the meeting* as a RECIPIENT participant, but if [12] is the appropriate question then *to the meeting* is to be interpreted as a circumstance of place. Arguably, both [11] and [12] could be appropriate questions to which [8] would be an answer, though we might regard [12] as marginally preferable. The paraphrase test is given at [13]:

[13] The manager has sent the meeting his apologies

This would appear acceptable, though it is difficult to make a clear judgement. What this discussion illustrates is that there is a blurring of the distinction between participant and circumstance with the third element in propositions with *send*. We need to be prepared to accept such indeterminacy in language, and to provide for it in our analysis and description.

What types of circumstance?

We noted that the example at [1] has two types of circumstance expressed: place (*on the bus*) and time (*last night*). These are given the labels **LOCATIVE** and **TEMPORAL**, respectively, and they are the two most commonly occurring circumstances in propositions. There are four further types of circumstance, which we shall review below: **PROCESS**, **RESPECT**, **CONTINGENCY**, **DEGREE**. Most of these, including LOCATIVE and TEMPORAL, have a number of subdivisions, which we shall also mention. As with the semantic role labels for participants (Chapter 2) we shall take those for circumstances from the *Comprehensive Grammar of the English Language*.

Locative

Circumstantial roles concerned with space are given the semantic label 'LOCATIVE'. This label, however, subsumes a number of subtypes of circumstance relating to space: **POSITION**, **DIRECTION** and **DISTANCE**. POSITION is a static notion, by contrast with the dynamic DIRECTION. It provides an answer to the question 'Where?' (i.e. Where is something situated or where did some event/action take place?). The examples at [14] to [16] below each contain a POSITION LOCATIVE circumstance:

[14] Kennan sat *on the edge of the bed*   [M05: 182]
[15] Her car was already *outside the door*   [K06: 130]
[16] Hal would sit *behind the shed door*   [P18: 8]

In [14] the POSITION LOCATIVE is 'on the edge of the

bed'; in [15] it is 'outside the door'; and in [16] 'behind the shed door'.

DIRECTION LOCATIVES refer to three different kinds of movement in space: movement from a **SOURCE**, movement to a **GOAL**, and movement along a **PATH**. The notions of Source and Goal are encoded in English in the now rather archaic question forms 'Whence?' (for Source) and 'Whither?' (for Goal); they have been replaced, except in highly formal or literary contexts, by the periphrastic forms 'Where from?' and 'Where to?', respectively. A PATH DIRECTION LOCATIVE is associated only with a periphrastic question form, such as '(By) which way?'. The examples at [17] and [18] illustrate contexts including SOURCE DIRECTIONALS:

[17] He rushed *from the house* without a word
[M01: 179]

[18] I walked quickly *out of the shade of the Forest trees*
[L09: 152]

The SOURCE DIRECTIONALS are 'from the house' in [17] and 'out of the shade of the Forest trees' in [18]. You will note that the verbs in these sentences (*rush, walk*) refer to movement: DIRECTION LOCATIVES are typically associated with movement verbs, either intransitive as in these two examples, or transitive verbs involving movement, e.g. *remove* in [19], where the SOURCE DIRECTIONAL is 'from his desk':

[19] Taking the sheet McNaught removed the feet from his desk   [M05: 38]

You may also note that the notion of Source is associated with particular prepositions (discussed later in the chapter), namely *from, out of,* etc..

We will now illustrate PATH and GOAL DIRECTIONALS together in the same sentence, at [20] and [21]:

[20] He threw himself *across the floor towards the entrance*
[L03: 18]

[21] She followed him *along the street opposite the church of the mammoth pillars towards the arid wastes of the Place de la Concorde,* and then *by devious dangerous routes towards the Seine*   [L20: 87]

In [20] the PATH DIRECTIONAL is 'across the floor', and the GOAL DIRECTIONAL is 'towards the entrance'. In [21] there are two PATH DIRECTIONALS ('along the . . . pillars' and 'by devious dangerous routes') and two GOAL DIRECTIONALS ('towards the . . . la Concorde' and 'towards the Seine'). The verbs in both sentences are transitive verbs involving movement (*throw, follow*). The prepositions associated with PATH are *across, along* and *by*, and with GOAL *towards, to, into, onto*, etc.

The third type of LOCATIVE mentioned earlier is **DISTANCE**. This circumstantial role refers to space expressions answering the question 'How far?'. The answer with the DISTANCE LOCATIVE may contain either an expression of a specific type of quantity with a word like *miles* (as in [22] below), or an expression with a vaguer term like *way* (as in [23]).

[22] You could see far over west and north *for many miles*   [N06: 112]
[23] I can walk *all the way* to the mine   [N07: 57]

Besides referring to type of quantity (*miles, way*) the DISTANCE expressions also contain a word referring to amount: *many, all*.

The following is a summary of LOCATIVE circumstances:

[24]   ┌Position (Where?)
              │   ┌Source (Where from?)
 LOCATIVE─┤DIRECTION ─┤Path (Which way?)
              │   └Goal (Where to?)
              └Distance (How far?)

[*Exercise 1*]

Temporal

Circumstantial roles concerned with time are given the semantic label 'TEMPORAL'. As with LOCATIVES, the TEMPORAL semantic role encompasses a number of circumstances of time: **POSITION**, **DURATION**, and **FREQUENCY**. POSITION in time is parallel to POSITION in space: it provides an answer to the simple question 'When?', which serves to place an action or event at a point or period in time. The sentences at [25] to [27] below contain POSITION TEMPORAL circumstances.

[25] *In the afternoon* I went out again   [K12: 47]
[26] He must have quite enjoyed himself with young
     Lee *during the afternoon*   [K02: 57]
[27] The journey ended *that evening*   [K22: 58]

The POSITION TEMPORALS are, respectively, 'in the afternoon', 'during the afternoon', and 'that evening'. The parallel between LOCATIVE and TEMPORAL POSITION is reinforced by the fact that many prepositions may be used for both types of Position, e.g.

[28] *at*   at home   at five o'clock
     in   in the house in the afternoon
     on   on the bus   on Saturday

For other kinds of POSITION, LOCATIVE and TEMPORAL circumstances use different prepositions: compare *in front of* (Locative): *before* (Temporal), *behind* (Locative): *after* (Temporal).

The notion of **DURATION** in time has some parallels with that of DISTANCE in space. Both are concerned with the measurement of extent, and the question 'How far?' for DISTANCE is matched by the question 'How long?' for DURATION. But in DURATION we make some finer distinctions which have no correspondence in the DISTANCE category. Besides giving the **GENERAL** information relating to the question 'How long?', DURA-TION may also be related to **ORIENTATION** in time, either **FORWARD** into the future or **BACKWARD** into the past. Duration with forward orientation corresponds to the question 'Until when?', and Duration with backward orientation to the question 'Since when?'. Look at the examples in [29] to [31].

[29] He was ill *for three days*   [N13: 66]
[30] Julian had acted very strangely *since the tragedy*
                                                            [L04: 144]
[31] It would probably last *until the evening*
                                                            [L11: 169]

The TEMPORAL expressions 'for three days' [29], 'since the tragedy' [30] and 'until the evening' [31] all relate to

DURATION. In the case of those in [30] and [31] there is an orientation to the duration, backward in the case of [30] with the preposition *since*, and forward in [31] with the preposition *until*. The TEMPORAL expression of duration in [29] is of the general type, with the characteristic preposition *for*.

The third subtype of TEMPORAL circumstance is that of **FREQUENCY**. Here the reference is not to point in time ('When?') or extent through time ('How long?'), but to the incidence of an event or action in time, relating to the question 'How often?' This question is typically answered by adverbs (see below) like *frequently* and *often*, as in [32] and [33]:

> [32] Frequently, the charge for these prescriptions is considerably higher than the cost at which they can be bought at the chemists [B10: 148]
> [33] I often come up myself when I'm out this way [P15: 49]

Another typical expression of FREQUENCY involves the use of the word **times**, either in the compound adverb **sometimes** or with a numeral or other expression of quantity, as in [34] to [36].

> [34] We spent our time *sometimes* with Max and Jill but more often alone, swimming [N13: 86]
> [35] He pulled the trigger *five times* [N19: 110]
> [36] He did this *several times*, much to the amusement of passers-by [P28: 79]

The sentence at [34] contains the FREQUENCY expressions *sometimes* and *more often*, referring to two different rates of occurrence.

We can summarise the types of TEMPORAL circumstance with the following diagram:

[37]

```
                 ┌ Position (When?)
                 │                                  ┌ backward (Since when?)
                 │              ┌ ORIENTATION ──────┤
TEMPORAL ────────┤ DURATION ────┤                   └ forward (Until when?)
                 │              └ General (How long?)
                 └ Frequency (How often?)
```

[*Exercise 2*]

Process

Circumstances of PROCESS relate to the question 'How?'
How did some event come about or was some action
performed? But the 'how' of an event or action may
encompass a number of different types of Process, namely
Manner, **Means**, **Instrument** and **Agentive**. They are
exemplified in that order at [38] to [41]:

[38] Dai, meanwhile, was pedalling *furiously* on the
road   [M04: 114]

[39] I was able *by means of a trick* to floor the first three
who attacked   [M03: 67]

[40] Together they knelt, prising *with their knives* round
the scab   [M06: 206]

[41] She was warned *by everyone* that it would never
stick to the walls   [K23: 178]

It is not always easy to determine in any particular instance
what type of PROCESS is being referred to. MANNER
PROCESSES may be more specifically questioned by 'In
what way?', and the answer will often be in the form of a
'manner' adverb ending in *–ly*, as in [38] (*furiously*) and in
[42] below (*sharply*).

[42] Megan Thomas spoke sharply to the conductor,
demanding an explanation   [M04: 85]

Characteristic of MANNER PROCESSES is their subject-
ivity: they represent the speaker's subjective assessment of
the way in which an event happens or an action is
undertaken. For that reason they are **gradable**. That means
that there can be degrees of a MANNER PROCESS, e.g.
an action may be done 'more' or 'less' *carefully*, 'very' or
'quite' *expertly*, and so on.

MEANS and INSTRUMENT PROCESSES, on the
other hand, are objective. They do not represent a speaker's
assessment of how something happened, but are verifiable
observations of the means by which an action or event
occurred. Expressions of MEANS and INSTRUMENT are
therefore not gradable, since they represent either/or
categories. For example, *more* or *less* could not normally be
added to 'by means of a trick' in [39], nor to 'with their
knives' in [40]. A MEANS PROCESS answers the specific

'how' question 'By what means?', and the INSTRUMENT
PROCESS answers the specific question 'What with?' A
MEANS refers to a technique used in an action, e.g.
'timbres and intervals' in [43] below, while INSTRU-
MENT refers to the thing used in order to carry out the
action referred to in the proposition, e.g. 'medicaments. . .'
in [44]:

[43] Henze obtains his musical characterisation by
     means of individual instrumental timbres and
     'personal' intervals   [C01: 36]

[44] (She) dressed our cuts and scratches with medica-
     ments from her little box   [M03: 114]

The final type of PROCESS – AGENTIVE – is
different from the other three in that it refers to a person. It
may be seen as the answer to the question 'By whom?' or
'By whose agency?', both of which, especially the use of
whom, mark it out as having personal reference. The
AGENTIVE is the person who carries out an action (see
Chapter 2), and we used that term to designate a semantic
role of participant. An AGENTIVE PROCESS is the
circumstantial counterpart to the AGENTIVE participant.
There is a direct grammatical ('transformational') relationship between [41] and [45], in which the AGENTIVE now
has a participant role. Compare also [46] and [47].

[45] Everyone warned her that it would not stick to the
     walls
[46] He was quickly surrounded *by a number of ex-
     Ministers*   [K03: 25]
[47] *A number of ex-Ministers* quickly surrounded him

The AGENTIVE PROCESS is typically introduced with
the preposition *by*, though this preposition may also
introduce other types of PROCESS.

We may summarise the types of PROCESS circumstance by means of the following diagram. (Note the use of
a MEANS PROCESS here!):

[48]

PROCESS (How?) ——
- Manner (In what way?)
- Means (By what means?)
- Instrument (What with?)
- Agentive (By whom?)

Respect

The rather broad and abstract category of RESPECT has a relatively minor circumstantial role. It has no subtypes. It relates to the question 'In respect of what?', and it is typically introduced by prepositional expressions such as 'concerning', 'in respect of', 'with respect to', 'so far as . . . is concerned'. We give a couple of examples at [49] and [50] below.

[49] *So far as Frank is concerned* there is a complete biography contained within the book   [E11: 178]

[50] It is our leanest Spring *in this respect* for ten busy years   [E15: 166]

In cases where a RESPECT circumstance is introduced other than by an expression containing 'respect' or 'concerning', it may usually be paraphrased by 'with respect to. . .'. For example, in [51] the RESPECT circumstance is 'talking of jobs', which may be rephrased as 'with respect to jobs'.

[51] Talking of jobs, he wanted to know whether the police had got any nearer to solving the crime
                                                                          [L14: 69]

The RESPECT circumstance provides a point of reference for the proposition in which it is placed. We may summarise this circumstantial role quite simply as:

[52] RESPECT – Respect (In respect of what?)

[*Exercise 3*]

Contingency

By contrast with RESPECT the semantic category of CONTINGENCY has an important circumstantial role, with a number of subtypes expressing various kinds of contingent circumstance, including **Cause**, **Reason**, **Purpose**, **Result**, **Condition** and **Concession**. Many of these types of CONTINGENCY are related to each other, differing only in perspective. For example, CAUSE, REASON and PURPOSE are all related to the question 'Why?' but answer it in slightly differing ways. PURPOSE is also related to RESULT, and CONDITION and CONCESSION are related, as we shall see.

CAUSE refers to a circumstance of CONTINGENCY which expresses an objectively identifiable cause or motive for an action or event. REASON, on the other hand, expresses a relatively personal or subjective view of a Contingency. PURPOSE includes a goal element in its expression of Contingency: it is a reason formulated in the terms of an intended outcome. The examples at [53] to [55] below illustrate respectively CAUSE, REASON and PURPOSE CONTINGENCY.

[53] The hand-over, due in September, was delayed *because of the Berlin crisis* [A05: 58]

[54] The play has since been banned in Eire *because of its outspoken nature* [A44: 124]

[55] She had paid a £50 deposit *so that he could have one for his birthday* [A35:197]

The CAUSE circumstance of CONTINGENCY in [53] is introduced by the preposition *because of*, and so is the REASON circumstance in [54], showing how closely related they are and how difficult it may sometimes be to distinguish them. The difference may be illustrated by the fact that we can paraphrase [53] as [56], but we could not paraphrase [54] in a similar way, but rather as [57].

[56] The Berlin crisis was the cause of the delay to the hand-over

[57] The outspoken nature of the play was the reason for its ban in Eire

The 'Berlin crisis' represents an objective cause of the 'delay', while the 'outspoken nature of the play' refers rather to a subjective reason for the 'ban'. The clause introduced by *so that* in [54] expresses a PURPOSE circumstance, but it could also be seen as a reason for 'paying a deposit', though with the added reference to a goal. It may be paraphrased by 'with the purpose that'.

The conjunction *so that* may also be used to introduce a RESULT circumstance of Contingency, as in [58].

[58] A shell dropped close, shattering a soldier's arm, *so that it hung by a thread* [F23: 128]

Here the *so that* clause could not be construed as a purpose of the action, but could be paraphrased rather by 'with the result that'. Similarly, this circumstance cannot be questioned by 'Why?', as may the first three types of CONTINGENCY, including PURPOSE. A RESULT Contingency answers the question 'With what result?', and it may be introduced by *so*, as well as by *so that*, as in [59].

> [59] The weather's getting chilly now, *so I'm going home*   [F12: 88]

Again, this is shown to be a RESULT CONTINGENCY because a paraphrase is possible by means of the periphrastic conjunction 'with the result that'.

We will turn now to the final two types of Contingency circumstance: **CONDITION** and **CONCESSION**, illustrated by [60] and [61] respectively.

> [60] Most British farmers will not be adversely affected *if Britain joins the Market*   [A21: 84]
> [61] *Despite the glitter and the globe-trotting*, she has kept a shrewd eye on the family business   [A37: 66]

CONDITIONS are typically expressed by clauses introduced by the conjunction *if*, and they answer the question 'Under what conditions?' There is a relationship between the Contingency circumstance of CONDITION and that of RESULT, in that a CONDITION may be viewed as an expression of the circumstances in which a particular result might have been achieved. Thus, in [60] the condition that 'Britain joins the Market' will achieve the result that 'British farmers will not be adversely affected'.

CONCESSION is related to CONDITION: it is a kind of disclaimer, expressing a condition that may obtain but has no effect on the result achieved. Thus in [61] 'glitter' and 'globe-trotting' occurred, but 'she' was still able to 'keep a shrewd eye on the family business'. CONCESSIONS may be seen as answers to the question 'Despite what conditions?'. They are typically introduced by the preposition *despite*, or by the conjunction *though*, as in [62].

> [62] Mr Harvey is extremely successful in his aims, *though he creates enemies in sport and in Fleet Street*
>   [A07: 187]

CONCESSIONS may also be seen as causes that might have obtained, and, had they operated, would have achieved a different result: the 'glitter and the globe-trotting' might have affected her ability to 'keep a shrewd eye on the family business'. It will be apparent, therefore, that there are a number of interrelationships between these different types of CONTINGENCY circumstance.

We will summarise the types of CONTINGENCY by means of the diagram at [63].

[63]
```
                      ┌Cause (Why? What cause?)
                      ├Reason (Why? For what reason?)
                      ├Purpose (Why? What for?)
CONTINGENCY ──────────┤
                      ├Result (With what result?)
                      ├Condition (Under what conditions?)
                      └Concession (Despite what conditions?)
```

Degree

This final semantic role of circumstance relates to the expression in English of the degree to which something happens or is the case. There are three broad types of Degree. The first is **Amplification**, illustrated at [64] below, which refers to a greater than neutral or a 'high' degree. The second type of Degree is **Diminution**, illustrated at [65], which refers to a less than neutral or a 'low' degree. The third is **Measure**, illustrated at [66], which implies neither a high nor a low degree.

[64] *Increasingly* arts graduates are being taken on as teachers without having any training   [B27: 130]

[65] The problems involved have *not* been *adequately* thought out   [B12: 85]

[66] It is not therefore possible to lower fares *appreciably*   [B10: 125]

High degree, or AMPLIFICATION, is signalled in [64] by *increasingly*; in [65] low degree, or DIMINUTION, is signalled by *not adequately*; and the signal of 'MEASURE' in [66] is *appreciably*. The circumstance of DEGREE can be viewed as an answer to the question 'How much?'

The adverbs *much* and *a little* may perhaps be seen at the representative expressions of AMPLIFICATION and DIMINUTION respectively, as in [67] and [68]:

[67] I shall look forward to it *very much*   [K10: 10]
[68] Julie tried to joke *a little* and then Kate came back
                                                    [K17:137]

With private states of emotion the adverb *badly* is typically used for AMPLIFICATION, e.g.

[69] He wanted *badly* to tell him how sorry he was for
     the hard, offhand way he had sometimes behaved
     to him   [K06: 135]

A further example of MEASURE, with the adverb *sufficiently*, is given at [70]:

[70] Mamma, poor darling, has *sufficiently* roused
     herself from her grief to be concerned for us
                                                    [K13: 187]

We may summarise the types of Degree circumstance with the following diagram:

[71]   ┌Amplification
        DEGREE (How much?)────────┤Diminution
                                  └Measure

[*Exercise 4*]

Adverbs

While situation types are particularly associated with the word-class of verbs (Chapter 1) and participants with that of nouns (Chapter 2), circumstances are not clearly associated with any one word-class. Most often, though, a circumstance is expressed by means of an adverb or a preposition, together with any other words that may accompany them. We will consider adverbs in this section, and prepositions below.

–ly adverbs

A glance through any dictionary will reveal that the items given the label 'adv' represent a rather heterogeneous class of words. It will be useful to us, for the purposes of this chapter, to distinguish three sets of adverbs. The first and largest of the sets contains adverbs which typically, though not exclusively, end in –ly and are derived from adjectives by means of this suffix.

[72] *adjective*   *adverb*
      faint   faintly
      frequent   frequently
      slow   slowly
      spiteful   spitefully
      sufficient   sufficiently

Adverbs belonging to this set most commonly express the PROCESS circumstance of MANNER. Thus, *slowly* implies 'in a slow manner', *spitefully* 'in a spiteful manner', and so on. But this is not the exclusive use of the –ly adverbs. We have seen *frequently* used to express the TEMPORAL circumstance of FREQUENCY, e.g. in the example at [32] (compare also *usually, generally, commonly*); and the example at [70] illustrates the use of *sufficiently* to express the DEGREE circumstance of MEASURE.

Other adverbs belonging to this set are derived from nouns by means of the suffixes –wise, –ward/–wards and –ways, e.g. in the adverbs *clockwise, skyward, eastwards, sideways*, etc., which express the LOCATIVE circumstance of DIRECTION, e.g. in

[73] From Frankfurt this useful insect has spread *eastwards* to Brno in Czechoslovakia and *westwards* as far as Fontainebleau   [E07: 32]

[74] She usually went upstairs heavily, lifting her knees *sideways* as if her feet were weighted   [K06: 68]

The suffix –wise has also come to be used more extensively in recent times to derive adverbs which express the RESPECT circumstance, e.g. *weatherwise* = 'in respect of the weather' or *familywise* = 'with respect to the family', 'as far as the family is concerned'. The example at [75] is taken from the *Longman Concise English Dictionary*.

[75] *Careerwise* it's a good idea

Simple adverbs

The second set of adverbs that we want to consider is a restricted group of mainly LOCATIVE and TEMPORAL adverbs, which have a simple (i.e. non-derived) form. The TEMPORAL adverbs in this group include

[76] always just never now often soon then

These adverbs may express TEMPORAL POSITION (*just, now, soon, then*) or FREQUENCY (*always, never, often*). We might also include the following TEMPORAL POSITION adverbs in this group:

[77] yesterday today tomorrow

These adverbs, though, are a little different in that they are sometimes used like nouns, e.g. in 'yesterday's paper', 'tomorrow's problems', where the *'s* genitive case marker suggests a noun status (see Chapter 2). Whereas circumstances are usually positioned peripherally in a sentence, at the beginning, or more commonly at the end, the adverbs at [76] generally occur within a sentence, especially those relating to FREQUENCY, e.g.

[78] They had *always* succeeded in the past   [K14: 163]

Other items in this set of simple adverbs include the DEGREE words *much* and *little* (though these may also belong to the word-classes of pronoun and determinative), the PROCESS adverbs *thus* and *so*, and the LOCATIVE words *here* and *there*. Some of these items have a substitute function; they are the adverb equivalent of pronouns. We might call them **pro-adverbs**, though they are more accurately 'pro-circumstances', since they substitute not only for adverbs but for prepositional expressions and even for clauses as well. *Here* and *there* are LOCATIVE pro-adverbs, *now* and *then* are TEMPORAL pro-adverbs, and *thus* and *so* are PROCESS pro-adverbs, e.g.

[79] Charlie and he sometimes went *there* for a meal
          and a dance   [K07: 197]

[80] Yes, I promise I'll give you an answer *then*
[K18: 120]

[81] To do so would reduce her bride-price and would *thus* be an injustice to her parents [K29: 109]

The item *there* in [79] presumably refers to a restaurant or other eating-place that has already been mentioned. Similarly in [80], *then* refers to a future time POSITION which has been under discussion. In [81] *thus* stands as a pro-adverb of a PROCESS circumstance for 'reduce her bride-price', i.e. 'an injustice to her parents' would be committed by 'reducing her bride-price'.

Adverb particles

The final set of adverbs we need to consider in this chapter is a restricted group of words referring mainly to the LOCATIVE circumstances of POSITION and DIRECTION. Typical members of this group are

[82] in   out   on   off   up   down   above   below
     before   after

Adverb particles of this type may often be viewed as a kind of abbreviated expression of a LOCATIVE circumstance, e.g.

[83] Have you let the cat out?
[84] Why did you climb up?

Usually the interpretation is possible either from the generally understood situational context (e.g. in [83] *out* means 'out of the house'), or from some previous sentence in the discourse or text (e.g. in [84] *up* relates to a place under discussion or where the questioner is currently positioned – 'up the tree' or 'up onto the wall'). The perspective of 'current position' is also implied in examples [85] and [86].

[85] There's another bus behind (i.e. this one)
[86] I've told you all this before (i.e. this moment/now)

Example [86] also illustrates that adverb particles may

express TEMPORAL POSITION as well as LOCATIVE POSITION, as in [85].

Another important function of adverb particles is to combine with a verb word to compose a **phrasal verb**. In many phrasal verbs the adverb particle retains its LOCATIVE meaning, e.g.

[87] take away   kneel down   send in   throw out

In others the combination has led to fusion and the phrasal verb now means something other than the sum of the meanings of its parts, e.g.

[88] give in (= submit)   take off (= mimic)
     carry on (= continue)   let down (= disappoint)

These two types of phrasal verb probably represent the end-points of a gradation from 'literal' [87] to 'idiomatic' [88], with many phrasal verbs placed somewhere in between, e.g.

[89] slow down/up   join in   stand out   blow up

It is their inclusion in phrasal verbs which has earned these adverbs the name of 'particle', which implies that they do not have a clear status as independent words.

Prepositions

Prepositions are used to realise nearly all of the types of circumstance which we have discussed in this chapter. Prepositions cannot occur on their own, they are accompanied; usually they are followed by another item, most often a noun. The term 'preposition', however, reflects the relationship in reverse; i.e. the preposition is 'put in front of' (pre-posed to) the noun. It is the preposition, though, which is the primary realisation of the circumstantial meaning and may therefore be seen as the central item in a 'prepositional phrase', e.g.

[90] in the garden   (LOCATIVE POSITION)
     after dinner   (TEMPORAL POSITION)
     despite the weather (CONTINGENCY CONCESSION)
     with a paintbrush   (PROCESS INSTRUMENT)

Having said this, there are many prepositions which may express more than one type of circumstance, and in these cases it is the following noun, or the more general context, which provides the interpretation, e.g. for *on*, *through*, *for*

[91] on the roof (LOCATIVE)
        – on Saturday (TEMPORAL)
      through the forest (LOCATIVE)
        – through the night (TEMPORAL)
      for three weeks (TEMPORAL)
        – for washing up the dishes (PURPOSE)

Locative prepositions

We will now review briefly the relationships between circumstances and prepositions, to illustrate both the range of circumstances expressed by prepositions and the range of words that belong to the word-class of preposition. Let us begin with prepositions expressing LOCATIVE circumstances. Prepositions expressing LOCATIVE POSITION include

[92] at   near   on   above   against   below   beside
     among   behind   in front of   inside   outside
     over   under

For example, 'inside and outside the vessel' in [93] and 'behind him' in [94]:

[93] By that time three-quarters of the men were hard
      at work inside and outside the vessel   [M05: 160]
[94] They followed the beaming Dan aboard, taking
      seats some rows behind him   [M01: 93]

Prepositions expressing LOCATIVE DIRECTION include

[95] Source: from   off   out of
     Path: down   past   round   across   along
              between   through
     Goal: into   to   towards   onto   over   under

For example, 'along the country highway' in [96] and 'from its hiding-place' in [97]:

[96] The tractor roared along the country highway at
      full throttle   [L03: 172]

> [97] He withdrew the tin box from its hiding-place
> [L04: 98]

Prepositions expressing LOCATIVE DISTANCE include

> [98] as far as   for

For example, 'as far as the cliff path' in [99]:

> [99] Chased him as far as the cliff path – and then lost
> him   [L16: 192]

Temporal prepositions

We will find that a number of the prepositions which we have identified as being associated with LOCATIVE circumstances are also used for expressing TEMPORAL circumstances: there are certain parallels between spatial and temporal orientation. Prepositions expressing TEMPORAL POSITION include

> [100] at   on   in   before   after

For example, 'on Monday' in [101] and 'in the morning' in [102]:

> [101] He went to the British Museum on Monday
> [L02:160]
> [102] We'll ring up the airport in the morning and get
> our reservations   [L05: 44]

Prepositions expressing TEMPORAL DURATION include

> [103] Orientation: from   since   until   up to
> General: during   for   throughout
> between

For example, 'until the evening' in [104] and 'during this period' in [105]:

> [104] It would probably last until the evening, he
> thought as he shaved   [L11: 165]
> [105] During this period he came in contact with no
> one   [L24: 154]

Circumstances of TEMPORAL FREQUENCY are not usually expressed by means of prepositions, but rather by means of adverbs, e.g. *often*, *usually*, or noun phrases (see below), e.g. *every day*, *six times*.

Process and Respect prepositions

The circumstances relating to space and time have a much larger number of prepositions associated with them than the other circumstances. In the case of PROCESS circumstances, we noted in our discussion of adverbs above that MANNER is usually expressed by means of an *−ly* adverb. For the other PROCESS and RESPECT circumstances the range of prepositions is quite limited. Prepositions expressing PROCESS circumstances include

[106] MANNER: in . . . manner (e.g. 'in a
                                  foolish manner') like   with
          MEANS: by   by means of
          INSTRUMENT: with   without
          AGENTIVE: by

For example, INSTRUMENT 'with his teeth' in [107], and MANNER 'with erratic and reckless fury' and AGENTIVE 'by a team of Sikhs' in [108]:

[107] Captain Cordora made a little clicking sound
          with his teeth   [N19: 202]
[108] They were driven with erratic and reckless fury
          by a team of Sikhs   [N11: 158]

Prepositions expressing the RESPECT circumstance are mostly phrasal and include

[109] in respect of   with respect to   with regard to
          concerning   with reference to   as for

For example, 'with regard to the refereeing' in [110]:

[110] With regard to the refereeing, the Polish official
          seemed to go out of his way to stop the
          exchanges on the slightest pretext when the
          action was getting exciting   [E17: 17]

Contingency prepositions

As we noted when we discussed contingency earlier in the chapter, some of the types of contingency are usually expressed by means of clauses, e.g. CONDITION by an *if*-clause, PURPOSE by a *so that* or *in order to* clause – which we will be discussing below. Prepositions expressing CONTINGENCY include

[111] CAUSE/REASON: because of   out of   from
through   for
on account of

PURPOSE: for (e.g. 'This machine is for washing dishes')

CONCESSION: despite   in spite of
notwithstanding

For example, 'in spite of or because of the confession' in [112] and 'on account of her remarkable likeness. . .' in [113]:

[112] In spite of or because of the confession Nan was feeling better   [K18: 21]
[113] A large part of her father's fondness for her was on account of her remarkable likeness to the mother she had hardly known   [N28: 128]

DEGREE circumstances are usually expressed by adverbs and there are no prepositions regularly associated with them. Prepositions are, though, clearly a very important means of expressing elements with a circumstantial role in a proposition. We need to consider finally two further ways by which circumstances are realised grammatically: noun phrases, which form a relatively minor way; and certain types of clauses, which are more important.

Noun phrases

For a limited number of circumstances, mainly TEMPORAL, we may use a noun with its accompanying words, i.e. a noun phrase (see Chapter 5). All three types of

TEMPORAL circumstance may in fact be expressed by a noun phrase, e.g.

[114] POSITION: last Thursday   that afternoon
                    next week
      DURATION: several years
                    the whole summer   all year
      FREQUENCY: each evening   every Friday
                    many times

Some of the POSITION phrases could alternatively be introduced by the preposition *on* (e.g. 'on that afternoon') and the DURATION phrases by the preposition *for* (e.g. 'for several years'). It is useful to see these expressions in context, and a couple of example sentences are given at [115] and [116].

[115] *The following Friday* I moved out of my flat
                                              [L07: 150]

[116] *All day* they were tormented by cruel, relentless
      sun   [N20: 66]

The only other circumstance that is regularly expressed by means of a noun phrase is LOCATIVE DISTANCE, where a number of quite restricted phrases involving nouns of measurement are used, e.g.

[117] several miles   a thousand feet   a long way

These may alternatively be introduced by the preposition *for* (as with TEMPORAL DURATION phrases), e.g. 'for a thousand feet'; though the meaning is different (compare 'She ran 100 metres' and 'She ran for 100 metres'). A contextualised example is given at [118].

[118] The lane skirted the quarry, leading downhill *for*
      perhaps another hundred yards before the hedges
      gave way on the one side to a high wall
                                              [L09: 32]

Clauses

A clause represents the grammatical expression of a proposition which is contained within another proposition. As grammatical expressions of propositions, clauses are equivalent to sentences (see Chapter 6), except for their 'dependent' status, as against the 'independent' status of sentences. But clauses also have a greater variety of forms than sentences. Adverbial clauses are discussed in detail in Chapter 8.

One function of clauses is to express certain types of circumstance, especially circumstances of CONTINGENCY, though also some TEMPORAL circumstances. Such clauses are usually introduced by a conjunction, e.g. *because*, *so that*, which indicates the type of circumstance being expressed. TEMPORAL clauses include those of POSITION introduced by the conjunctions *when*, *before*, *after* and *while*, those of DURATION introduced by *since* and *until* for backward and forward Orientation, respectively. Clauses introduced by *while* may on occasions represent a circumstance of GENERAL DURATION. Sentences containing TEMPORAL clauses are exemplified at [119] to [121]:

> [119] *When* you come back, find the stores and equipment sheets and bring them here
> [M05: 80]
> [120] Tom Dreyfus had a job on the machines in the Secretariat *while* Sally sulked at home
> [M02: 84]
> [121] The grub of the tigerfly is not a tigerfly *until* it changes
> [M06: 32]

CONTINGENCY clauses include those of: REASON introduced by the conjunction *because*, PURPOSE introduced by the conjunctions *so that*, *in order that/to* and *so as to*, RESULT introduced by *so that* or *so*, CONDITION introduced by *if* or *unless*, and CONCESSION introduced by *though* or *although*. CONTINGENCY clauses are exemplified in the sentences given at [122] to [125].

[122] She was standing halfway up the stairs, *so that* her
      head was on the level of his feet   [K06: 65]
[123] 'The opinion in the country,' Fritz said bitterly,
      'is that I am urging my father to abdicate, *in order*
      that I may step into his shoes'   [K13: 29]
[124] *Unless* my father is pacified, that is what it will
      come to   [K13: 69]
[125] *Although* neither of them wished to follow the
      sightseers, there seemed no alternative
                                                  [K04: 15]

[*Exercise 5*]

Grammatically in our discussion of circumstances we
have gone beyond the simple word-classes of adverb and
preposition announced in the title of this chapter. Prepositions, by definition, imply the presence of other items to
accompany them – principally nouns; and we have talked of
'noun phrases', i.e. nouns together with accompanying
elements, as well as of 'clauses' – whole propositions –
which also serve to express the semantic roles of circumstance.

In these first three chapters we have, though, identified
four main classes of word which bear the main semantic
load of sentences as expressions of propositions: verbs,
representing situation types; nouns, representing participants; adverbs and prepositions, representing circumstances.
In the next two chapters we investigate the ways in which
verbs and nouns in particular may be further specified by
other words which may accompany them.

Exercises

Exercise 1

Identify the LOCATIVE circumstances in the following
propositions and say what type of LOCATIVE each one is
(i.e. Position, Direction – Source, Path, Goal – or Distance).

1. Sam will have to come out of his kennel   [L01: 148]

2. The tumbler rose the whole way and the lock snapped open [N08:20]
3. He walked slowly back to the little side gallery which had been his prison [L03: 57]
4. Dan was lying on a long bench in the breakfast nook [M01: 30]
5. Marching out of the cabin he set forth towards the bow [M05: 110]
6. They were outside Santa Maria degli Angeli [K04: 123]
7. Rollison moved with astonishing rapidity through the crowds towards the little Frenchman [L20: 132]
8. Why had they troubled to bring her body all the way from Trento? [N01: 99]
9. We came to it riding muleback along the wooded slopes [M03: 132]
10. I got out, walked to the mouth of the alley and stood back under a shop awning waiting for him [N22: 38]

Exercise 2

Identify the TEMPORAL circumstances in the following propositions and say what type of TEMPORAL each one is (i.e. Position, Duration – Forward/Backward Orientation, General – or Frequency).

1. On a bright unclouded morning a few days after the visit to the Doria palace, the cardinal's coach left the villa [K04: 72]
2. She wouldn't get the telephone call until tomorrow [L05: 61]
3. That made me think, not once but three times [N11: 94]
4. Since his last stay there Alan had had it redecorated to suit the taste of his English patron [L11: 42]
5. He telephoned her early one morning, and asked her if she would come and have a drink with him that evening [K08: 90]
6. The Chancellor was repeating an argument which he had already developed for an hour before lunch [K03: 166]
7. 'Yes, of course,' they said every morning at the airline

office. 'It will stop tonight, planes will certainly be leaving tomorrow'   [K22: 116]

8. He felt its contours carefully, and determined to keep it there all evening   [K27: 61]
9. The process could, and often did, take several years
[R02: 11]
10. After a long debate far into the night we decided to leave it till morning and then decide   [L15: 103]

Exercise 3

Identify the PROCESS and RESPECT circumstances in the following propositions and say for each PROCESS circumstance what type it is (i.e. Manner, Means, Instrument or Agentive).

1. He stared at her blankly   [M01: 5]
2. The drinks were served by two young Malay girls
[K02: 84]
3. All human activity, as far as its final significance is concerned, is like feeding on the wind   [D03: 102]
4. McNaught consolingly lowered a hand   [M05: 133]
5. Cricket is an open-air game played with ball, bats and wickets   [B05: 82]
6. My attention was drawn to the above by a friend
[B24: 191]
7. The north of England is strong in this respect
[F42: 89]
8. My efforts to promote new trade were actively supported by the British Ambassadors   [B09: 205]
9. He dispersed a Communist rebellion with a whiff of grapeshot   [B16: 14]
10. Mr Lloyd has done this superbly with his budget
[B08: 8]

Exercise 4

Identify the CONTINGENCY and DEGREE circumstances in the following propositions and say for each what type of CONTINGENCY or DEGREE it is (i.e. Cause, Reason, Purpose, Result, Condition or Concession for Contingency, and Amplification, Diminution or Measure for Degree).

1. Chelsea moved well at the start, despite Villa's seventh-minute lead [A22: 83]
2. Dealing was banned on Friday because of lack of information about the bidder, who still has not made himself known [A13: 174]
3. I would write to the Bishop and if he told me to marry them I would have to consider resigning [A24: 229]
4. Conditions for factory workers and other trades have greatly improved, so why not for the landworker? [B24: 170]
5. I rushed downstairs telling Julie we were just playing a game, so that she would not get upset [A12: 45]
6. The complete course takes three of these sessions, so that this year was the second year of the course [A17: 104]
7. It's an uncomfortable condition because of the irritation [F31: 74]
8. Would it not be possible slightly to change the date of the Chelsea Flower Show so that it was not dominated year after year by the azaleas and rhododendrons? [B16: 124]
9. Not many people change sides during an election, though a little change can mean much [F10: 132]
10. I was uncertain whether I could control my voice sufficiently to produce the right sort of cry [K15: 93]

Exercise 5

Look at the following sentences, taken from *The Guardian* for 21 June 1988, and identify the circumstances. Say what grammatical form (adverb, prepositional expression, noun phrase, clause) each one has and what type of circumstance (LOCATIVE, TEMPORAL, etc.) it is.

1. A way has been cleared for big increases in the number of lorries travelling to and from Britain and the other European Community member states after 1992
2. Ethnic violence flared up again in Armenia over the weekend
3. Save today if you want more tax cuts tomorrow
4. By 1979, a high-speed, longer-range version had reached 300 mph on the Miyazaki test track by using superconductors

5. In the morning, tough black sports cars nip angrily around its snaking corners

6. At least 250 people were injured, mostly by rubber bullets, and ten were killed by the police

7. At least another 50 people are on death row in South Africa for their alleged involvement in political activities

8. They had previously pitched camp on a stretch of woodland despite injunctions granted to owners of land around the monument

9. Many travellers had hoped they would be allowed to walk peacefully to the stones and be admitted at the last moment by English Heritage as happened last year, after police reluctance to move in on the large woodland camp in Cholderton

10. As for the damage the Government claimed would result from publication here, Mr Gray said much of the evidence produced by Lord Armstrong . . . was couched in generalities. . .

CHAPTER 4

Specifying States, Events and Actions: Tense, aspect and modality

In Chapter 1 we generalised about the kinds of things which we talk about by introducing the notion of situation types. We recognised three broad types of situation – STATE, EVENT, ACTION – with various subtypes. States, events and actions are represented in the grammar of the language by verbs. When we use a verb in a sentence there are a number of additional pieces of information which we may or must specify. For example, we have to choose whether to use a verb in the present tense or the past tense (see Chapter 1); it must appear in one or the other. In this chapter we are going to look at these specifications of states, events and actions. They have broadly to do with the setting of situations in time, and with the possibility or necessity of situations.

Time

Time is an essential element in probably all actions and events. We specify when something took place relative to the time of speaking or writing, and we may specify other time-related factors, such as whether an event (or action) was instantaneous or lasted over a period of time. States, too, are specified for time, though some may be considered to be 'timeless', e.g.

> [1] Daffodils have a trumpet-shaped flower and are yellow

Equally, some events may be regarded as 'timeless' in that they express an unending regularity, e.g.

[2] Daffodils flower in the spring
[3] Water boils at 100°C at sea-level

Few actions can be 'timeless', not least given the mortality of human beings, unless we predicate them of humans (or animals) in general, or of God, as for example in the well-known harvest hymn:

[4] We plough the fields and scatter
    The good seed on the land,
    But it is fed and watered
    By God's almighty hand;
    He sends the snow in winter. . .

Here then 'ploughing' and 'scattering' are actions that 'we' humans do regularly, as 'feeding', 'watering' and 'sending' are God's regular actions – and are in that sense timeless, though they obviously take place in time. But then so do the events in [2] and [3], and states like [1] are also bounded by time.

Present

We usually orientate ourselves in time with reference to the moment of speaking or writing. For us that moment is 'now' or the **present**. We look backwards from that moment into the **past** and forwards from that moment into the **future**.

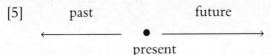

[5]   past   future

←—————————— ● ———————————→

                    present

We may illustrate these time 'zones' with the following examples:

[6] Martha *had* a headache (yesterday)
[7] Martha *has* a headache (now)
[8] Martha *will have* a headache (tomorrow)

According to the diagram at [5], 'present' is represented as a point on the time continuum: the present is ever fleeting, always becoming past. But the example at [7] implies a state which lasts longer than a fleeting moment. In reality we usually experience 'now' as a period of time that spans the 'moment of speaking', but which includes time just past and perhaps time about to become present as well.

There are certain kinds of commentary that do give a moment by moment account of present time actions and events – for example, the 'ball by ball' cricket commentaries on the radio:

> [9] Marshall comes in, bowls, and he's out, caught behind!

Such an association of present time with the present moment is unusual and is more or less restricted to sports and some other kinds of commentary, and to the language of demonstration, e.g. of cookery:

> [10] Now I add the flour and egg, and stir gently

Actions and events which take place in the present are generally conceived as being more like the state at [7], that is, as including the present moment within their time span, but not restricted to it, e.g.

> [11] Sheila and Hugh are fixing the boat   [K17: 19]
> [12] Very likely the olive trees are burning too
>   [K12: 26]

You will notice that the form of the verb, 'are fixing' in [11] and 'are burning' in [12], is different from that of the verbs expressing momentary actions in [9] and [10]. We will discuss these differences later in this chapter.

Past and future

The **past** represents a time span that looks back from the present moment 'now', while the **future** looks forward from the present. That, at least, is how we conceive of time in our culture, and how we represented it spatially in [5]: the past is where we are coming from – it is behind us – and the future is where we are going to – it is before us. We have incorporated this spatial perspective on time in sayings like those at [13] and [14].

> [13] Let's leave the past behind us
> [14] You've got your whole future in front of you

In some languages and cultures, not only may there not be

the same attention to time as in English and other European languages, but the spatial metaphors of 'behind' for past and 'in front' for future may be reversed. This has a certain logic, since there is a sense in which you can 'see' the past, whereas the future is not yet visible.

In English the notions of past and future time contrast with the present in that they represent spans of time rather than a moment in time. By past time we may be referring to a time just pre-present or we may be referring to a time remote from the present. Similarly, future may be just post-present or be located remotely in future time:

past   pre-present   post-present   future

←————————···—————— • —————————···—————→

present

These contrasts are illustrated at [15] and [16] for the past, and at [17] and [18] for the future.

[15] I am fifteen and have just completed my first real
     story   [K25: 11]
[16] My father built this road almost thirty years ago
                                                    [N14: 158]
[17] I do not even defend what I am about to tell you
                                                    [G09: 118]
[18] Maybe sometime later he will forgive you com-
     pletely   [N19: 215]

Pre-present is expressed by 'have just' in [15], and post-present by 'am about to' in [17].

Past time differs from future time in that we can probably 'see' further into the past than we can into the future, and we can talk about the past with more certainty than we can about the future. Much of what we want to say about the future is hedged about with qualifications and expressions of uncertainty, taking us into the realm of modality (see below). There may be uncertainty associated with the past – we can dispute about what may or may not have happened – but in general what we say about the past we state with a fair degree of certitude.

Point and period

As our discussion so far has implied, when we place actions, events and states in time, we express not just their location in the present, past or future. We may also express how the situation is distributed in time, or rather how we view the situation as distributed. We may choose to regard actions or events as taking up only a moment of time, as in [9], or we may view actions or events as lasting through a period of time, as in [11] and [12].

Some situations are inherently 'momentary' or 'durative'. States, for example, usually last for a period of time. Some actions and events take up the briefest moment of time, and we identified in Chapter 1 special situation types of MOMENTARY EVENT and MOMENTARY ACT, e.g. *trip*, *knock*, *catch*, *hit*. Other actions and events are inherently durative, for example ACTIVITIES and GOINGS-ON (like *sing*, *wash*, *celebrate*), but we may choose to regard them as taking place at a point in time. In [9], for instance, *come* and *bowl* may be categorised as ACTIVITIES, but here, in this discourse style of commentary, they are represented as MOMENTARY ACTS. Similarly, in referring to actions and events in past time, we may express them as either **punctual** (taking place at a point in time) or **durative** (taking place over a period of time). Compare *blow* in [19] and [20].

[19] It rained and blew for five days without stopping
                                                    [K22: 96]
[20] The whistle was blowing furiously   [K27: 106]

MOMENTARY ACTS and EVENTS may also be viewed as lasting through a period of time, e.g. in [21] and [22] below. In this case the MOMENTARY ACTS or EVENTS are seen as being repeated through a period of time, in a succession of moments. This is often called **iterative**.

[21] His heart was beating fast   [K04: 160]
[22] Now they were banging the stretched hide shields
                                                    [K09: 180]

Iteration may refer either to the succession of MOMENT-
ARY EVENTS or ACTS, as in [21] and [22], or to the
repetition of an ACTIVITY or GOINGS-ON in the nature
of an habitual action or event, e.g. indicated by *used to* in
[23] and by *would* in [24]:

[23] 'I used to play rugger,' said Armstrong   [K03: 83]
[24] The net curtain would stir and part very suddenly
     and somewhere in the room the ball would thud
     and then roll   [K23: 111]

Definite and indefinite

Besides indication of location in time (present, past, future)
and distribution through time (punctual or durative), we
can in English specify whether an action or event occurred
at some definite time or merely within some time period on
an unspecified occasion or series of occasions. The contrast
may be most clearly drawn for past time, e.g. in [25] and
[26]:

[25] Your father has met me but once in his life
                                                [K19: 91]
[26] Your father met me yesterday

The example at [25] locates the event in past time, but
leaves the point or period within the past indefinite. The
example at [26], on the other hand, refers to an event taking
place at a definite point in past time, with the point specified
by the adverb *yesterday*. You will notice that the forms of
the verb also differ: *has met* in [25], and *met* in [26].
    In the present we might draw a similar distinction
between [27] and [28]:

[27] Elizabeth is seeing him
[28] Elizabeth sees him on Tuesdays

Both these examples refer to habitual actions. In [27] the
time points within the present period are indefinite; in [28]
they are specified by the prepositional phrase 'on Tuesdays'.
Note that, while the verb forms differ in these examples (*is*

seeing as against *sees*), [28] would be equally possible with *is seeing*, with a slightly different meaning, implying a short-term rather than an established habit. *Sees* would not be possible in [27], however.

Reference to future time may equally be indefinite [29] or definite [30], with the definite reference carried by an adverb or other Temporal circumstance element alone.

[29] We'll be meeting again, no doubt   [N04: 123]
[30] I'll make them ready for you at nine o'clock
                                              [N24: 56]

The assertion at [29] implies 'sometime', while that at [30] specifies the 'sometime' as a definite time – *nine o'clock*.

Orientation

When we make reference to time, our point of orientation is usually the present moment – 'now'. In the spoken mode, this means the moment of speaking, and usually also of hearing. In the written mode it usually means the moment of writing, which is not the same as the moment of reading. For example, if you receive a letter from a friend which relates events that happened 'yesterday', you will have to calculate when 'yesterday' was by referring to the date of the letter. A similar situation may apply in spoken language if the spoken discourse is being recorded for later public transmission or reception by the hearer. In this case, and in the case of some written language, the encoder (speaker or writer) may take into account the displacement in time of the eventual reception of the message and make appropriate adjustments to the time references in the discourse or text.

With 'now' as the point of orientation we have identified two spans of time: before now or up to now, and after now or from now – which we have called 'past' and 'future' (see diagram at [5]). We have also noted that we can conceive of both time spans in terms of 'proximate to now' (pre- and post-present) and 'remote from now' (see examples at [15] to [18]). Another way in which we propose alternative conceptions of time is by shifting the point of orientation to within the past and future spans of time.

'Remote' past time, for example, may be viewed as split into two periods, effected by introducing a past point of orientation:

remote past

```
←——————————— • ——————————— • ——————————→
            past point          present
            of orien-
            tation
```

Consider the following example:

> [31] After he had finished doing so he dropped the
>   helicopter to five hundred feet   [N19: 87]

This sentence contains two propositions, both referring to
past time, but one ('After he had finished doing so')
referring to a time remoter than that in the second
proposition. A point in past time (when 'he dropped the
helicopter to five hundred feet') becomes a point of
orientation for another past time event. [32] gives a further
example in which this is the case:

> [32] Gloria had been waiting at the Hotel Roma when
>   punctually at 6 the call from Alastair came
>   through   [N01: 124]

In this example the past point of orientation is given in the
clause introduced by *when*, and the first proposition refers to
a state of affairs which preceded that point in past time. The
sentences at [31] and [32] are taken from narrative texts,
which are conventionally written in the past tense, that is,
with a past time orientation. It is not surprising therefore
that such texts should exploit the possibilities in English of
relating to each other events of varying remoteness by
means of different verb forms (e.g. *had finished* vs *dropped*).

A past point of orientation may serve not only as a
means of relating situations that are more remote in time,
but also to relate situations that are less remote. Consider
the following example:

> [33] Possibly he'd been responsible for the noise that
>   had woken him, Frank had decided; and now
>   within a short span of time he would have his
>   chance within his grasp. He waited until he heard
>   the door slam   [N09: 101–4]

As a narrative, the point of orientation within the text from
which [33] is taken is past (e.g. *waited*, *heard*). Some events

are indicated as being prior to that point (*'d been, had decided*). And one is indicated as being subsequent to that point (*would have*). The time of situations like *had decided* is sometimes referred to as **past in the past**, and that of situations like *would have* as **future in the past**:

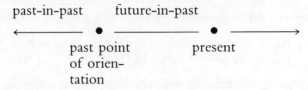

past-in-past   future-in-past

past point of orientation   present

We might expect to find a parallel situation in the future time period, but, as we have noted before, we tend not to make so many distinctions in the future as we do in the past. There is, though, a future point of orientation, which is used to relate future events that are seen as occurring prior to that point. Consider the example at [34]:

> [34] A good example of the advance in education is that there are now twice as many university students as in 1938, and it is anticipated that by 1970 the number will have more than trebled
> [B26: 72]

This sentence was written in 1961 ('now'). The second proposition, beginning with *and*, looks into the future to the year 1970, and then back from that future point of orientation to a situation preceding it – 'will have more than trebled'. The time of this situation is referred to as **past in the future**:

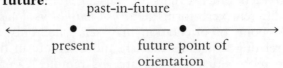

past-in-future

present   future point of orientation

There would appear to be no 'future in the future' corresponding to the 'past in the past'.

[*Exercise 1*]

Tense and aspect

The meanings associated with the notion of 'time', which we have been discussing so far in this chapter, are realised in the grammar of the language by the systems of **tense** and **aspect**. In this section we will consider first of all how tense and aspect are manifested in the forms of the verb. Then we will look more systematically at the relations between verb forms and the meanings we have discussed. Finally, we will comment on some of the relations between tense and aspect on the one hand, and Temporal circumstances and situation types on the other.

Verb forms

In Chapter 1 we noted that the distinction between present and past tense is encoded in the verb word in English by means of an inflection, e.g.

[35] PRESENT   PAST

stay, stays	stayed
swim, swims	swam
think, thinks	thought

Verbs have two present tense forms and one past tense form (except *be*, which has three present tense forms – *am*, *is*, *are* – and two past tense forms – *was*, *were*). For a few verbs the past tense form is identical to one of the present tense forms (e.g. *cut*, *hit*). It is noteworthy that in English there is no future tense manifested by inflections in the verb word. How future time is expressed in English and what the correlations are between tense forms and time meanings will be discussed below.

In addition to the inflectional forms of the verb word, English has a number of periphrastic forms of the verb. In the periphrastic forms the main verb is in one of the non-finite forms (see Chapter 1) and it is preceded by an **auxiliary verb**. One set of periphrastic forms expresses a 'progressive' or 'durative' aspect: they consist of the verb *be* as an auxiliary and the present participle of the main verb, e.g.

[36]   PRESENT PROGRESSIVE   PAST PROGRESSIVE

am/is/are staying	was/were staying
am/is/are swimming	was/were swimming
am/is/are thinking	was/were thinking

Another set of periphrastic forms express a 'perfective' aspect: they consist of *have* as an auxiliary verb and the past participle of the main verb, e.g.

[37]   PRESENT PERFECTIVE   PAST PERFECTIVE

has/have stayed	had stayed
has/have swum	had swum
has/have thought	had thought

The two aspects may combine in the same verb phrase to produce periphrastic forms such as:

[38]   PRESENT PERFECTIVE   PAST PERFECTIVE
       PROGRESSIVE   PROGRESSIVE

has/have been staying	had been staying
has/have been swimming	had been swimming
has/have been thinking	had been thinking

These forms consist of auxiliary *have*, inflected for tense, followed by the past participle form of the auxiliary *be* (because perfective auxiliary *have* is followed by a past participle), followed in turn by the present participle form of the main verb (because progressive auxiliary *be* is followed by a present participle).

We have now identified four forms of the verb phrase in English, which manifest categories from the tense and aspect systems.

[39] 1. simple present/past   stay(s)/stayed
      2. present/past progressive   is/was staying
      3. present/past perfective   has/had stayed
      4. present/past perfective   has/had been
         progressive   staying

You will note that the tense distinction between 'present' and 'past' is always carried by the first item in the verb phrase, whether it is the simple main verb (1) or one of the auxiliaries (2–4).

Meanings and forms

We are now going to bring together the meanings which we discussed in the first part of this chapter with the forms that are summarised at [39], though we shall need to introduce some additional material as well.

Present

We will begin with the notion of 'present' time, which we will take to include all time references that include the present moment within their compass. The most extensive of such references are the 'timeless' states, events and actions, illustrated by the examples at [1] to [4]: they are expressed by verbs in the simple present form. Similarly, temporary states which include the present moment are expressed by simple present forms of verbs, as exemplified by [7] and [40] following (with the state verb *live*).

[40] In Latin America, Jones and Robinson live in a constant state of revolt against each other
[R01: 116]

When we turn to events and actions which take place in present time, we find that the associated verb forms are different from those for states. The simple present is used for commentary and demonstration, as in the examples at [9] and [10], where the action or event is viewed as occupying a moment of time – the present moment. More usually, however, actions and events taking place in present time are expressed by the present progressive, as in [11] and [12], where the action or event is viewed as taking place over a period of time which includes the present moment, or as being in progress at the moment of speaking.

Another kind of action or event which includes the present in its time span is 'habit'. Habit is a type of iterative, expressing a repeated action, as in the following examples:

[41] It only goes when it's wanted   [L11: 10]
[42] He's eating at McDonald's in the evenings

The example at [41], with the simple present verb form (*goes*), refers to a habit which is relatively permanent or established, whereas the habit expressed in [42] with the present progressive verb form (*is eating*) implies that the habit is temporary. You could specify a time limit, such as 'while his wife is in hospital' or 'until his cooker has been mended'. The contrast between permanent habit and temporary habit in the present is realised grammatically by progressive aspect: the temporary habit has a progressive verb form.

Past

We will now turn to the expression of 'past' time. Actions and events that are viewed as occurring immediately before the present moment, in what we have called pre-present time, are expressed by the present perfective form of the verb, usually with an adverb like *just*, as in the example at [15]. Similarly, a state or a habit which began in past time, and is still going on at the present moment of speaking or writing, is expressed by the present perfective form of the verb, e.g.

[43] He *has been* too miserable to think about his future
                                                   [K13: 192]

[44] I *have* often *remembered* Innocencio's dialect version of the song   [K12: 10]

Such states and habits may also be expressed by the present perfective progressive form of the verb, when there is a particular focus on the duration of the state or habit, e.g.

[45] He *may have been feeling* ill for weeks and said nothing   [K06: 101]

[46] They *must have been meeting* fairly often
                                                   [K10: 55]

States, events and actions in the past which are viewed as having no connection with the present but are located at a definite point in past time, are expressed by the simple past verb form, as in the examples at [16] and [19]. To say that a situation is located at a 'point' in past time does not imply that it had no duration, but that the period of time is not under focus. If it is under focus, then the past progressive is used, as in [20] and

[47] I *was looking* down on the beach   [K12: 52]

In narrative texts, e.g. novels or reports, simple past is typically used to narrate the sequence of actions or events, which are then viewed as a series of points in time. The past progressive is often used in narratives for descriptive scene-setting, painting a backdrop against which the action takes place, e.g.

[48] The full moon *was just rising* over the rocks. Then he laid his hand on hers   [P02: 28]

These references to past time are definite. The point or period in time is either expressed by a TEMPORAL circumstance (e.g. 'almost thirty years ago' in [16]), or it may be deduced from the context, because, for example, the action or event is one of a series set in a particular past time context. If reference is to an indefinite point or period in past time, then the present perfective form of the verb is used, as in the examples at [25] and [49] to [52]:

[49] All this *has happened* before   [L12: 24]
[50] He *has done* so many things   [L07: 179]
[51] He *has robbed* me   [L08: 17]
[52] Why *has* he *mortgaged* this ranch?   [L05: 117]

In these cases the time reference is to some point in the period leading up to present time. In [51] and [52] it may be possible to detect what is sometimes called 'current relevance': the implication of these propositions is that a past action ('robbing', 'mortgaging') has consequences for and is relevant to the present state of affairs.

Corresponding to the expression of iteration in present time, we can identify a past habit also. It is most commonly expressed by the invariant auxiliary *used to*, as in the examples at [23] and [53]:

[53] The Caxtons *used to have* their holidays there
                    [L01: 9]

Used to is followed by the base form of the main verb: *play* in [23] and *have* in [53]. Alternatively, past habit is expressed by *would*, as in [24].

Finally in our discussion of the verb forms used to express past time, let us return to narrative, which, we noted earlier, is associated with the simple past. In some contexts, past time narration is made using simple present tense verb forms, what is sometimes called the 'historic present'. This is the tense form that is commonly used to retell the plot of a story, e.g.

> [54] The god Indra *sentences* a heavenly nymph guilty of an illicit love affair to become a mortal and be murdered by a Javanese queen before she *can return* to heaven. She *descends* and *becomes* incarnate in the wife of a Javanese headman. A prince hunting *sees* her and *weds* her, though he *is* betrothed to a princess. . .   [G40: 49–53]

Simple present tense verb forms are also commonly used for retelling narratives in informal conversation. The example at [55] is of someone retelling a dream she has had.

> [55] I *am* in a grocer's shop and just as I *come* out I *see* an aeroplane hovering in the sky. Suddenly it *starts* to fire at me and I *am wounded* in the left arm.
> [F12: 118–20]

The effect of using simple present verb forms for narration, which is essentially the retelling of past events, is to make the story more vivid and immediate. Some novelists use simple present verb forms instead of simple past forms at climaxes in their story, as a way of marking a sequence of events as climactic. There is a well-known example in Charles Dickens' *Tale of Two Cities*, when the condemned hero Darnay is escaping from Paris in a stagecoach:

> [56] The same shadows that *are falling* on the prison, *are falling*, in the same hour of the early afternoon, on the barrier with the crowd about it, when a coach going out of Paris *drives* up to be examined. . . . The papers *are handed* out, and read. . . .   [Dent 1906, reprint 1958, p. 350]

Future

In our discussion of verb forms earlier we did not list any forms for a future tense in English. This is because there are no future inflections of the verb in English, as there are in French (*je parlerai, tu parleras*, etc.). There are in fact a number of expressions for referring to future time in English. Probably the most frequently used expression, and the one which is sometimes regarded as a 'future tense', is the periphrastic form with the auxiliary verb *will*, as in [18] and the following:

[57] I will see you in the morning   [P01: 124]

Will is followed by the base form of the main verb, and it is often contracted to *'ll* in speech and informal writing.

[58] Then we'll go for a stroll along the beach
                                             [P02: 26]

Some speakers, especially in southern Britain, replace *will* by *shall* with the 1st person (*I*, *we*), e.g.

[59] I shall serve them with tomatoes and olives
                                             [P08: 3]

Some speakers will pedantically insist on the *shall/will* distinction, but the use of *shall* for future reference is probably getting less common (compare [30]). The future expression with *will* is often regarded as the most neutral expression of future time in English, but it is not always completely neutral. It may have overtones of prediction [60] or, with 1st and 2nd persons, it may express willingness or intention in addition to simple futurity [61].

[60] Regis Road pavements *will soon be crowded* with
     late-homers   [P01: 85]
[61] I *will be* brief   [P01: 60]

Another common expression of future time, used especially in an informal style of speaking and writing, is *be going to* followed by the base form of the main verb, e.g.

[62] He flew over from Barcelona and *is going to stay*
     two days   [P02: 69]

The meaning overtones of this future expression are said to be 'future fulfilment of the present'. It tends to be used when the future event is seen as relatively close to the present. We noted earlier the expression of immediate future or 'post-present' with the periphrasis *be about to* followed by the base form of the main verb (example at [17]). A further example follows at [63].

[63] What I *am about to relate* passed in a series of flashes
                                             [M03: 74]

In addition to these expressions specifically relating to the future (*will*, *be going to*, *be about to*), we also find the simple present and the present progressive being used with future reference. With these forms, the fact that the future is being referred to is indicated either by the general context or by the presence of an appropriate Temporal circumstance.

> [64] When I *wake* up *tomorrow* let me remember my real name   [N25: 58]
> [65] *Tonight* I *am flying* back to Rome   [N22: 113]

The simple present with future reference is said to have overtones of 'definiteness'. One of its common uses is in timetable announcements:

> [66] The train for Newcastle *departs* from Platform 5 at 10.25

The present progressive is said to have overtones of 'future arising from present arrangement or plan'. This expression of the future may combine with *will* to give a form that has overtones of 'future as a matter of course' (see examples at [29] and [67]).

> [67] I'*ll be joining* you in a minute or two   [P01: 109]

The future action or event is seen as happening in the normal course of events.

Past in past

There are two kinds of meanings associated with the notion of past-in-the-past time, both of which relate to a past point of orientation and both of which are expressed by the same periphrastic verb form – the past perfective. The first kind of meaning relates to the ordering of events relative to each other in past time: one event can be indicated (by means of the past perfective) as occurring prior to another (expressed by the simple past), as in the examples at [31] and [68]:

> [68] It *had passed* him at the temporary bridge over the Tartaro at a few minutes past ten on the previous night   [N01: 76]

The second kind of meaning associated with past-in-the-past is the past orientation equivalent of the present perfective meaning of 'state or habit beginning in the past and lasting up to the present'. With the past perfective the state/habit begins in the remote past and lasts up to the past point of orientation, which is often expressed in a clause introduced by *when*, e.g.

[69] He *had been* with Anna's sister, Adriana, *when* I went to tell her the news   [N22: 10]

As with the present perfective, the focus on the duration of a state or habit may be added with a progressive form, as in the examples at [32] and [70]:

[70] It had gone round and round and then people *had been screaming* and the wheel had come slowly apart   [L06: 123]

Past and future
We have two final meanings to discuss, which link past time and future time. One we have termed 'future in the past', illustrated at [33], where an event looks forward in past time from a past point of orientation. It may be expressed by a periphrastic verb form with auxiliary *would* and the base form of the main verb, as in [33], though this form is rather formal. More commonly, the past form of *be going to* or the past progressive is used to express this meaning, as in [71] and [72]:

[71] No doubt there *was going to be* a return journey
                    [L13: 156]

[72] It was August the eleventh, and Fay *was arriving* from Delhi   [N11: 61]

The other meaning we have termed 'past in the future', illustrated at [34], where an event looks back in future time from a future point of orientation. It is expressed by the periphrastic verb form with the future auxiliary *will* followed by the present perfect (auxiliary *have* followed by past participle) of the main verb. There is a further example at [73].

[73] And if there is one thing certain about this programme, it is that long before the material promises are realised the whole concept *will have become* irrelevant, overtaken by events; or, to use Mr Krushchev's own favourite expression, life

itself *will have shown up* the startling insufficiencies
of his present thinking   [B15: 168–173]

Form and meaning

By way of summary we will now reverse the direction of
our discussion and list the verb forms together with the
meanings (concerned with time) which they typically
express.

simple present	timeless situations, present states, commentary, permanent habit, narrative, future
simple past	definite past
present progressive	present actions/events, temporary present habit, future
past progressive	definite past period, future-in-past
present perfective	pre-present, state/habit up to present, indefinite past (possibly with current relevance)
past perfective	past-in-past, state/habit up to past point
present perfective progressive	state/habit up to present (+ limited duration)
past perfective progressive	state/habit up to past point (+ duration)
used to + main verb	past habit or state
will + main verb	future
will + present perfective	past-in-future
be going to + main verb	future, future-in-past
be about to + main verb	post-present, post-past
would + main verb	future-in-past

Relations with TEMPORAL circumstances

Both the tense/aspect system connected with verbs and
TEMPORAL circumstances are concerned with the location
of situations in time and their distribution through time.

Their function in a proposition is usually complementary. Sometimes the reference to time is made exclusively by means of tense/aspect, e.g. for indefinite past time or for 'timeless' present. In other instances, the TEMPORAL circumstance is essential in order to specify the time reference of the tense/aspect, e.g. for present progressive, whether the reference is to future time as opposed to present time. In yet other instances, the TEMPORAL circumstance makes more specific the point or period of time expressed by tense/aspect, e.g. for definite past or for habit. Consequently, we find that particular kinds of TEMPORAL circumstance are associated with particular tenses/aspects.

Not surprisingly there are particular sets of TEMPORAL expressions for each of the three time zones, e.g.

[74] past: yesterday last week   ten years ago
     present: now   at this moment
     future: tomorrow   next week   in five years

Some TEMPORAL expressions, though, are interpretable as having past or future reference only in the appropriate context. For example, *today* or *this afternoon* may refer to past or future: compare [75] and [76]:

[75] I met them this afternoon   (past)
[76] I'm meeting them this afternoon   (future)

There are also TEMPORAL expressions which are typical of the present perfective meaning of state/habit up to the present, e.g.

[77] since last month   for twelve years

These expressions could not be used with the simple past in its definite past meaning. Other TEMPORAL expressions may be used with both present perfective and simple past, but are interpretable as indefinite or definite past respectively. Some TEMPORAL expressions of this kind are given at [78], with example sentences at [79] and [80].

[78] recently   this week   today
[79] I've only met him today   [P02: 137]
[80] She only arrived today   [P02: 37]

Lastly we may note a correlation between iterative verb meaning and TEMPORAL expressions of frequency, such as

[81] daily   every week   once   six times   often

Such expressions correlate with a number of verb forms, since iteration is realised in several ways and differently in present and past tense. Some verbs are inherently iterative in meaning, like *hammer* or *scratch*, whose iteration may be made specific by a TEMPORAL expression such as *six times*.

[82] I saw you scratch that spot six times

Momentary verbs may be made iterative by being used with a TEMPORAL expression of frequency, e.g. *punch*, *knock*.

[83] They punched him six times

Similarly, habit may be realised in the present by a simple present or present progressive form and in the past by a past progressive or the auxiliary *used to*, often with a TEMPORAL frequency expression, e.g.

[84] They used to meet/were meeting every day in the park
[85] They meet/are meeting every day in the park

Here, then, the TEMPORAL expression either reinforces the habitual meaning (e.g. with *used to*) or indeed creates it (e.g. with present progressive). Both the tense/aspect system and TEMPORAL expressions make a contribution to the signalling of time meanings and relations.

Relations with situation types

The meaning which a verb form may have in a particular context arises not just from the nature of the verb form itself (present or past, progressive or perfective), nor just from the verb form together with the contribution of any associated TEMPORAL circumstances. Another major factor in interpreting the meaning of verb forms, especially progressive aspect, in any proposition is the situation type to which the main verb refers. Take, for example, a TRANSITIONAL EVENT like *arrive*. In the simple present form [86], with an obligatory TEMPORAL, the verb has future (or possibly habitual) meaning. In the present progressive without a TEMPORAL [87] the transition is interpreted as being under way. To indicate that it is complete we use the present perfective form [88], implying 'current relevance'; and to report it as a past event, we use the simple past [89].

[86] The bus arrives at 3 o'clock
[87] The bus is arriving
[88] The bus has arrived
[89] The bus arrived at 3 o'clock

The particular meanings of these forms arise from the fact that *arrive* belongs to the subtype of TRANSITIONAL EVENTS. So, the present progressive means 'in transition', the present perfective means 'transition complete'.

In a broader context, some verbs regularly occur in progressive forms, while others do not. In general, verbs referring to actions and events may have progressive forms, and verbs referring to states may not. You do not, for example, find verbs such as *know* or *like* (private states) or *belong* (quality) or *seem* (temporary state) in the progressive form. There are some exceptions to this generalisation, however. Verbs referring to stance (e.g. *sit, stand, hold*) regularly occur in the progressive with meanings similar to those for activities: compare [90] and [91].

[90] He *stood* near the gas cooker   [K06: 20]
[91] He *was standing* rigidly in the centre of the room
                                                     [K02: 173]

This characteristic of stance verbs identifies them as intermediate in status between state and non-state.

Some of the other types of state verb may also be used in the progressive, usually with rather specialised meanings. For example, *be* in the progressive [92] has the meaning 'are behaving'; *hope* [93] has the overtone of 'tentativeness'; but with bodily sensation verbs like *ache* [94] there is little or no difference in meaning between progressive and simple forms.

[92] 'For once, I'*m being* practical,' he said   [P22: 31]
[93] You'*ll be wanting* a wash   [P21: 117]

[94] His head *was aching* with strain   [P09: 119]

With actions and events we also find that the meaning of the progressive may differ according to the situation type. We saw earlier how the progressive had a specialised meaning with TRANSITIONAL EVENT verbs like *arrive*. In the case of MOMENTARY ACTS and EVENTS like *hit* [95] the progressive implies or focuses on repetition.

[95] Foster *had always been hitting* his native servants
                                                           [N10: 41]

For processes like *grow* [96] the progressive focuses on the process being under way.

[96] She *was growing* cold and numb with shock
                                                           [M01: 48]

Similarly, for activities and goings-on, it is often the action or event in progress or having duration that is the particular connotation of the progressive.

It is then not easy to provide a simple meaning or list of meanings for particular verb forms, unless we couch them in fairly general terms, as we did earlier (p. 94). There is an interaction between verb form, TEMPORAL circumstance, situation type and context, which makes this area of English grammar particularly difficult to describe – or to understand, as any learner of English as a foreign language will tell you.

[*Exercise 2*]

Possibility and necessity

We have so far in this chapter considered the ways in which situation types are specified in relation to time. We turn now to a different kind of specification, but one which may also be realised grammatically in the verb phrase. It concerns the specification of a situation in respect of the notions of possibility and necessity. This may relate to a speaker's (or writer's) assessment of the possibility or necessity of a state, event or action [97] or to possibility/ necessity relating to the situation itself [98].

[97] The gateway to the right *might have* been the entrance to another sort of world   [L09: 93]

[98] No innocent passer-by *must pay* the price of my stupidity   [L12: 186]

In [97] the writer thinks that it is possible that 'the gateway' is 'the entrance to another sort of world'. In [98] the writer denies that the 'passer-by' (a participant in the situation) is under obligation (necessity) to 'pay the price'.

Speaker's assessment

The speaker (or writer) adds to the proposition an attitudinal component, giving the hearer (or reader) an assessment of the possibility, likelihood, probability, etc. of the situation occurring or obtaining. The speaker intrudes on what is said and embellishes it with a personal opinion about it. This may be expressed lexically by words which refer explicitly to prediction, possibility or opinion, e.g. 'I predict that. . .', 'I think it is possible that..', 'In my opinion there is a likelihood that. . .', etc. Alternatively, it may be expressed grammatically by means of the modal auxiliary verbs like *can, might, must.*

What kind of assessment can a speaker or writer make? First of all there is an assessment of **possibility**, as given in the examples at [99] and [100]:

[99] It was *possible* that the notary *might* have come out the afternoon of the funeral   [L05: 166]

[100] He *may* be the man who murdered Alice
          [L07: 39]

The possibility of the proposition is expressed in [99] both lexically (by the adjective *possible*) and grammatically, by the modal auxiliary verb *might*. In [100] it is expressed solely by the modal *may*. Without the addition of the speaker's assessment, the examples would read:

[101] The notary came out the afternoon of the funeral

[102] He is the man who murdered Alice

The items *possible, might, may* allow the speaker to draw back from the assertion of the proposition and be tentative or uncertain about it, express it as a possibility rather than as an assertion.

Secondly, a speaker may express the **necessity** or **certainty** of a proposition, as in the examples at [103] and [104]:

> [103] Many of your cases *must* be really deserving ones
> [L23: 23]
> [104] The job here *ought to* be finished in a matter of days
> [L05: 43]

The necessity of the proposition is expressed in [103] by the modal auxiliary verb *must*, and in [104] by the modal *ought to*. As plain assertions, these propositions would read:

> [105] Most of your cases are really deserving ones
> [106] The job here will be finished in a matter of days

While [106] is a more neutral expression of the proposition than [104], it is not entirely so, since the modal auxiliary *will*, used here as an expression of 'future', has an overtone of prediction. In a sense it is impossible to be neutral about the future: talking about the future invites an assessment from the speaker about the likelihood or certainty of an event taking place. This is why we noted earlier (p. 90) a range of overtones for the expressions of future time in English.

We may recognise **prediction** as a third kind of speaker's assessment, though it is perhaps a type of necessity or certainty with future reference. [106] above, and [107] following, serve as examples.

> [107] Graham *will* surely agree   [L21: 169]

Possibility and necessity represent the broad categories of speaker's assessment. There are, though, numerous degrees of possibility – probability, likelihood, etc. – and we are able in English to express a series of quite fine gradations in our assessment of the possibility of propositions. Compare examples [108]–[114], which are ranked on the scale from 'possible' to 'necessary'.

> [108] It might be unwise to draw attention to it
> [L19: 86]
> [109] You may be in serious danger from Hardy
> [L07: 67]

[110] I could produce his confession and he'd go to gaol   [L02: 133]

[111] It would probably last until the evening, he thought as he shaved   [L11: 169]

[112] There ought to be a better way of doing things   [L01: 160]

[113] 'Something will turn up one day, you'll see,' Roddy said confidently   [L04: 159]

[114] This must be the original ark   [L07: 157]

In all these examples the speaker's assessment is expressed grammatically by means of modal auxiliary verbs: *might, may, could, would, ought to, will, must.*

There is one further kind of intrusion that the speaker (or writer) can make in respect of the possibility of the proposition. The speaker can speculate or hypothesise and express a proposition as hypothetical. Consider the examples at [115] and [116]:

[115] You said that if Rose would have consented, she might be alive today   [L05: 208]

[116] I wondered stupidly what would happen if I dropped it   [L12: 163]

The hypothesis in each example is expressed by the modal *would*. The speaker is thus enabled to hypothesise about what is possible given certain conditions, to manipulate reality and experience by means of language to speculate on the 'mights' or 'might have beens' of life.

Possibility/necessity relating to the situation

We considered in the previous section the expression of possibility and necessity in relation to the encoder of the proposition. We now turn to the expression of possibility and necessity in relation to the participants in the proposition, in particular in relation to an AGENTIVE participant in an action. The possibility of an AGENTIVE performing an action may be related to the participant's **ability**, to the participant's having **permission**, or to the participant's **willingness**, as illustrated in [117] to [119] respectively.

[117] I *can* put him into a hypnotic sleep very quickly   [L16: 74]

[118] You *can* go, but I'll want you again   [L22: 177]
[119] It's shameless, horrible! I *will* not do it   [L08: 4]

Ability and permission are expressed by modal *can* in [117] and [118], while willingness is expressed by modal *will* in [119]. In [120] to [122] below the same notions are expressed more explicitly by the adjectives *able* [120] and *willing* [122], and the form *be allowed* [121].

[120] Of course he won't be able to work at all with his right hand or arm   [L23: 36]
[121] It finally ended with him being allowed to use the farmhouse phone   [L03:178]
[122] He's willing to pay   [L17: 94]

The other kind of possibility in respect of the situation is a circumstantial possibility, as illustrated in [123] and [124].

[123] 'I didn't dream clothes *could* make so much difference,' she said   [L05: 35]
[124] He *could* only have said such a thing because he did not know the whole truth   [L07: 75]

In both these examples modal *could* expresses circumstantial possibility. They might be paraphrased with the opening 'Circumstances are such that. . .'.

Necessity in relation to the situation is expressed in terms of various kinds of obligation, as illustrated by the examples at [125] to [129].

[125] 'You *must* get rid of that coat,' he said urgently
[L02: 107]
[126] You'll *have to* buy all my clothes for me
[L05: 36]
[127] Jane knew that she *ought to* feel pity for the McGregors   [L21: 99]
[128] Lea knew she *should* have held her ground
[L06: 175]
[129] She had *been obliged* to take a job some considerable distance away   [L24: 65]

In [125] and [126] the obligation expressed by modals *must* and *have to* is an externally imposed one, in these cases by the speaker or the circumstances. Circumstances would also seem to be responsible for the necessity expressed by *obliged* in [129]. In the case of [127] and [128], where the necessity is expressed by *ought to* and *should*, the obligation arises more from the participant's own moral conviction than from any external source.

Modality

Meanings of possibility and necessity are expressed grammatically by choices from the system of **modality**. Modality is realised first of all by the set of modal auxiliary verbs, listed at [130], which form part of the verb phrase in English (examples at [131]).

> [130] can   could   may   might   will   would   shall
>   should   must   ought to

Modal auxiliary verbs have only the forms listed at [130]; they have no distinct 3rd person singular present tense form, nor any non-finite forms (infinitive or participle). Moreover, the past tense form (*could* for *can*, *might* for *may*, etc.) only exceptionally operates like the past tense of other verbs: it is, in each case, to all intents and purposes, a distinct modal verb. Indeed, *must* and *ought to* have no past tense forms.

Where they occur, modal verbs are always the first item in a verb phrase:

> [131] can find   will have found
>   may be found   must be finding
>   should have been finding

They are followed by the base form of the main verb or auxiliary *have/be* which immediately follows them (*find* in 'can find', *have* in 'will have found'). Modal verbs may not co-occur, i.e. no more than one may occur in any verb phrase; and they may not occur in non-finite verb phrases. If more than one possibility/necessity meaning has to be expressed in a single proposition, then one of the other expressions of modality (e.g. adverb or adjective) is used instead of the second modal, as in the example at [120], where predictive *will* is accompanied by *be able to* to express ability. Similar substitutions have to be made in the case of non-finite verb phrases, e.g. in [121], where the present participle phrase contains *allowed to* as an expression of permission, rather than *can* or *may*.

Alternative realisations of modality are lexical, including semi-modal verbs like those at [132], modal adverbs like those at [133], adjectives like those at [134], and nouns like those at [135].

[132] have (got) to   need
[133] certainly   maybe   perhaps   possibly   probably   surely
[134] certain   likely   necessary   possible   probable   sure   able   allowed   obliged   willing
[135] likelihood   necessity   possibility   probability   ability   capability   obligation   permission   willingness

Forms and meanings

The speaker's assessment of possibility is expressed by *may, might, maybe, perhaps, possibly*, etc., further illustrated at [136] and [137]:

[136] I *maybe* lent it to someone and they haven't returned it   [L11: 233]
[137] *Perhaps* your readers *may* have forgotten these statements   [B27: 158]

Notice how in [137] the modal adverb *perhaps* and the modal verb *may* reinforce each other.

The speaker's assessment of necessity is expressed by *will, should, must, certainly, probably, surely, likely, necessary,* etc., further illustrated at [138] and [139].

[138] She *probably* didn't think you'd really tell Hilary about the man in Dallas   [L05: 192]
[139] It *must surely* be in the character of a Sleeping Beauty   [L13: 187]

Notice how *must* and *surely* reinforce each other in [139].

Ability of the AGENTIVE participant is expressed by *can, able, capability,* etc.; permission is expressed by *can, may, allowed, permission,* etc.; and willingness by *will, willing,* etc. A further example of each is given at [140] to [142] respectively.

[140] This is complicated; but I *can* handle it

[L16: 125]

[141] She *was 'allowed'* to accompany him to Scotland Yard   [L24: 25]

[142] Mr Lloyd has emerged – a Chancellor *willing* to grapple with the economy   [B08: 31]

Circumstantial possibility is expressed by *could, possible,* etc., further illustrated at [143]:

[143] You know that it'*s possible* – with the right subject – to virtually turn back the clock

[L16: 72]

Obligation is expressed by *shall, should, ought to, must, have (got) to, need, obliged, necessary,* etc., further illustrated at [144] to [146]:

[144] I shall *have to* give a week's notice at the flat

[L07: 131]

[145] Are they only *obliged* to offer service where profitable to them?   [B09: 102]

[146] It is *necessary* to repeat it here for the purpose of clarifying what happened subsequently

[L24: 44]

[*Exercise 3*]

Exercises

Exercise 1

For each of the following propositions say (where relevant): which time zone (past, present, future) is being referred to; whether the situation is viewed as occurring at a point in time (punctual) or over the period of time (durative); for the past, whether reference is to a definite or indefinite time; whether the point of orientation is other than present (i.e. past or future).

1. When he first sees the light machine-guns being assembled his stomach goes cold   [K09: 113]
2. I haven't seen any signs of her carrying on with anyone

[L14: 83]

3. Mr de Freitas became MP for Lincoln in February 1950 and his term will have extended to 13 years and eight months by October 1963 [B22: 45–6]
4. The newspapers had carried a story about it [N16: 138]
5. I'm boarding the yacht tonight [K18: 93]
6. They were going to have an open quarrel any minute [P03: 189]
7. She had, moreover, a reasonable endowment of intelligence [R03: 172]
8. As the argument between the landowner and the saint is warming up a very fierce-looking felon, chained, is brought on by an escort of gaolers [R04: 170]
9. My husband and I, Nanny and the children will be homeless next January unless you sell or let us that six-bedroomed Georgian country house [R05: 170]
10. It was the voice of two geese, and they were to plague us for many a month [R08: 6]

Exercise 2

Label the form of the verb in each of the following sentences (e.g. present perfective progressive), and identify any other items (e.g. Temporal circumstance) which contribute to the time meanings.

1. It was already after six when I awoke, and the sun was nearly setting beyond the west window [K02: 51]
2. As she was about to mount a wide and shallow flight of marble stairs, she became aware of someone watching her intently [K04: 17–18]
3. Doria was continually stopping on the way [K04: 35]
4. She was wondering whether Olimpia had been watching her talk with Orsini [K04: 29]
5. She had never loved him [K04: 98]
6. Nor had she told her parents that she was coming [K05: 14]
7. When are we going to see you? [K05: 60]
8. Her mother had been watching for her arrival [K05: 97]
9. She looked back and her parents were still waving to her [K05: 144]

10. 'I've changed nothing,' he said, 'except I've got my own books.' [K08: 101]

Exercise 3

In the following sentences identify the item(s) expressing modality and describe the possibility/necessity meaning associated with them.

1. He could always turn on the charm when it suited him [L01: 14]
2. How then can Gillian possibly have committed this murder? [L24: 182]
3. You should tell the police [L19: 92]
4. Maybe she thought she could trust me [L12: 6]
5. It must have been no easy task getting it into place [L08: 140]
6. He had been pressing to be allowed to build his 'wall' [B21: 196]
7. I'll probably be around [L17: 12]
8. Mr Ferguson might be able to tell you [L11: 140]
9. It would seem that he must somehow pass his inheritance on to her [L08: 60]
10. Surely he cannot begrudge them to people less fortunate than himself [B24: 109]

CHAPTER 5

Specifying Participants: Determinatives and modifiers

In Chapter 4 we have examined the ways in which the situation types that we talked about in Chapter 1, and the verbs which realise them, may be specified in English. We are now going to consider how participants, and the nouns which realise them, which we talked about in Chapter 2, may be specified. There are two broad types of specification that participants may have: identification, and classification and description. **Identification** provides a means of identifying which and what *general* type of participant is being referred to, and of keeping track of a participant through a text. **Classification** and **description** provide means of making specific the type of participant *being talked about* and of giving information about a participant's characteristics or features.

Identification

We begin our examination of identification by making a distinction between a participant which refers to a class of things and one which refers to an instance or member of the class. Sometimes we want to talk about things as a class: a species of animal, or a kind of furniture – and we say that the participant has **generic** reference [1]. Alternatively, and more commonly, we are talking about a particular member of the species or article of furniture [2] – and we say that the participant has **specific** reference.

> [1] Executive councils are responsible for the general practitioner, the dentist, the supply of drugs
> [B14: 172]

[2] A curious advertisement appears on page nine, paid
for by that curious body Moral Re-Armament
[B01: 91]

In the example at [1], *executive councils* are being referred to
as a class, and so are 'general practitioners' and 'dentists'.
Notice, though, that the generic reference of *executive
councils* is realised simply by the plural form of the noun
councils, whereas 'general practitioners' and 'dentists' have
generic reference by virtue of being in the singular with a
preceding *the*, but not referring to a particular GP or dentist.
In the example at [2] all the participants (*advertisement*, *page*,
body) have specific reference; in each case a particular
member of a class is being referred to.

Definite and indefinite

Participants with specific reference may be further specified
as having definite reference or indefinite reference. You will
remember that we used these terms in Chapter 4 to refer to
the difference between the past time reference of the simple
past tense and the present perfect tense (see examples [25]
and [26] there): the meaning of the terms is parallel. A
participant with definite reference is one which speaker and
hearer (or writer and reader) can identify uniquely from the
knowledge which they share about the world they inhabit
and the ongoing communication that they are engaged in.
A participant with indefinite reference cannot be thus
uniquely identified. Compare the examples at [3] and [4].

[3] But *the leaves* gave off a warm, soaking smell, *the
pain* in his head lifted   [K03: 100]
[4] *A flying saucer* was tilting and dipping over the War
Memorial   [M01: 116]

In [3], the participants *leaves* and *pain* are specified as
definite, by means of *the*: they are identified as known or
uniquely recognisable to reader and writer from the
preceding context, which has mentioned the leaves and the
pain already. This may be contrasted with *flying saucer* in
[4], which is specified as indefinite by means of *a*, and is
thus identified as not present in the reader's and writer's
shared knowledge or not previously mentioned in the

context. The 'definite article' *the* typically realises definite reference, and the 'indefinite article' *a* (or *an* before a word beginning with a vowel letter) typically realises indefinite reference.

As we have implied, the definite reference of a participant – its unique identification in the shared knowledge of speaker and hearer – may arise in a number of ways, which we may categorise as either situational or contextual. The **situation** may comprise the immediate situation in which the communication is taking place, and reference is made to something visible to speaker and hearer, or at least common knowledge to them [5]. Or the situation may comprise the more general shared cultural knowledge of speaker and hearer – the institutions, organisations, systems, traditions, etc., of a culture [6].

[5] Now tell me, have you been to *the aquariums* yet?
[P08: 160]
[6] At half-past nine, in an interval between calls, *the telephone* rang. It was *the police station*   [P26: 135]

In [5] we may assume that the aquariums are known as a place to be visited in the neighbourhood, and that the speaker and hearer know of them: the reference to the aquariums is therefore definite and to the immediate situation. In [6] the definite reference of *telephone* and *police station* is attributable rather to their existence in the more general situation of life within British culture, and therefore assumed to be known and identifiable by all readers of this text.

Whether to specify a participant as definite or indefinite is a choice of the encoder, who does so on the basis of their assessment of the knowledge which is shared with hearers or readers. Encoders can be mistaken about the extent of this shared knowledge. In conversation, a hearer can ask for clarification. In written texts, the more remote in time that they were encoded, the more difficult they may be to decode, because the extent of shared knowledge, especially of a cultural kind, has become less between reader and writer.

The other ways in which definite reference may arise we have called **contextual**. A participant is specified as having definite reference because it occurs, usually by previous mention, in the verbal context. The mention may be either direct, by repetition of the participant concerned, or indirect, by inference from a previous mention. Consider the examples at [7] and [8].

[7] There was *a* large new roundabout and a sign. . . At one time she had watched the workmen constructing *the* roundabout   [P03: 7, 15]
[8] I noticed *a* little gate at *the* side of *the* house, which doubtless led into *the* garden   [K15: 100]

In the example at [7] the first mention of *roundabout* (line 7) is specified as indefinite reference, while the second mention (line 15) is definite, because it can now be assumed to be shared knowledge from the context. In [8] we must assume that the *house* has been mentioned before, while *gate* is specified as indefinite (on first mention); *side* and *garden*, however, are specified as definite, because it may be inferred that houses have sides and gardens, and these items are therefore indirectly present in the context.

Possession

Another way in which a participant may be identified is by the relation of possession. Possession is usually by human participants, or at least by animates, though it is not restricted to these. Possession is another means of identifying which participant we are talking about. Consider the examples at [9] to [11].

[9] *Hilary's lawyer's* secretary is a close personal friend *of mine*   [L05: 127]
[10] We piled all *my* things into *his* car   [L07: 152]
[11] Kennan found *the bullet's* exit point   [L03: 96]

In [9], *secretary* is identified as 'belonging to' the lawyer, and *lawyer* in turn as 'belonging to' Hilary. In [10], *things* are identified as 'belonging to' me, and *car* as 'belonging to' him. And in [11], *exit point* is identified as 'belonging to' the bullet. It will be clear that possession is interpreted quite widely, to include not just personal possession (*my*, *his* in [10]), but all manner of relationships of belonging and association. You will also note that the possessor in [11] is inanimate (*bullet*).

Possession is marked, as the examples at [9] to [11] illustrate, either by means of a possessive identifier (see below) or by means of a genitive inflection (*'s*) on a noun. There is a third way, illustrated in the example at [9]: *of mine*. The preposition *of* often introduces a noun in a relationship of 'possession' to the preceding noun. This is the usual way of indicating possession for inanimates. [11] might be rephrased as [12].

[12] Kennan found the exit point of the bullet

Conversely, [9] might be rephrased as [13].

[13] Hilary's lawyer's secretary is my close personal friend

However, [13] could imply that I have only one 'close personal friend', while [9], because it allows the use of the indefinite *a* with *friend*, implies that I have several. [9] thus exploits the flexibility in the expression of possession in English to advantage. Two further examples to illustrate the use of *of*-phrases for possession are given in the sentence at [14].

[14] All Aristotle was excited at the time, not by the prospect *of the U.S. President's visit*, but by a great storm in the photosphere *of the sun*   [M02: 104]

The first *of*-phrase could not be expressed in any other way (!'the U.S. President's visit's prospect'), but the second could be rephrased using the *'s* construction: 'the sun's photosphere'.

Quantity

We have seen that participants may be specified for reference (generic/specific, definite/indefinite), and they may be specified for possession. A third kind of specification is quantity. A participant is specified for amount or number. If the participant is a mass (uncountable) noun, quantity will relate to an amount [15]; if it is a countable noun, it will relate to number [16].

[15] There was *a lot of* noisy talk and laughter
[P18: 145]

[16] She thought of all the *many* years of life he was to
    miss   [P17: 91]

In both of these examples, the expression of quantity (*a lot of*, *many*) is indefinite. It does not give a precise specification of quantity, either of the amount of 'talk and laughter' or of the number of 'years of life'. Besides indefinite expressions of quantity, of which there are quite a few, there are also definite expressions of amount [17] and number [18].

[17] His 'statement of basis of claim' ran to *three sides of*
    foolscap   [L23: 81]

[18] The *two* girls followed their mother downstairs
                                                      [P05: 86]

In [17], the amount of the mass noun *foolscap* (i.e. 'foolscap paper') is made definite by the quantifying expression of measure 'three sides of'; and in [18], the number of the countable noun *girls* is made definite by the numeral *two*.

We may summarise the various types of identification which specify participants in English by means of the following diagram.

[19]

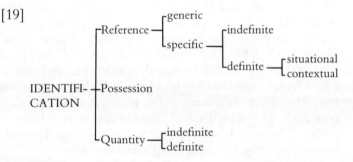

We turn now to the grammatical realisation of these meanings.

Determinatives

The identification of participants in terms of reference, possession and quantity is realised grammatically by a set of items, called 'determinatives', which accompany nouns. The class of determinatives is quite restricted, and is made up of four subclasses: **articles, demonstratives, possessives,** and **quantifiers**.

Articles

The articles are: *a/an*, indefinite article; *the*, definite article. The definite article is used to express definite specific reference with both singular and plural countable nouns and (singular) mass nouns, e.g.

[20] the box   the boxes   the flour

The indefinite article is used to express indefinite specific reference with singular countable nouns. For plural countable nouns and mass nouns, no article is used for indefinite specific reference, e.g.

[21] a box   boxes   flour

All three articles – definite, indefinite and zero – may be used for generic reference, e.g.

[21] No man can tame the tongue/a tongue/tongues

The use of the indefinite article (*a tongue*) implies that the noun represents any member of its class (of tongues). Zero article (*tongues*), used generically with plural countable nouns and (singular) mass nouns, views the class (of tongues) as an undifferentiated whole. The definite article (*the tongue*), used with singular countable nouns, implies that the noun represents the prototype of its class (of tongues). This use of the definite article is associated with a rather formal or literary style. It is also typically used with nouns referring to musical instruments, e.g.

[23] Kirsten plays the clarinet

The definite article also occurs with countable nouns in the plural in two special cases: nationality nouns ('the Germans', 'the Japanese'); and nouns derived from adjectives referring to groups of people ('the elderly', 'the dead').

We may summarise the use of the articles for generic and specific reference as follows:

[24]   GENERIC   SPECIFIC

                              INDEFINITE   DEFINITE

count sg	a/the tongue	a box	the box
count pl	tongues/the Germans	boxes	the boxes
mass	money	flour	the flour

The articles cannot, thus, uniquely identify a noun as generic or specific: the context and content of the proposition in which it functions also plays a part. Within specific reference, however, indefinite and definite are uniquely identified, since *the* is restricted to definite reference and *a*/'zero' to indefinite reference.

Demonstratives

The subclass of determinatives called 'demonstratives' contains the following members:

[25] this   these
     that   those

These is the plural form of *this*, and *those* the plural of *that*. *This/these* and *that/those* are distinguished by a category of 'proximity': *this* implies proximate (to the speaker), while *that* implies non-proximate or distant (from the speaker): see the diagram at [86] in Chapter 2 and the associated discussion there. Proximity may be situational [26] or contextual [27].

[26] The first batch of around 50 mantis hatched from *this* egg-case on June 20   [E07: 91]
[27] All *these* minor problems must be worked out as each mill is photographed   [E10: 91]

We may imagine the speaker of [26] pointing to the particular 'egg-case' present in the situation, while in [27] the 'minor problems' have been discussed in the preceding sentences of the text. In both these examples the demonstrative has the 'proximate' meaning, which occurs more commonly than the non-proximate *that/those*, illustrated at [28].

[28] Now, the descendants of *those* slaves have multi-plied, and *those* tiny islands are bursting at the seams   [B26: 98]

Demonstratives substitute for the definite article in definite specific reference, but they add a 'pointing' or 'deictic' function. Their proximate/non-proximate distinction is paralleled by other pairs of deictic items in the language, e.g.

[29] here – there   now – then

Mostly these point to the situation, though *here* can sometimes be used contextually, e.g.

[30] The economy, Berlin, the Common Market – *here* are three issues whose gravity. . .   [B12: 169]

Possessives

The members of the subclass of determinatives called 'possessives' also substitute for the definite article in definite specific reference, but with the additional meaning of possession, belonging or association. Possessives include: the restricted set of 'possessive identifiers', given at [31] (compare the possessive pronouns given at [72] in Chapter 2); genitive nouns; and some *of*-phrases.

[31] my   our   your   his   her   its   their

Like personal pronouns (see Chapter 2), possessive identifiers show distinctions of person (1st, 2nd, 3rd), of number (singular, plural) and in the 3rd person singular of gender (masculine, feminine, neuter).

[32]

| | | NUMBER | |
		singular	plural
	1st	my	our
	2nd	your	your
PERSON	3rd ⎧ masc.	his	⎫
	⎨ fem.	her	⎬ their
	⎩ neut.	its	⎭

You will note the similarity in form between these items and the possessive pronouns (mine, ours, yours, his, hers, its, theirs – see p. 41), but the difference in function: like other pronouns, the possessive pronouns substitute for nouns; whereas possessive identifiers, like other determinatives, accompany nouns and contribute to their specification and identification.

Possessive identifiers of 1st and 2nd person have exclusively situational reference, with *my/our* referring to the speaker(s)/writer(s) and *your* to the hearer(s)/reader(s). The 3rd person possessives may, like demonstratives, have either situational [33] or contextual [34] reference.

[33] Look at the colour of *her* hair
[34] In some perverse way *their* brief quarrel had forged a bond between them   [L04: 69]

We might suppose [33] spoken in the street about a female present in the situation, while in [34], *their* (like *them*) refers to persons previously mentioned in the text.

We may regard **genitive nouns** as kinds of 3rd person possessive identifiers, though, unlike these, they are not restricted in number. The sentence at [33] for example, might read as in [35] or [36].

[35] Look at the colour of *Lydia's* hair
[36] Look at the colour of *that girl's* hair

In [35] the possessive is a proper name, the most common kind of genitive; while in [36] it is the noun *girl*, further specified by the demonstrative identifier *that* with situational reference. Genitive nouns are useful when a possessive identifier would be ambiguous in the context or when a more explicit identification is required.

[37] She thought of *Tim's* cunning sidelong look, *his wife's* hostile air of concealed knowledge
[L21: 100]

His instead of *Tim's*, and *her* instead of *his wife's* may well not be adequate to unambiguously identify whose 'look' and 'air' are being talked about.

Of-phrases have a number of functions and meanings, one of which is to be an alternative expression to genitive nouns of possession, belonging, etc., especially where the noun being specified is inanimate. Consider the example at [38].

[38] The ditch at *the wall's* foot was frilled with cow-parsley   [L09: 78]

There is a certain strangeness about the genitive of *wall*, and many English speakers would probably find [39] more natural.

[39]   The ditch at the foot *of the wall* was frilled with cow-parsley

Following are two further examples of *of*-phrases with possessive meaning.

[40] The more serious scenes *of the opera* were in fact often uninteresting   [C01: 46]
[41] Günther   Rennert's   imaginative   production cleverly conveyed the crazy, precarious atmosphere *of the Alpine inn inhabited by the Poet's court*
                                                       [C01: 66]

The example at [40] could be rephrased as [42].

[42 *The opera's* more serious scenes were in fact often uninteresting

But [41] could not be similarly rephrased, since it would produce a highly unwieldy sequence:

[43] . . . the Alpine inn inhabited by the Poet's court's crazy, precarious atmosphere

The choice of an *of*-phrase in [41] is required not just by the inanimateness of the noun *inn*, but also by the fact that *inn* is accompanied by further specification after it.

Quantifiers

A final set of determinatives is the group of items specifying quantity. There are two subgroups of quantifier: **numerals** and **indefinite quantifiers**. Numerals give precise numbers of countable nouns and are of two types: **cardinal** and **ordinal**. Cardinal numerals comprise the series at [44], with an example at [46]; and ordinal numerals comprise the series at [45], with an example at [47].

[44] one   two   three   four   five   etc.

[45] first   second   third   fourth   fifth   etc.

[46] Those *five* members remain members of the
Labour Party   [B26: 129]

[47] The *third* article excluded any allegorical interpretation of the Gospel   [D01: 27]

To express precise amounts of mass nouns, we have to use
various appropriate phrases of measurement, as in the
example at [48].

[48] Into a champagne glass put *a lump of* sugar, *an
eggspoonful of* brandy, and on the sugar literally *one
drop of* angostura bitters   [E19: 139]

Sugar, *brandy* and *angostura bitters* are mass nouns. In this
recipe their precise amounts are specified by means of the
expressions 'a lump of', 'an eggspoonful of' and 'one drop
of', respectively. The measurement expressions contain
countable nouns (*lump*, *eggspoonful*, *drop*), which may
themselves be specified by numerals ('three lumps of
sugar').

Indefinite quantifiers are imprecise in their specification
of number or amount, but there is a considerable range of
them, with several gradations of quantity. We seem to want
to talk vaguely about quantity very often. Indeed, we
sometimes use or modify expressions with numerals so that
they are made to sound vague; e.g. 'a couple of' rarely
means just 'two', and we modify numerals or expressions
like 'half a dozen' with *about* or *or so*.

[49] In *about 18 months or so* he will have to make it
clear to the Conservative Party whether. . .
                                                     [B08: 67]

Indefinite quantifiers themselves can be categorised into four
types: universal, assertive, non-assertive and negative. The
typical **universal** indefinite quantifier is *all*, which can be
used with plural countable nouns [50] and with mass nouns
[51]. It may be the only determinative [50], or it may
precede another determinative like *this* [51].

[50] It would obviously be wrong to refuse *all* political
advertisements with which we disagree [B01: 100]

[51] I think someone should put a stop to *all this* idle gossip about the pupils   [B23: 180]

All is the only universal indefinite quantifier for mass nouns. For plural countable nouns there is also a quantifier used to encompass two of a noun: *both* [52]. With singular countable nouns, *each* and *every* are used as universal quantifiers [53].

[52] He held *both her* hands tightly behind her back
                                                    [P04: 21]
[53] The costs of *each* section of the Health Service are scrutinised as though they were isolated problems
                                                    [B14: 193]

Assertive indefinite quantifiers specify a positive but indefinite number of amount of a noun. The typical assertive quantifier is *some*, which may be used with plural countable nouns [54] and with mass nouns [55].

[54] *Some* east European churches had been members already   [B03: 6]
[55] To this there will be *some* opposition   [B03: 148]

Other assertive indefinite quantifiers used with countable nouns (plural) include those listed at [56], and examples of those used with mass nouns are given at [57].

[56] many   several   a few   few
[57] much   a little   little

Also included in this type of quantifier are several expressions with *of*, such as:

[58] plenty of   a lot of   a number of   a (large/small) quantity of

Quantifying expressions with *of* may then be followed by another determinative, and those listed at [56] and [57] may also enter an *of*-construction and so be followed by *the* etc.

[59] *Several of* your correspondents on this subject have put forward the view that. . .   [B11: 71]

The **non-assertive** indefinite quantifier *any*, which may be used with both countable (singular and plural) [60] and mass [61] nouns, occurs in negative [60] and interrogative [61] sentences to deny the specification of quantity.

[60] It won't make *any* difference   [K18: 159]

[61] Does it have *any* control over the Indian airmen who are going to drop the bombs?   [B13: 168]

Corresponding to the universal quantifier *both* (see [52]), there is a non-assertive quantifier *either*, used with (singular) countable nouns.

[62] Some formal subject teaching must go on in *either* case   [B19: 34]

Parallel to the non-assertive quantifier *any* is the **negative** indefinite quantifier *no*, and corresponding to *either* is *neither*. These are used in positive sentences (i.e. without *not* in the verb phrase) to assert the absence of quantity, e.g.

[63] Let her tell men like Strauss that he shall have *no* bases or 'facilities', *no* help in his quest for atomic arms   [B06: 75]

We may summarise the types of indefinite quantifier in the following table:

[64]

	COUNTABLE NOUN	MASS NOUN
UNIVERSAL	each/every + sg all/both + pl	all
ASSERTIVE	some, many several, a few	some, much a little
NON-ASSERTIVE	any/either	any
NEGATIVE	no/neither	no

[*Exercise 1*]

Classification and description

Besides identifying a participant in terms of its reference, possession and quantity, we may also wish to distinguish a participant from other members of its class or to mention descriptive information about it. Consider the examples at [65] and [66].

[65] He wondered if she would be wearing mama's blue dress with the lace on the collar   [P18: 114]

[66] She had watched her grow into a likeable, happy
little girl   [P29: 68]

The participant *dress* in [65] is distinguished from other
members of the class of dresses by the classification *blue*: it
belongs to the subclass of dresses which are blue. The
phrase 'with the lace on the collar' seems to be adding
further descriptive information about the dress, and we may
note that the dress is identified as 'belonging to mama'
(*mama's*). In [66], we might regard *little* as constituting a
classification of *girl*, but *likeable* and *happy* as providing
further description. As we shall see, classification and
description are not always easy to distinguish.

Classification

Colour adjectives like *blue* and **size** adjectives like *little*
frequently function as classifiers of participants.

[67] A *small* boy in a *blue* blazer was walking along the
pavement   [P26: 30]

Here the *boy* is classified by size (*small*), and his *blazer* by
colour (*blue*). These are two of the ways in which we choose
to distinguish one person or thing from another. There is no
readily available and widely agreed analysis of the types of
classification made of participants in English, though we
might begin to derive such an analysis from the *Longman
Lexicon of Contemporary English* (1981), a dictionary com-
piled by Tom McArthur on a lexical field model. All we can
do here is suggest some of the categories that might be used
in describing English classifiers.

We have noted colour and size as common means of
classification. Others might include **shape** [68], **material**
[69], **function** [70], **appearance** [71].

[68] . . . leaving four stunted growths of stone,
projecting from a *square* tower   [K24: 153]
[69] Nelly had a green *velvet* dress and a hat with
pansies on it   [P18: 142]
[70] Her *riding* skirt was creamy and expensive-looking
[N14: 107]
[71] You'll marry a darned *attractive* girl   [K07: 99]

In [68], the shape adjective *square* classifies *tower*; and we may also note in this example that *growths* is classified as *of stone* (material) and *stunted* (size). In [69], *dress* is classified first by its material (*velvet*) and then by its colour (*green*). In [70], *skirt* is classified by *riding*, indicating its function; it is also described in terms of colour (*creamy*) and appearance (*expensive-looking*). In [71], *girl* is classified by *attractive*, indicating appearance.

There are yet further ways in which we choose to classify participants, including by **time/age** (*early, late, young, old*) [72], by **place** (*local, foreign*) [73], by **temperature** (*cold, cool, warm, hot*) [74], by **speed** (*slow, fast*) [75], and no doubt many another category.

[72] Juarez was a *young* man of the slim athletic type
                                                    [N19: 4]
[73] He would get on with the *local* workmen
                                                    [N25: 107]
[74] He remembered those *hot* sandy beaches and the *warm* middle sea, so many years ago   [N24: 62]
[75] He had been complaining about the *slow* rate at which I had been feeding him the designs of British consumer goods   [R04: 57]

It is clear from some of the examples that a participant may be classified in a number of ways at the same time. A further example follows at [76].

[75] a big black crocodile bag   [K08: 40]

Here, the *bag* is classified for material (*crocodile*), colour (*black*) and size (*big*) – in that order: the classifier nearest to the participant noun represents the first stage of classification, and so on.

Distinguishing between classification and description is not always easy. The categories discussed in this section probably generally function as classifiers, though *creamy* (colour) in [70], for example, might be analysed as description rather than classification, because it has an overtone of evaluation.

Description

Description adds information about a participant that is in some sense gratuitous. It does not represent an attempt by speaker or writer to identify a participant or to assign it to a class of objects. Rather it is an attempt to add colour and substance to the description of a participant, often with an overtone of evaluation, or indeed with an explicit evaluation. Categories of description might be said to include: **manner** (e.g. *careful, easy*) [77], **emotion** (e.g. *glad, cheerful, annoyed, happy, disappointed*) [78], **evaluation** (e.g. *good, bad, excellent, enjoyable, important, delightful*) [79] and [80]. Probably this last category is too large and ought to be subdivided.

[77] The *careful, precise* pen of the former short-story writer could have made his parable shorter
[C09: 89]
[78] The warmth of their welcome in India and Pakistan are *happy* memories [B01: 54]
[79] The author's many *excellent* photographs make an integral and illuminating contribution [C14: 81]
[80] Ben Hawthorne has the *important* role of the son in 'The Glass Menagerie' [C15: 83]

In [80] the participant noun *role* is classified by the *of*-phrase 'of the son', and in addition we are told that the writer thinks that this role is 'important', thus adding further descriptive information. In [77], *pen* is not classified by *careful* and *precise*: these are not types or classes of pen. Rather they describe the pen (or its use) and provide a reason for the statement that is made about 'his parable'. In this example, however, *short-story* does classify *writer*: a 'short-story writer' is a type of 'writer'. The following are some further examples of description:

[81] the uncultured, nagging, parsimonious, penurious household [K01: 41]
[82] his pleasant, open face [K03: 89]
[83] through sticky, intolerable tropics [K16: 180]
[84] the makeshift, toiling lives [K23: 62]
[85] Steve awakened early and switched on the radio, which he kept tuned to CBO [M01: 105]

In [85], the participant *radio* is described by the expression following it, introduced by the relative pronoun *which*. It is perhaps now appropriate to turn to a consideration of the grammatical means by which classification and description are realised in English.

Modifiers

The class of items which realise meanings associated with the classification and description of participants we will call 'modifiers'. Modifiers relate, therefore, to nouns. Nearly all our examples of modifiers given so far have been **adjectives**, probably the most frequently occurring type of modifier. Other types of modifier include: **participles**, **nouns** and **relative clauses**, which we will consider in turn. But we begin with adjectives.

Adjectives

The word-class of adjectives is a large one: we have many ways in which we want to talk about the characteristics and attributes of nouns, or in which we want to make more precise who or what we are talking about. Adjectives commonly occur as modifiers before nouns in English, in the 'attributive' position [86], but they also occur after verbs of quality or temporary state in the 'predicative' position [87].

[86] Trembled when he touched her *long warm* fingers
[K21: 126]

[87] The grass was very *warm*　　　　　[K11: 10]

A few adjectives are restricted to either one or the other position. For example, *former* and *main* occur only in attributive position [88], while *asleep* and *awake* occur only in predicative position [89].

[88] It added infinitely to her *former* resentment
[K20: 47]

[89] The forester seemed to be fast *asleep*　　　[K11: 19]

We could not say 'her resentment was former' or talk of 'the fast asleep forester'. The vast majority of adjectives may occur in both positions. Many adjectives also occur in a third position: after indefinite pronouns ending in −*thing*, −*body* or −*one*, e.g.

[90] She'd said something *vague* and gone to bed
[L06: 177]

Another important characteristic of most adjectives is that they are 'gradable'. There are grades or degrees of the quality or description referred to by the adjective, and we can express this gradability grammatically. Adjectives can be inflected for **comparative** and **superlative** degree, e.g.

[91] long   longer   longest
    warm   warmer   warmest

Longer and *warmer* are 'comparative' forms, and *longest* and *warmest* are 'superlative' forms. Comparative and superlative degrees of adjectives may also be expressed periphrastically by means of the modifying adverbs *more* (comparative) and *most* (superlative), e.g.

[92] versatile   more versatile   most versatile
    polite   more polite   most polite

Adjectives of a single syllable in length, like *long* and *warm*, usually form their comparative and superlative by means of the −*er*/−*est* inflection. Adjectives of three syllables or more in length, like *versatile*, usually form their comparative and superlative periphrastically by means of *more*/*most*. With adjectives of two syllables in length there is often a choice: *polite*, for example, could form comparative *politer* and superlative *politest*. The inflection is most readily used with two-syllable adjectives ending in an unstressed vowel /ə/ or syllabic /l/, e.g.

[93] funny   funnier   funniest
    gentle   gentler   gentlest

There are one or two adjectives which have irregular inflections for comparative and superlative, most notably

[94] good   better   best
    bad   worse   worst

The gradability of adjectives enables us to compare entities for particular qualities. We may compare them for sameness of quality, using a construction 'as adjective as', with the adjective in its base form [95]. We may compare them for higher degree, using the comparative form of the adjective followed by *than* [96]/[97]. Or we may compare them for lower degree, by using *less* (the antonym of *more*), plus the base form of the adjective, plus *than* [98].

[95] Miss Murdoch's publishers claim that 'A Severed Head' is *as exciting as* 'Treasure Island' [C11: 147]

[96] Food is *more important* than the social revolution
[B21: 60]

[97] Could anything be *neater*? Or anything *more true* than this? [C08: 119]

[98] Nor need they be *less concerned* than Mr Victor Gollancz [B02: 61]

Note the use of periphrastic *more* with the single-syllable adjective *true* in [97], perhaps for stylistic variation.

The use of the superlative form of adjectives enables us to assert that an entity has a quality to the highest degree, e.g.

[99] He has been the *greatest* influence from the past on contemporary Greek poetry [C12: 90]

[100] Mr Bennett is one of the *most musical* of our younger composers [C01: 79]

A further way in which the gradability of adjectives may be exploited and expressed is by means of modifying adverbs (other than *more/most*). An important set of such adverbs is called **intensifiers**, and they are of two kinds: **amplifiers** [101] and **downtoners** [102].

[101] extremely terribly entirely highly very etc.

[100] fairly quite relatively hardly pretty etc.

Amplifiers imply that something is at a higher degree than the norm expressed by the adjective [103]/[104], while downtoners imply that something is at a lower degree than the norm [105]/[106].

[103] His future is obviously *extremely* bright
[A32: 26]

[104] They operate along unorthodox but *highly* effective lines [A20: 131]

[105] Elliot will have to pass a *pretty* stiff midweek tryout [A23: 11]

[106] On the whole, 'Song Without End' is *fairly* accurate [C17: 122]

Two other groups of modifying adverbs perform a similar function to intensifiers. They are **emphasisers** like *really*, *just*, *indeed* [107], and **viewpoint adverbs** like *artistically*, *theoretically*, *dramatically*, *musically* [108].

[107] No one has mentioned the *really* outstanding characteristic of Miss Murdoch's new novel [C11: 32]

[108] Thomas Hemsley's performance as the Poet's private doctor was *dramatically* shrewd and *musically* well-conceived [C01: 60]

Participles

As modifiers of nouns, present and past participles of verbs function very much like adjectives. Indeed, they are sometimes regarded as adjectives when they modify nouns. A present participle attributes a quality of action to the noun, which is viewed as undertaking the action, as *retreating* of *legs* in [109]. A past participle views the noun as having undergone the action expressed by the participle, as *prefabricated* of *buildings* in [110].

[109] . . . the cripple's envy at his straight, *retreating* legs [K24: 129]

[110] various *prefabricated* buildings [K05: 5]

Thus the present is an 'active' participle and the past a 'passive' participle. Participle modifiers probably occur more often in attributive position; in predicative position they cannot always be clearly distinguished from progressive or passive verb forms. For example, [111] could be expanded as [112], leading to a passive verb interpretation, or as [113], leading to an adjective interpretation.

[111] She was annoyed

[112] She was annoyed by the continuous hammering

(related to the active 'The continuous hammering annoyed her')

[113] She was annoyed with them

Some participles, however, have taken on meanings as adjectives which allow them to be used unambiguously in predicative position, e.g. *depressing* in [114]; while there are others that we think of more as adjectives than participles in any position, e.g. *tired* in [115].

[114] So once again the metaphysics were *depressing*
[M02: 191]

[115] . . . a haven of safety and comfort for *tired* rowers
[M05: 31]

One interesting development with participle modifiers has been that of hyphenated expressions composed of an adjective, adverb or noun with a participle, e.g. *particle-scarred* in [116], *fast-disappearing* in [117].

[116] She lay in the Sirian spaceport, her tubes cold, her shell *particle-scarred*
[M05: 13]

[117] She looked down at the *fast-disappearing* earth
[M04: 110]

On this pattern, however, other participle-like adjectives have been coined, especially with a past-participle form, that are not derived from verbs, e.g. *tight-lipped* in [118], i.e. 'with tight lips' or 'with lips shut tight'; *empty-minded* in [119], i.e. 'with an empty mind'.

[118] Megan Thomas sat *tight-lipped*, nursing the sleeping Cadwallader
[M04: 129]

[119] . . . the *empty-minded* receptiveness that prepared the way for the second stage
[M01: 57]

Noun modifiers

Nouns may also be modified by other nouns, in attributive position. If such a noun modifier occurs, it immediately precedes the participant noun being modified, e.g. *metal* modifies *box* in [120].

[120] He pointed at a *metal* box on the wall
[M05: 210]

A number of modifiers referring to 'materials' are nouns, e.g. *velvet* in [69], but they are not restricted to these by any means, as the examples at [121] to [124] show.

[121] I had to send back our *bedroom* furniture in the second year [M02: 87]

[122] Dan was lying on a long bench in the *breakfast* nook [M01: 30]

[123] The *enemy* tigerfly had been at it [M06: 174]

[124] The latter suggested barefaced theft of *government* property [M05: 93]

In [121], *bedroom* modifies *furniture*, indicating its usual place or purpose; in [122], *breakfast* modifies *nook*, to indicate the usual purpose or function of the nook; *tigerfly* in [123] is modified by *enemy*, giving an evaluation; and *property* in [122] is modified by *government*, to indicate possession.

Sometimes noun modifiers become so closely associated with their following nouns that they come to be regarded as having the status of a single word (compound noun), e.g. *bus stop* in [125], *registration number* in [126].

[125] They followed him to a city *bus stop* on Carling Avenue [M01: 180]

[126] I tried to read the *registration number* [M04: 170]

The example at [125] illustrates a further point about noun modifiers: there may be more than one present in a phrase. Here, *city* modifies *bus stop*, or *city* modifies *bus* and *city bus* together modifies *stop*, depending on your interpretation. Similarly in [127], *feeding* modifies *centre* and this construction is in turn modified by *space-navy*, which is itself a compound noun.

[127] You got a certificate with three credits from the *space-navy feeding centre* [M05: 199]

Other modifiers

In addition to the modifiers we have considered so far, there are a number of phrasal and clausal expressions which may modify nouns. We will simply illustrate some of them at this point, as they will be discussed in more detail in Chapter 7. In [85] we noted one such modifier, a **relative**

clause introduced by the relative pronoun *which*. In this case, a whole clause gives descriptive or classificatory information about a noun. Classificatory relative clauses are often referred to as 'restrictive' relative clauses, and descriptive ones as 'non-restrictive'. Consider the further examples at [128] and [129].

[128] The rotations proceeded by rhythmic jerks, *which were timed to a painful throb that bumped in his head*
[M01: 19]

[129] This was the Senator *who had annoyed the United States* [M02: 135]

In [128], the noun *jerks* is modified by the non-restrictive relative clause 'which . . . head', and within that clause *throb* is modified by the restrictive relative clause 'that . . . head'. In [129], *Senator* is modified by the restrictive relative clause 'who . . . States'.

Another type of clausal modifier is the non-finite clause, usually with a present [130] or past [131] participle.

[130] Little to be seen, only a few lone stars, and the distant earth, *brooding in her shroud of mist*
[M04: 128]

[131] I was able by a trick *practised in equally repugnant circumstances* to floor the first three [M03: 67]

In [130], the noun *earth* is modified by the non-finite clause 'brooding . . . mist'; and in [131], *trick* is modified by 'practised . . . circumstances'.

Finally, and very commonly, a noun may be modified by a prepositional phrase, as in [132] to [134]:

[132] . . . a sly reference *to the long break in Mo-American affairs* [M02: 42]

[133] Leap on your bicycle and scour the countryside *between here and the Traveller's Joy* [M04: 70]

[134] I guess Sally made a mistake *about me* [M02: 92]

In [132], the noun *reference* is modified by the prepositional phrase 'to the . . . affairs', and within that phrase *break* is modified by 'in . . . affairs'. In [133], *countryside* is modified by 'between . . . Joy'; and in [134], *mistake* is modified by 'about me'.

You will note that all these phrasal and clausal

modifiers come *after* the noun which they modify: they are **post-modifiers**, whereas adjectives, participles and noun modifiers are usually **pre-modifiers**, occurring *before* the noun.

[*Exercise 2*]

Noun phrase

We conclude this chapter with a review of the kinds of specification associated with nouns and their position in relation to the noun and to each other. A noun with its associated specification we will term a **noun phrase**. A noun phrase may be viewed as having potentially three parts:

[135] pre-modification – NOUN – post-modification

The pre-modification consists of determinatives, adjectives, etc. Pre-modifiers occur in the order:

[136] determinatives – adjectives/participles – noun modifiers

Within the set of determinatives, articles, demonstratives and possessives precede quantifiers. Articles, demonstratives and possessives do not co-occur; they are mutually exclusive. Possession may be expressed in addition to one of the other forms of identification, but by means of the periphrastic *of*-phrase, as in the example at [9] (*of mine*). Quantifiers may occur on their own ('many people') and they may co-occur, though there are restrictions on co-occurrence, the most common types being:

[137] ordinal + cardinal   the first six
                                                  passengers
           ordinal (esp. *first/last*
               + indefinite quant   the first few miles
       indef quant + cardinal
           (esp round numbers)   several hundred fans

A small group of quantifiers, notably *all*, *both* and *half*, may occur before an article/demonstrative/possessive ('all the suggestions', 'both his sisters'). We may now expand the list of premodifiers in [136] to [137].

[138] all/both/half – article/demonstrative/possessive – quantifier(s) – adjectives/participles – noun modifier(s)

We noted earlier (p. 123) that adjectives are ordered among themselves, if two or more co-occur, e.g. 'size' before 'colour'. It is very unusual for all, or even most, of the premodifiers to co-occur in a single noun phrase, and the extent to which nouns are modified depends on the type of text (e.g. journalistic, narrative, casual conversation) and on the personal style of the encoder. The following are some examples from journalistic texts:

[139] the higher health charges   [A01: 161]
     (Art – Adj – NMod – N)
[140] General de Gaulle's official welcome   [A02: 9]
     (PossNP – Adj – N)
[141] his thirty-ninth birthday   [A03: 8]
     (Poss – ordinal – N)
[142] a European space satellite project   [A03: 149]
     (Art – Adj – NMod + NMod – N)
[143] five leading Communists   [A06: 47]
     (cardinal – participle – N)

Among post-modifiers we have noted adjectives after certain indefinite pronouns ('nothing new'), and more generally phrasal and clausal modifiers of nouns, such as prepositional phrases, participle clauses and relative clauses.

[*Exercise 3*]

Exercises

Exercise 1

Identify the means by which the nouns in the following sentences are 'identified' (articles, demonstratives, possessives, quantifiers) and supply an appropriate label (e.g. definite article, cardinal numeral, proximate demonstrative).

1. Then I'd like to go to all the theatres and look round the shops   [P29: 104]
2. I saw a blackbird's nest stuffed into a hole in the coping
                                                                      [L09: 79]
3. She had plenty of leisure to dwell upon those vanished days   [P23: 192]
4. There was some colour too in his tanned face
                                                                      [P16: 120]
5. In those forty years the Legion has achieved much
                                                                      [B25: 178]
6. Is there any reason why the centigrade countries should not change to fahrenheit?   [B03: 171]
7. I was there when that third astronaut went up
                                                                      [C06: 44]
8. Sam wanted one last cool glass before going to his room   [N10: 76]
9. We can imagine how the reader of Zechariah's day might pause at this ninth verse in amazement
                                                                      [D11: 123]
10. In spite of all their bluster, they let many a big fish through the net   [B05: 151]

Exercise 2

Identify the items (words, phrases, clauses) which are used to classify and describe nouns in the following sentences, and supply an appropriate label (e.g. colour adjective, participle, relative clause).

1. Round a bend in the road they came upon a low and elegant little house   [K19: 3]
2. Landis could not possibly have missed seeing the small attractive figure of Joy   [N05: 27]
3. He tried to control his fury and his hammering heart by taking a deep, slow breath   [N29: 160]
4. Bill had set off in his sixteen-foot yawl with Bueno Buch, a strapping young Pomo Indian, to row for him
                                                                      [N03: 84]
5. To them are added some excellent photographs of the finished weave   [C14: 191]
6. Two other important aspects of income taxation worry people   [B07: 78]

7. One had monstrous wings which trailed about him like
   a carpet   [M06: 7]
8. It's not often you get the chance of wearing a nice red
   dress instead of your old blue trousers   [P14: 92]
9. There was blue trout next, then a young chicken that
   had been cooked in wine and herbs   [P10: 24]
10. He drove down the lighted streets, his passage con-
    trolled by traffic lights that blinked green and red in
    their proper intervals   [M01: 98]

Exercise 3

Identify the noun phrases in the following sentences and
make a description of their structure.
1. The bus stop was a deserted island on an empty street
                                                       [M01: 181]
2. McNaught dumped himself in the pilot's seat
                                                       [M05: 122]
3. You soon discover the Hungarians are the biggest eaters
   in Europe   [B21: 21]
4. A belt of trees helped to absorb the noise of the traffic
                                                       [P03: 6]
5. Luckily I have a guest room in my apartment
                                                       [L05: 45]
6. She had two patches of red high on her cheek bones
                                                       [P21: 64]
7. When you have become proficient in these stitches,
   attractive articles can be made from the directions
   included in this book   [E01: 190]
8. These young people seem to have acquired a healthier
   slant on life   [R05: 124]
9. Morris said something wicked under his breath
                                                       [L17: 130]
10. London-born Stokowski, now 79, has a reputation for
    highly individual interpretations   [A10: 153]

CHAPTER 6
Propositions: Sentences

We are gradually building up a picture of the grammar of English through the meanings associated with grammatical categories and classes. We have concentrated so far largely on individual elements of grammar: words and parts of words (inflections). These we have related to situation types (verbs), participants (nouns) and circumstances (adverbs and prepositions), and to various kinds of specification of these major categories, e.g. auxiliary verbs and modal adverbs for situation types, adjectives and determinatives for participants, and so on. We have gone beyond the individual account of isolated classes of words in our treatment of specification as having a structural relationship with the item that is specified. The term 'noun phrase', for example, which we used in the previous chapter, implies a unit which has internal syntactic structure, e.g. in the way that determinatives and nouns relate.

In this chapter we come to what is sometimes regarded as syntax proper: the structure of sentences, or in semantic terms the structure of propositions. Following our practice so far, it is with propositions that we begin, and how propositions represent the combining of various elements – situation types, participants, and circumstances – that we have discussed in earlier chapters. Then we will investigate how the meanings associated with propositions are realised in the grammar of the sentence in English.

Propositions

A proposition is composed of a situation type together with
its associated participants and circumstances. A proposition
contains only one situation type. (Combinations of propositions will be dealt with in Chapters 7 to 9.) Consider the
examples at [1] to [3].

[1] Each short chapter contains suggestions for further
reading   [C14: 12]
[2] Many of George Herbert's poems have become
much-loved hymns   [D05: 89]
[3] I will bring you out from under the burdens of
Egypt   [D04: 183]

The proposition at [1] refers to a STATE situation type of
stance, represented by the verb *contain*. Associated with
contain are the participants *chapter* and *suggestions*, together
with their specifications. The proposition at [2] contains an
EVENT situation type of process, represented by the verb
become, which is specified for aspect by *have*. Relating to
become are the participants *poems* and *hymns*, each of which
has associated specification. The proposition at [3] contains
an ACTION situation type of accomplishment, represented
by the verb *bring*, which is specified by the modal auxiliary
will, indicating future intention. Combined with *bring* are
the (unspecified) participants *I* and *you* and the circumstance
of place introduced by the 'compound' preposition *out from
under*.

Semantic dependencies

We have noted before (p. 23), and the examples at [1] to [3]
illustrate this, that a proposition as a whole constitutes an
instance of a situation type, even though we have taken the
verb word as representative of the situation. In other words,
a situation includes participants and circumstances as well as
the state, event or action – the whole proposition therefore.
The reason why the situation type can be said to stand for
the whole proposition is because it, to a large extent,
determines how many and what type of other elements
must or may be present in the proposition. Or, to put it

another way, the participants and circumstances in a proposition are **dependent** on the situation type.

At the beginning of Chapter 3 we viewed a proposition as suggesting a kind of drama in which certain participants were present and certain kinds of setting (circumstance) were possible. So, in [3], the accomplishment action *bring* suggests a 'bringer' (*I*), a 'person/thing brought' (*you*), and 'somewhere' from or to which it is brought (*out from under*). Alternatively we may say that a proposition with *bring* will include an AGENTIVE participant, an AFFECTED participant and a LOCATIVE SOURCE or GOAL circumstance. *Bring* determines the presence of these elements; they are 'dependent' on *bring*.

The elements are, however, dependent on the situation type word in different ways. Consider the further examples with *bring* as the situation type at [4] to [7].

[4] I've brought you lovely, lovely presents
[K28: 82]
[5] You must bring George here, one day   [P20: 136]
[6] Mr Redfern very kindly brought me home in his car   [P05: 78]
[7] Mr Weir brought you?   [P21: 94]

All these propositions express the same sense of *bring*: transporting a person/thing from one place to another, with the orientation towards 'here' (by contrast with *take*, which is oriented towards 'there'). But these propositions contain a variable number of elements, though some are constant. The AGENTIVE participant occurs in all the propositions: *I* in [3] and [4], *you* in [5], *Mr Redfern* in [6], and *Mr Weir* in [7]. The AFFECTED participant occurs in all: *you* in [3], *presents* in [4], *George* in [5], *me* in [6], and *you* in [7]. A LOCATIVE circumstance occurs in some of the propositions: as a SOURCE in [3] (*out from under*), as a GOAL in [5] (*here*) and [6] (*home*). In [4] there is also what appears to be a GOAL (*you*), though we might prefer to regard this element as a RECIPIENT participant. This illustrates both the close relationship between RECIPIENT and LOCATIVE GOAL, and the blurring of the distinction between participant and circumstance in situation types like *bring*. The proposition at [7] contains only an AGENTIVE and an AFFECTED participant, but a LOCATIVE GOAL of 'here' is implied: the inherent 'here' orientation of *bring* means that the LOCATIVE GOAL may be omitted from the proposition if it is unambiguously *here*.

From this discussion it will be clear that a proposition referring to the situation type *bring* will contain three elements in addition to the ACTION: (1) AGENTIVE, (2) AFFECTED, (3) LOCATIVE (SOURCE/GOAL) or RECIPIENT. The third element may be omitted under certain contextual conditions, viz if it is 'here'. We may say therefore that these elements are semantically **obligatory** with *bring*, which determines their presence and on which they are dependent. What then of the elements that we have not yet accounted for in the propositions at [5] and [6]: *one day, very kindly, in his car*? They are, respectively, a TEMPORAL circumstance, a MANNER circumstance, and a MEANS circumstance. These elements are clearly not obligatory, since they do not occur in the other examples; nor could we say that they have been contextually omitted, as with the 'here' of [7]. They are circumstantial elements which are **optional**. They are still dependent on *bring*, since they must be semantically compatible with the situation type. But they are not required or determined by *bring*; they are not necessary for the proposition to make sense. Consider now, though, the proposition at [8], which like [5] contains a TEMPORAL circumstance.

[8] Ivy is bringing you your breakfast *as soon as she can manage it*   [P24: 148]

The TEMPORAL circumstance is itself a proposition – 'as soon as she can manage it' (see Chapter 8). If we omit it, then the proposition either seems to be incomplete or it implies 'now'. However, its obligatoriness does not arise from the situation type *bring*, but rather from the tense/aspect – present progressive – of the proposition, which, as we saw in Chapter 4, may refer either to a specified future time or to the present moment, which is usually not specified. In this context it refers to future time, and so a TEMPORAL circumstance has to be given. The tense/aspect requires temporal clarification, not the situation type.

We have now ascertained that a proposition, as a combination of a situation type, participants and circumstances, may contain obligatory and optional elements.

Obligatory elements are required for the proposition to make sense, though omission is possible according to context. Optional elements are, like obligatory ones, dependent on the situation type, but they are not required for any particular instance of the proposition. Participants are always obligatory elements; circumstances are most often optional, but a LOCATIVE circumstance especially may be obligatory with some situation types.

Our discussion has suggested how we might describe the syntax of propositions, in terms of dependencies; but, with its concentration on one item (*bring*), it has perhaps implied that this must be done uniquely for each verb word. This is true to an extent, in that the lexical description of verbs would include an indication of their syntactic operation (as in the *Longman Dictionary of Contemporary English*, 1987). But the notions of dependency are generalisable and we will find that verbs or verb senses group together into classes on the basis of their semantic/syntactic operation. Like *bring* in the sense discussed, for example, are senses of *take, send, carry, transport, fetch, lift, convey, dispatch*. These would be regarded as a subclass of action accomplishment verbs, defined by their syntactic operation and the semantic compatibilities between them and their associated obligatory participants and circumstances.

Semantic compatibilities

In our discussion of *bring* we noted that the usually obligatory elements determined by the verb are: (1) AGENTIVE, (2) AFFECTED, (3) LOCATIVE (SOURCE/GOAL) or RECIPIENT. The action of bringing is performed by an animate, usually human being – AGENTIVE; it is performed on a thing (*your breakfast* [8]) or on a person (*me* [6]) – AFFECTED; and it is performed in respect of a person (*you* [4]) – RECIPIENT, or in respect of a place from or to which the AFFECTED is brought (*home* [6]) – LOCATIVE. These are the normal semantic compatibilities as illustrated in the propositions at [3] to [8]. We have to allow, though, for the possibility that other compatibilities may operate. Consider the propositions at [9] and [10], which appear to be similarly structured to [3] and [6].

[9] An hour's riding brought us to a trail that we figured would lead us to the miners' camp
[N06: 122]

[10] A sharp rap on the door brought a frown of impatience to his face
[L10: 90]

The proposition at [9] contains an AFFECTED (*us*) and a LOCATIVE GOAL (*trail*). The action is not performed, however, by an AGENTIVE, but rather by an EVENTIVE (*an hour's riding*). The EVENTIVE implies an AGENTIVE ('*We* rode for an hour'), but it is the whole action of riding which performs the bringing. In [10] the normal semantic compatibilities have been stretched even further. The instigator of the action (*rap*) and the participant that is brought (*frown*) should probably both be analysed semantically as EVENTIVE participants, though we might argue that a distinction needs to be made between the EVENTIVE as INSTIGATOR and the EVENTIVE as AFFECTED. The question is whether we are dealing here with an extension of the sense of *bring* illustrated by the propositions at [3] to [8], in which there is some stretching of *bring*'s semantic compatibilities, or whether we are dealing with another sense of *bring*, marked by the different semantic compatibilities. There is no obvious answer to this question; it will probably depend on the exercise of the linguistic analyst's informed judgement.

What is clearly emerging is that verbs, or subclasses of verbs, constrain their environments semantically in different ways and determine varying sets of semantic compatibilities. This can be illustrated by the propositions at [11] to [14].

[11] Then we climbed a promontory   [M03: 176]

[12] A wide range of plants grow quite well in plastic pots   [E07: 183]

[13] In New York the Security Council is meeting at 11 a.m. today   [A21: 9]

[14] He talked of a Berlin crisis later this year
[A04: 60]

Here are four propositions representing further situation types: *climb*, an accomplishment; *grow*, a process; *meet*, an activity; *talk*, an activity. Each has its own set of semantic compatibilities and their variants, which it shares with other verbs in the same semantic subclass.

Climb, illustrated by [11], takes an AGENTIVE – human (*we*) or other animate – that performs the action, and a LOCATIVE (*a promontory*) referring to what is climbed. We might suppose that someone who goes climbing as a leisure 'activity' could say in response to the question, 'What do you do in your spare time?': 'I climb'. In this case, *climb* refers no longer to an accomplishment, but to an activity, and the LOCATIVE is excluded from *climb*'s obligatory elements. The LOCATIVE is also excluded in examples like [15].

[15] The bus climbed and went quietly into orbit
[M04: 174]

Here the sole participant (*bus*) is no longer AGENTIVE but AFFECTED, and *climb* is not an ACTION but an EVENT, specifically a process. The same structure would also be applicable to plants climbing, since we can no more attribute intentions to plants than we can to buses.

This brings us to *grow* in the proposition at [12], which is clearly a process, here with an inanimate participant undergoing the process of growing. The question is whether *grow* requires any further element than the AFFECTED participant (here *plants*). It may occur with just this element, e.g.

[16] These facilities are growing   [E34: 30]

But if we omit the MANNER circumstance (*quite well*) and the LOCATIVE (*in plastic pots*) from [12], the proposition seems incomplete. The completeness is restored if we add the LOCATIVE, though not if we add only the MANNER circumstance; which suggests that the LOCATIVE is here obligatory. It is doubtful, though, whether it is determined by *grow*: it would appear to be the quantifying phrase 'a wide range of' which requires the LOCATIVE, since 'Plants grow' makes sense more easily than does 'A wide range of plants grow'. The essentially optional nature of the LOCATIVE would appear to be confirmed by [17], which does not contain a LOCATIVE, only an omissible MANNER circumstance.

[17] The pigs will grow rapidly enough   [E37: 30]

A number of circumstantial elements are thus compatible with *grow*: expressing where things grow, the rate at which they grow, the extent to which they grow, and so on. None of them, though, is required for a proposition containing *grow* to make sense.

Turning now to *meet* in [13], which we have assigned to the activity situation type, we find that it requires an AGENTIVE participant (*the Security Council*) and a TEMPORAL circumstance (*at 11 a.m. today*) as obligatory elements; the LOCATIVE (*in New York*) may be omitted and the proposition still makes good sense – compare [18].

[18] They meet next Thursday   [A32: 69]

However, the TEMPORAL circumstance may be omitted, when the time may be deduced from the context. Such, we may assume, is the case for [19] and [20].

[19] The two men met alone in the Prime Minister's
     study   [A28: 220]
[20] There, on the Dow Agrochemicals Ltd stand, he
     will meet Ted Moult   [A42: 221]

Both these examples, however, contain LOCATIVES ('in . . . study', 'there on . . . stand'). The kind of information that we might expect to provide about a meeting would normally include both when and where it takes place: in that sense, both TEMPORAL and LOCATIVE expected in a proposition with *meet*, though under certain conditions of omissibility. The proposition at [20] illustrates a further interesting point about *meet*: it may require two participants, an AGENTIVE (*he*) and an AFFECTED (*Ted Moult*), instead of just an AGENTIVE as in [13]. The rule seems to be that if the meeting is reciprocal or mutual – there must after all be at least two parties to a meeting – then the proposition contains only an AGENTIVE, whose noun is plural in number. If, on the other hand, one party takes the initiative and the other has a passive role, then there are two participants, AGENTIVE and AFFECTED, respectively.

A similar semantic compatibility may apply to *talk*, though not relevantly to [14]. Compare [21] and [22], however.

[21] The two men talked alone   [A04: 24]
[22] I talked to him yesterday   [A10: 138]

The proposition at [21] represents the reciprocal version, with a plural noun as AGENTIVE, and [22] has AGENTIVE and AFFECTED, with an instigator and a more passive participant. *Talk* may, however, have only an instigator (singular noun as AGENTIVE), as in [14]; and it may additionally have the matter talked about present in the proposition (*crisis* in [14]) as an AFFECTED participant. We may note that, although time and place could well be specified for the activity of talking, the expectation that they will be expressed is not as high as it is for *meet*.

From our discussion of these further examples it will be clear that language is highly complex in the area of semantic compatibilities within propositions and that it is not just the verb word which governs what other elements may be present (e.g. tense/aspect have an influence on TEMPORALS). It almost seems as if each verb word needs its own investigation and description for its semantic operation in syntax, a description that is partly covered in dictionaries and more adequately in some than in others.

Functions of propositions

We turn now from the internal semantic-syntax of propositions to the roles that propositions may take on in the domain of discourse. Traditionally four general functions have been recognised for propositions, illustrated by the examples at [23] to [26]:

[23] His partner sat opposite him   [A07: 174]
[24] Why did you come in here?   [P24: 52]
[25] Frances, bring the sherry, please   [K08: 64]
[26] What a time it's taken to reach Glasgow!

                                            [P29: 4]

The proposition at [23] is a **statement**, as have been most of the examples so far in this book. The proposition at [24] is a **question**, conventionally marked in writing by a question mark. The proposition at [25] is a **command**, and the one at [26] is an **exclamation**, both of which may be marked in writing by an exclamation mark.

These different functions of propositions correspond to different roles that speakers or writers may take on *vis-à-vis* their addressees. They may take on a stating role, a questioning role, a commanding role, or an exclaiming role. The extent to which these roles are available to a speaker/writer will depend on their social position in respect of the addressee. For example, issuing a command such as [25] requires you to be in a position of power over your addressee. The functions of the propositions at [23] to [26] are marked by particular typical forms of sentences – declarative, interrogative, imperative, exclamative – which we will discuss below (p. 162). Suffice it to note at this point that the functions are not always manifested by these typical sentence forms. For example, [27] is phrased in the typical form of a question, but it functions more as an exclamation than a question,

[27] But how could I ever trust you?   [P04: 99]

Similarly, the question in [28] has rather the function of a kind of command, as the response given indicates.

[28] 'Will you pour your own, please, and one for me?'
James did so.   [K08: 66]

We often phrase 'polite' commands, or requests, in the form of a question: it brings the interlocutors onto a more equal footing in the power relationship, and it is a means by which you can get a social equal to do something.

We have suggested that there are four general types of function that propositions may have. A closer and more detailed investigation of the functions of propositions would want to identify a number of subtypes of each of these general functions. For example, the category of statements might include more specifically apologies, promises, threats, information, and so on; questions might be subdivided into requests for information, requests for confirmation, requests for action, and so on. Here we are straying from the area of grammar proper into **pragmatics**, a branch of Linguistics which is concerned with the functions of language in situational context (see Levinson 1983, Leech 1983).

[*Exercise 1*]

Sentences

Elements of propositions (AGENTIVE, AFFECTED, LOCATIVE, etc.) are realised grammatically by members of word-classes (noun, verb, adverb, etc.) together with their appropriate specifications. Propositions are realised by sentences. We can, therefore, discuss the internal structure of sentences in terms of the combinability of classes of word, in the same way that we discussed the structure of propositions in terms of the combinability of semantic elements (situations types, participants, circumstances). On this basis, a sentence represents the combination of a verb, corresponding to a situation type, and a number of nouns, adverbs, etc., according to the syntactic dependency relations contracted by the verb.

A sentence may be viewed as consisting of a number of slots. One of the slots will be filled by the verb. The verb then determines how many further slots will occur in a given sentence. The verb *give*, for example, opens up three further slots in the sentence in which it occurs.

[29] Someone had given John a drum   [K28: 24]

Here, three nouns fill the slots in the sentence opened up by *give*: *someone*, *John*, *drum*. *Fetch* in [30] opens up two slots, filled by *I* and *things*; and in [31] *smile* opens up only one slot.

[30] I'll fetch my things   [P11: 19]
[31] The registrar smiled   [K24: 66]

As our previous discussion would lead us to expect, the syntax of these verbs is of course much more complex than these isolated examples would suggest. What they do serve to point up, though, is that a syntactic description which deals only in the number of slots in the structure of a sentence is not very revealing. We need a way of talking about the interrelationships between the elements in a sentence.

Syntactic functions

We can begin to describe the syntax of sentences by labelling the slots with terms which will indicate the function of the items in the slots within the structure of the sentence as a whole. The constant in the structure of sentences is the **Predicator** slot: this is the slot which is filled by the verb word and its accompanying specification (auxiliary verbs). Virtually every sentence in English has a Predicator slot, and we have identified the verb word that fills this slot as the one on which all other items in the sentence are dependent: the Predicator is the prerequisite for a sentence.

Subject

The other slot that is obligatory in most sentences is that of Subject. A minimal sentence, like [31], is composed of a Subject and a Predicator. The Subject occurs to the left of the Predicator in the typical form of statements (declarative), but it inverts with part of the Predicator phrase in most interrogatives: compare [32] and [33].

> [32] *His grandfather* had spoken of a massive oak door
> [L08: 104]
> [33] Have *you* spoken to them? [K03: 174]

The Subject in [32] is *his grandfather*, and in [33] it is *you*. The Subject *you* in [33] has inverted with the perfective auxiliary *have* to form an interrogative (see further below), while in [32] the Subject is in its usual position to the left of the Predicator phrase.

The Subject is the sentence element that usually realises the 'doer' of an action (AGENTIVE), the 'undergoer' of an event (AFFECTED) or the entity that is in some state (AFFECTED, EXPERIENCER, RECIPIENT). A further grammatical characteristic of the Subject is that the noun or pronoun functioning in this slot 'agrees' with the verb. Specifically, this applies in English only to the present tense and only to 3rd person Subjects (except for the verb *be*). Compare [34] and [35].

> [34] Mr Hardaker *knows* Jimmy Hill is on my list of contributors [A07: 196]

[35] Not many people *know* that his decision . . . was
made at Oldham [A39: 215]

In [34] the singular Subject noun (*Mr Hardaker*) is matched
by the *–s* inflection on *knows*, which is absent from *know* in
[35] because the Subject (*not many people*) is plural in
number. For the present tense of *be* there is a person/
number agreement between Subject and Predicator as
follows:

[36] 1st singular I   am
     3rd singular he/she/it   is
     2nd singular you   ⎫
     all plural   we/you/they ⎬ are
                            ⎭

[37] I *am* a very wealthy woman [P07: 189]
[38] The view *is* well worth the scramble [P15: 27]
[39] Those birds *are* ready [P18: 109]

Object

Many verbs (e.g. *fetch* in [30]) open up an Object slot in
addition to a Subject slot, for example

[40] We have held *eleven meetings* [H02: 27]
[41] The Church rebukes *the poor monk* for his miracle
[C02: 41]
[42] The next morning he hears *the evidence against his
erstwhile host* [C03: 148]

The verbs in these sentences are *hold*, *rebuke* and *hear*, and
they have the Objects *meetings*, *monk* and *evidence* respectively. Omission of any of these makes the sentence in which
they occur ungrammatical. The Object represents the
AFFECTED participant in these propositions, the first two
of which are ACTIONS with an AGENTIVE as Subject
(*we*, *Church*), and [42] is a PRIVATE STATE with a
RECIPIENT as Subject (*he*). You will note that [41] and
[42] each contain a circumstance, which is optional: 'for his
miracle', a REASON; and 'the next morning', a
TEMPORAL. Objects usually occur to the right of the
Predicator in all types of sentence.
Some verbs may take two Objects, e.g.

[43] He brought *them their drinks* [K29: 128]
[44] He rarely told *her his plans* [K10: 26]

A distinction is sometimes drawn between the **Direct** Object and the **Indirect** Object. The Indirect Object in [43] is *them*, and in [44] it is *her*. In these examples the Indirect Object has the semantic role of RECIPIENT, and it could be expressed alternatively by a prepositional phrase with *to*, e.g.

[45] He brought their drinks *to them*

Indirect Objects with the role of Recipient are expressed only by the prepositional phrase after some verbs (e.g. *report, divulge, explain*).

[46] Jim had explained the job *to Willie*   [N24: 146]

Indirect Objects also regularly have the semantic role of BENEFACTIVE, when the alternative prepositional phrase is introduced by *for*: compare [47] and [48].

[47] His new employer found *him* a new flat   [H09: 34]
[48] His new employer found a new flat *for him*

A verb may, then, have up to two Object slots opened up by it. If only one Object occurs, it is a Direct Object, most usually with an AFFECTED participant role. The second Object is termed an Indirect Object; it is positioned before the Direct Object if it is a noun (or pronoun) and after it if it is a prepositional phrase; it most often has the participant role of RECIPIENT (including BENEFACTIVE).

Complement
Some verbs, referring mainly to temporary states and qualities, open up a Complement slot in sentence structure, instead of an Object slot, for example:

[49] She is *young and inexperienced*   [K19: 176]
[50] Prussia might become *a republic*   [K13: 74]

The Complement in [49] is 'young and inexperienced', and in [50] it is 'a republic'. The Complement occurs to the right of the Predicator, in the same position as the Object, but it differs in function from the Object. In sentences such as those at [49] and [50], the Complement has a direct relationship with the Subject of the sentence, in a way that the Objects in [40] to [44] do not. The Complement refers back to and says something about the Subject: semantically it has the role of ATTRIBUTE (see Chapter 2, examples at [3] and [4]) and describes a quality or state associated with the Subject. It is in this way that Complements differ from Objects, which refer to entities that are usually referentially quite distinct from the Subject. The exception to this is where an Object is a reflexive pronoun [51] or refers to a part of the Subject's body [52]; but even in these cases the Object does not have the semantic role of ATTRIBUTE, but of AFFECTED.

> [51] Rose didn't kill *herself*   [L05: 147]
> [52] Simon laid *his hand* on it   [L08: 137]

Another type of sentence structure in which the verb opens up a Complement slot is one which also has an Object slot, for example

> [53] You made me *angry*   [K18: 176]
> [54] He thought himself *a luckless individual*   [L10: 71]

In [53] the Object is 'me' and the Complement is 'angry'; in [54] the Object is 'himself' and the Complement is 'a luckless individual'. The Complement in these structures is positioned after the Object, and it is with the Object that it has the relationship of attribution, not with the Subject.

It will be noted that the Complement slot may be filled either by an adjective ([49] and [53]) or by a noun ([50] and [54]). Subject and Object slots are associated with nouns, the Complement slot with noun and adjective. Just as nouns may be specified by means of both adjectives and noun modifiers (Chapter 5), so when the attribution is made in the form of a proposition, the appropriate sentence slot – the Complement – may be filled by a member of either word-class.

Adverbial

Many sentences contain a functional slot which is labelled 'Adverbial'. In many cases the Adverbial slot is filled by syntactic elements with the semantic role of circumstance: such Adverbials are said to have the function of **Adjunct**. There are three further types of Adverbial – **Subjunct**, **Disjunct** and **Conjunct** – but we will concentrate on the more commonly occurring Adjunct function first.

A small number of verbs open up an Adjunct slot in the

structure of the sentence in which they function as Predicator. This is the case, for example, with the verb *put*:

[55] Rob put his hand *in the water* [P10: 57]

Put, with the meaning of 'transfer an object from one position to another', opens up a Subject slot, an Object slot and an Adjunct slot (filled by 'in the water' in [55]). By saying that *put* opens up an Adjunct slot, we imply that a sentence having *put* (with this meaning) as Predicator would normally be ungrammatical unless an Adjunct (with the semantic role of LOCATIVE circumstance) is present.

Adjuncts are, however, not usually obligatory in this way. Consider the sentences at [56] to [58].

[56] *In the morning* I had my breakfast *in a corner of the hotel dining room* [N15: 124]

[57] He might easily have been listening *outside the door* [P04: 58]

[58] *Outside Gaby's room* he said, 'I wonder what time band call will be?' [P10: 145]

In [56] there is a Temporal Adjunct, i.e. an element ('in the morning') with the syntactic function of Adjunct and the semantic role of TEMPORAL circumstance. It is not an obligatory element of [56]; the verb *had* does not require it for the sentence to be grammatical. It will, though, have a significant function in the text from which this sentence is taken, in keeping track of the time orientation of the text. From the perspective of the sentence, however, it is an optional, gratuitous element.

The same is true of the Locative Adjuncts in [56], [57] and [58], 'in a corner of the hotel', 'outside the door' and 'outside Gaby's room', respectively. The verbs *had*, *listen* and *say* do not require them to be present, though they are no doubt essential in marking spatial orientation in the texts from which these sentences are taken. In fact, as our discussion earlier in the chapter on semantic compatibilities indicated, circumstantial elements, and thus Adjuncts, cannot always be clearly assigned to either the obligatory category or the optional category. Sometimes we find an Adjunct which we have to consider to be more-or-less obligatory or more-or-less optional; this is particularly the case with verbs whose meaning includes a reference to motion and is associated with a Locative of Direction, e.g.

[59] As she spoke Ralph Batley came *into the kitchen*
[P21: 185]
[60] Nelly had thrown a stone *at it*   [P18: 126]

In [59] the verb *come* could be said to open up an Adjunct slot for a LOCATIVE DIRECTIONAL circumstance. On the other hand, the sentence without the Adjunct could be considered grammatical, even if with a feeling of incompleteness. The same is true of the Adjunct in [60] with the verb *throw* as Predicator, which seems to require or at least expect an Adjunct, though it is not altogether impossible to omit it.

Perhaps one distinguishing factor between obligatory and optional Adjuncts is the tendency for obligatory Adjuncts to be positioned normally to the right of the Predicator in the structure of the sentence, while optional Adjuncts may frequently occupy more than one position, notably initial (as in [56] and [58]) and final (as in [57]). Optional Adjuncts composed of a single word (usually an adverb) may also occur medially in a sentence, e.g. *usually* in [61] and *often* in [62].

[61] The older people *usually* stay here and have coffee
[P02: 42]
[62] They *often* had such a rendezvous   [P03: 213]

Optional Adjuncts are positionally mobile in a way that Subjects, Objects and Complements are not.

Let us turn now to the other more minor kinds of **Adverbial**, and first of all to **Subjuncts**. These may be illustrated in the sentences at [63] to [65].

[63] *Visually*, it is inventive and often lovely. *Dramatically*, it is a hotchpotch   [C10: 16]
[64] B.E.A. will fight any proposal to raise fares, *especially* at such short notice   [A15: 20]
[65] Its cost could *virtually* be ignored, and, indeed, it must *literally* be so by many in Budapest
[B21: 54]

The Subjuncts in [63] are *visually* and *dramatically*; in [64] it is *especially*; and in [65] there are two, *virtually* and *literally*. Subjuncts do not function as full elements of sentence structure in the way that Adjuncts do. Neither do they represent slots opened up by the verb. Their function is generally subordinate to one element or another in the sentence, though one group of Subjuncts functions in respect of a sentence as a whole. These are the **Viewpoint** Subjuncts, like *visually* and *dramatically* in [63]. They are to be interpreted as a comment by the speaker or writer on the perspective or viewpoint from which the proposition is to be regarded as valid. They can usually be expanded to the phrase 'From a . . . point of view', which is why they are termed 'viewpoint' Subjuncts.

The group of Subjuncts which are subordinate to some element or other in the sentence divides into a number of types. The term for the group is **Item** Subjuncts. We can distinguish five types.

1. **Subject-oriented**. Usually positioned initially in a sentence, they are subordinate to and comment on the Subject of the sentence. Adverbs functioning as this type of Subjunct include *bitterly, sadly, wisely, rightly*, e.g.

[66] Mr Kessler *rightly* regards [it] as superficial
[C13: 69]

2. **Time**. These are subordinate to the Predicator and are usually positioned within or before the verb phrase. This type includes the adverbs *yet, just, still, already, never, seldom*, e.g.

[67] The Heffer Gallery have *just* opened an exhibition of the works of Stanislas Reychan   [C15: 191]

3. **Emphasisers**. Subordinate to a variety of elements, in whose proximity they are positioned, these Subjuncts have a modality function and include the adverbs *really, actually, definitely, literally* (see example at [65] above).

4. **Intensifiers**. These relate to the degree of some element and may be either (a) **amplifiers**, e.g. the adverbs *completely, absolutely, terribly, enormously* or (b) **downtoners**, e.g. the adverbs *almost, nearly, somewhat, merely, virtually* (see example at [65] above), e.g.

[68] The result, if not *completely* satisfying, is remarkable   [C17: 178]

[69] *Somewhat* to my surprise, I received a long answer to this statement from Mr Krushchev   [G75: 13]

5. **Focusing**. Drawing the reader's/hearer's attention to a particular element, they are positioned immediately before the focussed item. This type includes the adverbs *precisely*, *simply*, *especially* (as in the example at [64] above).

Subjuncts may be regarded as a kind of encoder's comment, adding some observation to particular elements in the proposition. The second minor type of Adverbial – **Disjuncts** – have a similar role. In the case of Disjuncts, however, the Adverbial is, as their name implies, syntactically detached – or 'disjoined' – from the sentence; and they have as their scope the whole sentence. They are usually positioned initially or very early in a sentence; they are often marked off from the sentence by commas in writing or a separate intonation unit in speech.

Speakers and writers may make two kinds of comment, in the form of Disjuncts, on the sentences which they encode. They may comment, firstly, on the **Style** or the form of what is being said. A Style Disjunct has the effect of defining the conditions under which the encoder takes authority for what is said. Style Disjuncts include those listed at [70], two of which are illustrated at [71] and [72].

[70] candidly   bluntly   frankly   seriously   truthfully strictly   personally   generally

[71] *Personally*, I would prefer beech, which retains its beautiful golden-brown leaves in the winter
                                                                                   [E08: 81]

[72] It should, *strictly*, be only applied to those judges who have demonstrated a working knowledge of all breeds   [E32: 36]

Style Disjuncts may usually be expanded to the paraphrase '. . . speaking' or 'To speak . . .'.

The second type of Disjunct comments on the **Content** of the sentence and often reflects the attitude of the encoder to the proposition and to its truth value. Content Disjuncts include those listed at [73] and exemplified at [74] and [75].

[73] admittedly   indeed (see [65])   undoubtedly
      apparently   arguably   presumably   reputedly
      amazingly   remarkably   disappointingly
      regrettably   strangely

[74] *Admittedly*, extensive rent control has severely
      limited the number of 'true' rents available to the
      valuer   [E28: 34]

[75] But I have known a good conductor insist on
      what was *arguably* a 'correct' fast pace when the
      singer was incapable of singing at that pace
                                                  [G43: 103]

With these Disjuncts, the encoder intrudes on what they are
saying and invites the hearer/reader to interpret the
proposition expressed by the sentence in a particular way.
The encoder is directing the decoder's understanding and
interpretation of what is said.

The third minor type of Adverbial is the **Conjunct**. It
too, like the Disjunct, is more or less detached from the
sentence in which it is included. It is frequently positioned
as the first or second item in a sentence, and bounded by
commas or in a separate intonation unit. As its name
implies, the Conjunct has the function of 'joining together'.
A Conjunct joins the sentence containing it to the preceding
sentence or sentences in a text or discourse and specifies the
kind of relationship obtaining between it and what comes
before. There are a number of types of Conjunct,
established on the basis of the conjunctive relationship
implied.

1. **Listing**. This Conjunct indicates that the proposition is part of a list and, in some instances, what its
   position in the list is. Adverbial expressions with
   this function include *first of all*, *secondly*, *finally*,
   equally, *moreover*, *in addition*, e.g.

[76] *Finally*, the crux of this matter is surely not wages,
      but spending power   [B09: 71]

2. **Summative**. The sentence containing this Conjunct
   is a summary or conclusion in respect of what has
   previously been said, perhaps a list of evidence or set
   of arguments. Adverbs having this function include
   altogether, *in conclusion*, *therefore*, e.g.

[77] *In conclusion*, it is interesting to note that Sheffield United. . . [B24: 58]

3. **Appositive**. This Conjunct identifies the sentence containing it as a reformulation or specification of what precedes. Adverbs indicating apposition include *in other words, namely, for example*, e.g.

[78] *In other words*, they should carry on as they have been doing [B24: 223]

4. **Resultive**. The sentence containing this type of Conjunct expresses a result or draws a conclusion from previous propositions. Adverbs with this function include *accordingly, consequently, hence*, e.g.

[79] *Consequently*, the councils have more responsibility [B26: 196]

5. **Inferential**. This type of Conjunct identifies its sentence as drawing an inference from what has previously been said. Adverbs indicating inference include *else, in that case, otherwise*, e.g.

[80] *In that case*, why were farmers not allowed by the Board to load potatoes. . .? [B16: 116]

6. **Contrastive**. A sentence containing this Conjunct marks the proposition as being in contrast or opposition to a preceding proposition. Adverbial expressions with a contrastive function include *however, on the other hand, instead, nevertheless, alternatively, by comparison*, e.g.

[81] The versifiers do not display a high degree of technical competence. They are, *however*, bold in the use of rhyme to a degree that would astonish Mr Ogden Nash [C12: 119]

7. **Transitional**. This final Conjunct type indicates that the sentence containing it represents an interpolation or a transition from one part of the text to another. Adverbs of transition include *incidentally, meanwhile*, e.g.

[82] His 'holiday', *incidentally*, has consisted of working on his farm [A40: 35]

It will be clear that Adverbials, like the word-class of adverbs, play a set of diverse roles in the meaning and structure of a sentence. Some Adverbials – Adjuncts – function as part of the propositional content of the sentence, either as items required by the verb, or more usually as items adding gratuitous circumstantial information. Other Adverbials – Subjuncts and Disjuncts – add comment and observations from the speaker/writer, which colour the meaning or direct the interpretation of the sentence. Still other Adverbials – Conjuncts – have a textual function (see Chapter 10), making links of various kinds between sentences in a text or discourse.

We can summarise the discussion of Adverbials with the diagram at [83].

[83]

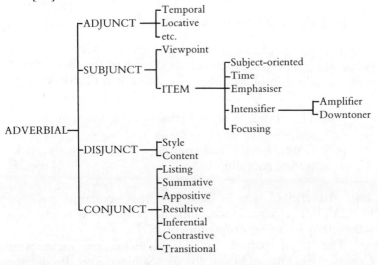

[*Exercise 2*]

Complementation

The elements required by the verb in a sentence are said to be its **complementation**, that is, the elements needed to make the sentence 'complete'. Sometimes the term 'complementation' is used to refer only to the elements occurring to the right of the verb – not the Subject, therefore. We have used the term 'Complement' (see p. 149 above) to refer to one of the functional slots opened up by the verb, i.e. one kind of complementation. We will use the term 'complementation', then, to refer to all those elements required by the verb: Subject, Object, Complement, Adverbial (where these are obligatory).

As we look at the kinds of sentence structures created as verbs attract to themselves the elements necessary to 'complete' them, we find that a number of basic patterns of complementation emerge, which we can describe using the functional labels we have discussed in the preceding sections. The first of these complementation patterns contains just the element Subject in addition to the Predicator (**1. SP**), e.g.

[84] *The chief in the white coat was talking* excitedly
[K09: 181]
[85] But today *the sun has broken through* [K05: 47]

This pattern is commonly used to express activities [84] or events [85]. The second pattern is similar to the first, except with the addition of an obligatory Adverbial (**2. SPA**), e.g.

[86] The couple – were sitting – on a low couch
[L11: 44]
[87] Goldie Lord – was running – back down the rock-walled corridor [L03: 26]

The Adverbial most often has the semantic role of LOCATIVE circumstance, and the proposition refers to a stance [86] or an accomplishment [87].

The third pattern of complementation includes a Complement in addition to the Subject and Predicator (**3. SPC**), e.g.

[88] Abby – didn't seem – discouraged [L06: 92]
[89] She – had become – a beauty [L05: 33]

The proposition expressed by sentences with this pattern commonly refers either to a state (quality or temporary state) [88] or to a process [89] in which the resultant attribute is realised as a Complement.

The fourth pattern of complementation contains an

Object in addition to the Subject and Predicator (**4. SPO**),
e.g.

> [90] He – crossed – the coast (a few miles south of
>   Ancona)   [N01: 168]
> [91] You – know – a great deal about me   [N04: 106]

Accomplishments [90], private states [91], and momentary
and transitional acts are situation types typically expressed
by this complementation pattern. The fifth pattern bears the
same relationship to the fourth as the second pattern does to
the first: it has additionally an obligatory Adverbial
(**5. SPOA**), e.g. (two instances of the pattern in this
example)

> [92] (Then) Jessie – placed – a bowl of porridge – on
>   the table (and) – pushed – Helen's own horn spoon
>   – towards it   [N28: 181]

As in the second pattern, the Adverbial most often expresses
a LOCATIVE circumstance, and the pattern is typical of
accomplishments involving sending or propelling or
moving some object.

The sixth pattern of complementation contains two
Objects in addition to the Subject and Predicator
(**6. SPOO**), e.g. (two instances)

> [93] He – gives – us – the gen (and) we – give – him –
>   the publicity   [N04: 131]

The propositions expressed by sentences with this pattern
commonly refer to accomplishments of transferring goods
from one person to another.

The seventh complementation pattern also has an item
in addition to Subject, Predicator and Object: a Complement (**7. SPOC**), e.g.

> [94] He (still) regards – spectacles – as faintly ridiculous
>   [R09: 24]
> [95] Stark fear – turned – the Italian's skin – yellow
>   [L10: 167]

As with the Complement in the third pattern, it may refer
to a state that the Object is in, often with a private state
verb of evaluation [94], or the Complement may refer to the

result of a process happening to an Object, with an accomplishment verb [95].

We have identified seven patterns of complementation, listed at [96] below. They represent the basic patterns underlying the great majority of English sentences, the models or templates on which the sentences of English are structured.

[96] 1. S P
2. S P A
3. S P C
4. S P O
5. S P O A
6. S P O O
7. S P O C

There are two traditional terms used to describe complementation patterns: **transitive** and **intransitive**. A transitive pattern is one that contains an Object, thus patterns 4 to 7. An intransitive pattern is one that does not contain an Object, thus patterns 1 and 2 and, perhaps, 3 though it does not fall readily into either category. In *A Comprehensive Grammar of the English Language* (see Introduction), 3 is termed a **copular** pattern: the Predicator is a 'copular' verb, most typically *be*, which links or 'couples' the Subject and Complement.

Obligatory and optional

The complementation patterns discussed above contain the elements that, for a particular Predicator, may be regarded as obligatory. For example, if the Predicator is the verb *give* in the pattern **SPOO**, then the Subject and both Objects must normally be present for the sentence to be grammatical.

[97] We'll give you a nice one [N10: 60]

In this example, *we* is the Subject, *you* and *a nice one* the two Objects, and none could normally be omitted. The sentence could be added to, however, by optional Adverbial elements, e.g.

[98] We'll *probably* give you a nice one *tomorrow at the fair*

The sentence now contains three Adverbials – a Content Disjunct (*probably*), a Temporal Adjunct (*tomorrow*) and a Locative Adjunct (*at the fair*) – in addition to the Subject and Objects. But, as [97] demonstrates, the Adverbials are all optional elements.

We discussed the obligatory and optional status of elements earlier in the chapter, under the heading of 'semantic dependencies'. There, obligatoriness was discussed in terms of a proposition making sense. We are now discussing it in terms of a sentence being grammatical. The two perspectives are, of course, complementary. Judgements about whether a sentence is grammatical or ungrammatical depend on the assessment of the sense or nonsense that a sentence makes, or on imagining a context in which a sentence might occur. Say, for example, that we omit the Indirect Object from [97]

[99] We'll give a nice one

A first reaction might be to declare [99] ungrammatical, and to ask 'Who'll be given a nice one?' But if we imagine [99] said in the context of donating prizes for a competition or items for a charity auction, then it begins to sound more grammatical.

Even less readily omitted from the **SPOO** pattern is the Direct Object. In 'We'll give you', for example, *you* must be interpreted not as an Indirect but as a Direct Object, in a context such as that envisaged for [99]. However, [100] contains only an Indirect Object (*to Oxfam*)

[100] We give to Oxfam

An appropriate context for [100] might be as a reason for not putting anything in the collecting tin of an alternative charity.

The obligatoriness of the elements in the complementation patterns listed at [100] must, therefore, be viewed in the light of the influence of context on whether a sentence is judged grammatical or not. The patterns represent the model or the norm.

Sentence types

In our discussion of propositions we identified four functions that propositions may have in on-going discourse: statement, question, command and exclamation. We also noted that each of these functions was typically associated with a sentence type: declarative, interrogative, imperative and exclamative, respectively – though the association is not on a strict one-to-one basis. We will now discuss these sentence types. The **declarative** sentence type, to which the great majority of our examples belong, is the type by which all the others are described. It typically has the Subject to the left of the Predicator, which is then followed by the Object(s), Complement or obligatory Adverbial as appropriate to the pattern. The order of elements may be varied for contextual purposes (see Chapter 10), and there are a few patterns that regularly have Subject after Predicator, e.g.

[101] Here comes *the train*

But the rule for declaratives is Subject before Predicator, even when one of the other elements has been moved to initial position in the sentence, e.g.

[102] This entrance *you* cannot use

Here *this entrance* is Object of the sentence, but Subject *you* still precedes the Predicator *cannot use*.

The **interrogative** sentence type has two subtypes, both of which involve some rearrangement of items in the (declarative) sentence. One type is termed the **yes/no** or **polar** interrogative, illustrated at [103]: the polar interrogative expects the answer either 'Yes' or 'No'. The other type, illustrated at [104], is the **wh–** or **information-seeking** interrogative: it begins with a *wh–* word asking for some piece of information.

[103] Will he ever reach the bay?   [K12: 68]
[104] What was he talking about?   [K11: 79]

In both cases the Subject inverts with the leftmost auxiliary verb of the Predicator, *he* with *will* in [103] and *he* with *was* in [104]. In *wh*–interrogatives, the interrogative word (*what* in [104]) is positioned initially, whatever may be the function that it has in the sentence (*what* is Object in [104]). With 'yes/no'-interrogatives, Subject/auxiliary inversion always occurs; with *wh*–interrogatives, it occurs unless the interrogative word itself functions as Subject, when there is no change from the declarative order, e.g.

[105] Who fired the shot? [L14: 196]

The **imperative** sentence type differs from the declarative type in having no Subject.

[106] Get back in the trucks! [K14: 14]

The imperative sentence normally begins with the Predicator, which is realised by the base form of the verb (see Chapter 1): *get* in [106]. The Predicator may, however, be preceded by a form of address (e.g. a name), indicating the person (or animal) to whom the command is directed [107]. It is, though, usually set off from the imperative sentence proper by a comma in writing and by having a separate intonation pattern in speech.

[107] *Harold*, let him go. [N14: 197]

The **exclamative** sentence type usually begins with the word *what* or the word *how*.

[108] *What* a fuss-box the man was! [N02: 179]
[109] *How* unimaginative you all are! [K11: 122]

The *what* introduces a noun phrase ('a fuss-box' in [108]), while the *how* intensifies an adjective or adverb ('unimaginative' in [109]) or indeed the whole sentence, e.g.

[110] How dare she accuse me of poisoning your mother! [L22: 204]

The exclamative element is placed initially and may function as Subject, Object, Complement or Adjunct in the sentence (C in both [108] and [109]). After that, the sentence follows the normal declarative order of elements.

Negation

We have illustrated the various sentence types in the preceding section with examples that have positive polarity. With the exception of the exclamative type, sentences may also have negative polarity. Polarity implies the expression of two opposites: here the opposition is between asserting that something is the case (positive polarity) and denying that something is the case (negative polarity). Negation is of two main types: negation of the whole sentence, and negation of some element or part of the sentence (local negation).

Sentence negation may be achieved either through the negation of the verb [111] or through the use of words with a negative meaning, e.g. *no* in [112], discussed below.

> [111] He would *not* have attempted to run away from his captors   [P01: 50]
> [112] He gave her *no* chance of any private conversation that evening   [N02: 55]

Negation of the verb is by means of *not*, placed after the first auxiliary verb of the Predicator (*would* in [111]). In informal language, auxiliary and negator often coalesce and *not* contracts to *n't*.

> [113] isn't, weren't, can't, wouldn't, mustn't, haven't

If the Predicator contains no auxiliary but only a main verb, and if the main verb is *be*, then it is negated in the same way as an auxiliary [114]. Otherwise a dummy auxiliary *do* is inserted to carry the negator [115].

> [114] You *aren't* the type who is tough enough to change him   [P02: 147]
> [115] I *didn't* see his face   [P03: 83]
> [116] I saw his face

The positive form of [115] would be [116]. Because the Predicator has no auxiliary verb, *do* has been put in to provide an auxiliary for *not* to attach to.

Words with negative meaning comprise those that are obviously negative like *no* in [112], as well as words like *seldom* or *hardly*, which also give the sentence a negative polarity, e.g.

> [117] I *hardly* expected it to explode so soon
> [N05: 192]

which is equivalent to 'I didn't expect it to explode so soon'.

Local negation affects some element or part of a

sentence, rather than the whole sentence. It is most frequently realised by *not*, as in the following examples:

[118] It's a *not* uncommon problem
[119] Three million beggars existed on what they could scrape from a *not* very good soil   [E22: 66]

In [118] a double negative occurs with *not* and the negative form of the adjective *common*. The *not* counteracts the negative force of *un–* and has the effect of making an understatement. In [119] the *not* relates to the intensifying adverb *very* and has the effect of 'toning down' the force of the following adjective.

In some contexts, local negation is realised by *no* or some other element with negative meaning.

[120] There were *no* more than ten superstitious pictures and a cross   [D05: 80]
[121] Here was a goal with *no* mystical nonsense about it   [D09: 177]

In [120] *no* combines with a comparative quantifier *more*, again to provide a form of understatement. In [121] *no* is contained within a prepositional phrase and negates the noun (*nonsense*) which the preposition (*with*) introduces.

Semantic and syntactic analysis

In this book we have proposed a number of ways in which the structure of a sentence may be analysed. We began with a semantic analysis and proposed a set of labels for situation types, participants and circumstances (which we have usually put in capital letters). We went on to syntactic analysis, with labels for classes of word and, in this chapter, labels for the syntactic function of groups of words in sentences. All these sets of labels contribute to the description of a sentence. Which of the labels are used on any particular occasion of analysis will be determined by the purpose of the analysis: stylistic or literary, for studying language acquisition or learning, for making diagnoses of language disorders, and so on. The argument of this book is that syntax and semantics interweave in the structure of language, and that a 'grammatical' description really has to take account of both aspects.

We will now give some examples of sentence analysis starting with [122].

[122] This verse contains the same Hebrew word four
       times   [D03: 28]

Let us analyse firstly the proposition expressed by the sentence. The proposition manifests the situation type *contain*, which is a **STATE**. The situation type *contain* normally involves a 'container' (**AFFECTED** participant) and 'entity contained' (**ATTRIBUTE** participant). If we apply this expectation to the sentence at [122] we can identify *this verse* as **AFFECTED** participant, *contain* as the **STATE** situation type and *the same Hebrew word* as the **ATTRIBUTE** participant. This leaves *four times* unanalysed: it is an expression of frequency ('how often'), and may therefore be labelled as a **TEMPORAL** circumstance of frequency. Syntactically, the **Predicator** *contain*, expressing the situation type, enters a transitive structure: the AFFECTED participant thus has **Subject** function and the ATTRIBUTE **Object** function; the TEMPORAL circumstance will have **Adjunct** function. The Subject consists of the **noun** *verse*, which is expanded (modified) by the **demonstrative determinative** *this*. The Predicator consists of the **verb** *contain* in the '3rd person singular present tense' form. The Object consists of the **noun** *word*, which is expanded/modified by a number of items: the **adjective** *Hebrew*, the **adjective** *same*, and the **definite article determinative** *the*. The Adjunct consists of the **noun** *times* in the plural form, which is expanded/modified by the **numeral** *four*.

We could set out this analysis in the following way, taking a line for each stage of the labelling:

[123]

This verse	contains	,the same Hebrew word	four times
AFFECTED	STATE	ATTRIBUTE	TEMPORAL
Subject	Predicator	Object	Adjunct
dem noun	verb	defart adj adj noun	num noun
	3sgpres		plural

We will now take some further examples and proceed directly to the display of the analysis.

[124]

He	is standing	in front of television cameras	[C03: 187]
AFFECTED	STANCE	LOCATIVE	
Subject	Predicator	Adjunct	
pron	aux. verb prog	prep noun.mod noun	
3sgmasc	3sgpr pres.part	plural	

[125]

He	has written	the present novel	[C09: 13]
AGENTIVE	ACCOMPLISHMENT	RESULTANT	
Subject	Predicator	Object	
pron	aux.perf verb	defart adj noun	
3sgmasc	3sgpres past.part		

[126]

Many readers	will dislike	it	[B01: 105]
RECIPIENT	PRIVATE STATE	AFFECTED	
Subject	Predicator	Object	
quant noun	aux.modal verb	pron	
plural		3sgneut	

[127]

The original	was written	on a roll	[D01: 32]
RESULTANT	ACCOMPLISHMENT	LOCATIVE	
Subject	Predicator	Adjunct	
defart noun	aux.pass verb	prep indefart noun	
	3sgpast. past.part		

[128]

Vicky	smiled	wryly	[K13: 172]
AGENTIVE	ACTIVITY	MANNER	
Subject	Predicator	Adjunct	
noun	verb	adverb	
	past tense		

The abbreviations used in [123] to [128] and elsewhere are explained as follows:

adj	= adjective
aux	= auxiliary
defart	= definite article
dem	= demonstrative
indefart	= indefinite article
noun.mod	= noun modifier
num	= numeral
pass	= passive
past.part	= past participle
perf	= perfective
poss	= possessive
prep	= preposition
prep.phr	= prepositional phrase
pres.part	= present participle
prog	= progressive
pron	= pronoun
quant	= quantifier
ref	= reflexive
3sgmasc	= 3rd person singular masculine
3sgneut	= 3rd person singular neuter
3sgpast	= 3rd person singular past tense
3sgpres	= 3rd person singular present tense

[*Exercise 3*]

Exercises

Exercise 1

What elements are required in propositions with the following situation types? Are any of the elements contextually omissible?

1. sneeze
2. abandon
3. steal
4. paint
5. complain
6. catch

Exercise 2

Analyse the following sentences into their syntactic elements: SPOCA.

1. She couldn't scream because of the gag in her mouth
                                                    [P04: 20]
2. What a nice person he must be   [N18: 190]
3. How many railway employees read books on philosophy?   [K05: 129]
4. She put the key in the lock   [N16: 154]
5. His eyes appeared enormous   [L23: 18]
6. She came home early from the party   [P04: 120]
7. I called myself a louse   [L12: 27]
8. Maxwell is a fine chap   [K18: 90]
9. Members made a path for him   [K03: 24]
10. I have explained this to him   [N22: 115]
11. They both carried rifles in the crooks of their arms
                                                    [P11: 170]
12. This year the Economic Consultative Council should
    meet in Accra   [A02: 105]

Exercise 3

Give a semantic and syntactic analysis of the following sentences, using the model illustrated at [123] to [128].

1. He was not on the seat   [P01: 116]
2. Hit him!   [K11: 23]
3. She put bread on the table   [N21: 73]
4. The chief in the white coat was talking excitedly with
    Father Felix   [K09: 181]
5. MacCleod appeared in the doorway   [L11: 209]
6. He pushed the case and the lamp into the boy's hands
                                                    [P21: 32]
7. They had become stone quarries   [K04: 138]
8. Once his father had shown him a small automatic pistol
    from the war   [K06: 170]
9. She was carrying a big black crocodile bag   [K08: 40]
10. Occasionally the brothers danced round the mother
                                                    [C11: 123]

CHAPTER 7

Propositions as Participants and Specifiers: Embedded clauses

Propositions in propositions

Our discussion of the structure of propositions has so far seen them as composed of situation types and participants, represented by single words (verbs, nouns) together with their specification. We are now going to extend our discussion to propositions which themselves contain other propositions. Consider the following examples.

[1] I decided *that I must wait no longer*   [K15: 75]
[2] She saw *that they were collecting dandelions and nettles*
          [K10: 65]

The proposition at [1] has the situation type *decide*. This accomplishment situation type is associated with two participants: the 'decision-maker' and the 'thing-decided'. The decision-maker participant has the AGENTIVE semantic role. The thing-decided may be seen as a RESULTANT: it issues from the action of deciding. But usually, as in [1], the thing-decided has the form not of a single word but of a proposition, in this case having the activity situation type *wait*. We may analyse the semantic structure of [1] as follows:

[3] AGENTIVE – ACCOMPLISHMENT –
    RESULTANT: Prop [AGENTIVE – ACTIVITY –
    TEMPORAL]

Similarly, the proposition at [2], with the private state situation type *see*, has a proposition as one of its participants. The first participant with *see* has the RECIPIENT role, the second the AFFECTED role.

[4] RECIPIENT – PRIVATE STATE – AFFECTED:
      Prop [AGENTIVE – ACTIVITY – AFFECTED]

The propositions at [1] and [2] both have the included proposition as their second participant. This is the most usual position in which to find a proposition participant, though they may occur as first participant with some situation types, e.g.

[5] It was unlikely *that either of them had ever been inside his pantry*   [P11: 113]

This example needs a little rearranging to illustrate the point being made:

[6] *That either of them had ever been inside his pantry* was unlikely

The situation type of this example is the temporary state *be unlikely*, which is associated with a single participant: the 'state of affairs' that is in the state of being 'unlikely'. The 'state of affairs' has the semantic role of AFFECTED participant. In [6] this AFFECTED participant, the first and sole participant in the proposition, is itself a proposition, having the situation type *be*, representing a temporary state. We may analyse [6] as:

[7] AFFECTED:Prop [AFFECTED – STATE – LOCATIVE] – STATE

Sentences like [6] usually undergo the syntactic process of 'extraposition' (discussed below, p. 181) to give the corpus example at [5].

We have now introduced the topic of this chapter and we will proceed to elaborate it, first by considering the typical semantic structures that contain included propositions, and then by discussing the grammar of 'embedded clauses', as they are called in syntax.

Direct and indirect speech

What people say and think is often expressed in an included proposition which is a participant of a situation type of communication or cognition. What is said or thought may be represented either as the actual words which were spoken or thought – **direct speech** [8] – or as if the words were being reported – **indirect speech** [9].

> [8] '*The men won't like this,*' remarked Pike feebly
> [M05: 77]
> [9] Tarrant thought *that he had hidden his perturbation*
> [L02: 88]

As so often with direct speech, what is said in [8] precedes the other elements of the proposition, while in the indirect thought of [9] a more neutral order occurs.

With situation types of saying and thinking, one of the participants – the sayer or thinker – has the semantic role of AGENTIVE, while the other may be considered to have the role of RESULTANT. What is said or thought results from the action of speaking or thinking. The RESULTANT participant in such propositions ('The men won't like this' in [8] and 'that he had hidden his perturbation' in [9]) is frequently a proposition itself, which may be expressed in either direct or indirect form, with appropriate grammatical adjustments. Compare [10] with [8], and [11] with [9].

> [10] Pike remarked feebly *that the men wouldn't like that*
> [11] '*I have hidden my perturbation,*' thought Tarrant

You will note a number of changes (e.g. *won't* to *wouldn't*, *this* to *that*, *have* to *had*, *my* to *his*) that occur as a consequence of transforming direct speech into indirect speech.

In the examples at [8] and [9] we have given sentences which illustrate included propositions representing statements. Speech and thought may have the function of asking a question or issuing a command, as well as that of making a statement. We therefore find RESULTANT participants with the appropriate speaking/thinking situation type consisting of propositions representing questions and commands also, e.g.

> [12] '*Where were these found?*' he asked   [P12: 147]
> [13] '*Will you bring Peggy, too?*' she asked   [P20: 142]
> [14] Alan asked Field *if he knew where a boy named Cobbold lived*   [P26: 72]
> [15] She wondered *what would do it*   [K10: 188]

The propositions at [12] to [15] all contain included question propositions: in [12] and [13] they are direct questions, in [14] and [15] they are indirect questions. In [12] and [15] they are information-seeking questions (*When?* in [12], *What?* in [15]); in [13] and [14] they are polar questions, expecting the answer 'yes' or 'no'. Note the changes which occur when these examples are changed from their original form (direct or indirect) into the alternative.

[16] He asked where they were found
[17] She asked whether I would bring Peggy too
[18] 'Do you know where a boy named Cobbold lives?' Alan asked Field
[19] 'What will do it?' she wondered

An included indirect polar question [14]/[17] begins with either *if* or *whether*. An included indirect information-seeking question begins with the same *wh*–word that introduces the direct form of the question: compare [12] and [16], [15] and [19].

Situation types of commanding, such as *order* [20] or *tell* [21] typically have three associated participants: the person issuing the command (AGENTIVE), the person receiving the command (RECIPIENT) and the action being commanded (EVENTIVE).

[20] She ordered Cecil *to summon the council*
                                          [K20: 160]
[21] I told her *to file it*   [N11: 108]

In each case, the action commanded has the form of an included proposition: 'to summon the council' in [20], and 'to file it' in [21]. It is interesting to compare [21] with [22], also with a *tell* situation type, but where *tell* is now an 'informing' rather than a 'commanding' accomplishment situation type. You will note, too, that the structure of the included proposition is different: an infinitive clause for the command, and a *that*-clause for the statement.

[22] He told him *that the bird could be taught to talk*
                                          [P18: 52]

Other included propositions

The reporting of what people say or think is perhaps the single most common use of included propositions. But there is quite a range of situation types where one of the participants may have the form of an included proposition. With saying and thinking situation types it is typical for one of the participants to be in the form of an included proposition, whereas with other situation types an included proposition may be no more typical than a noun. We will consider a selection of situation types where included propositions may commonly occur as one of the particip-ants.

Starting and stopping

Situation types referring to the beginning, ending or continuing of some action or process may frequently have as their second participant an included proposition referring to the action or process that is starting or finishing.

[23] The percolator in the living room started *making bubbling noises* [L12: 89]

[24] After a week she stopped *writing letters* altogether [P22: 176]

[25] She suddenly began *to talk about bicycles* [K16: 156]

[26] Bell continued *to squint into the distance* [N14: 72]

These situation types have one participant which has either an AGENTIVE role as instigator of the beginning, etc. of the action, as in [24] (*she*), [25] (*she*) and [26] (*Bell*), or an AFFECTED role as the entity beginning, etc. to undergo a process, as in [23] (*the percolator*). The action or process that is begun, etc. has an EVENTIVE role and has the form of an included proposition, either with the structure of a present participle (*–ing*) clause [23]/[24] or with the structure of an infinitive clause [25]/[26]. (The different types of clause are discussed later in the chapter, p. 178.)

Liking and preferring

The private state situation types of liking, preferring or hating usually have a RECIPIENT as first participant and an AFFECTED as the second. The AFFECTED participant represents the 'thing liked/preferred/hated', often a person or object (food, book, film, etc.). The 'thing liked' may also, however, be an action, event or state, that is an EVENTIVE participant, when it becomes an included proposition, as in the following examples:

[27] I like *to wrestle sometimes*   [N23: 197]
[28] She likes *wearing it*   [K03: 109]
[29] He naturally preferred *to carry it with the sealed packet to Slade*   [N09: 43]
[30] He hated *having to hurt her*   [P12: 2]

In these examples, the RECIPIENT is represented by *I*, *she* and *he* respectively; and the EVENTIVE included proposition is represented by the infinitive clause 'to wrestle sometimes' [27], 'to carry it . . . to Slade' [29] and by the present participle clause 'wearing it' [28], 'having to hurt her' [30].

Be likely, obvious

Propositions with situation types such as *be likely*, *be obvious*, *be probable* (we will consider '*be* + adjective' as representing the situation type) typically contain a single participant, which refers to a state-of-affairs that is characterised as 'likely', 'probable', etc. This participant usually has the semantic role of EVENTIVE and appears as an included proposition.

[31] It is likely *that they will take off for Majorca on Monday*   [A10: 210]
[32] It is obvious *that very few fish would be caught*   [E06: 84]
[33] It is probable *that the estuary would never have gained any commerce*   [A44: 204]
[34] It seems likely *that they will have future dealings with one another*   [F08: 108]

The EVENTIVE participant in each of these examples is

represented by a *that*-clause, which has undergone the process of extraposition, giving it final position (discussed further below, p. 181). You will note that in the example at [34] the verb is no longer *be* but *seem*: this alternation could be used as an argument for regarding *be likely* etc. as a 'verb + adjective' construction rather than as a multi-word verb. In that case, *likely* would be analysed as an ATTRIBUTE participant. The argument is reinforced by the fact that the adjective may be modified by an 'intensifying' adverb, e.g. *quite* in [35] following:

> [35] It is *quite* likely that the mill will still be standing or even have been restored [E10: 82]

Alternatively, the adverb *quite* may be considered to be a Circumstance of EXTENT (compare 'I quite like him'), and *be likely* retains its integrity.

Consenting and refusing

The typical proposition with a situation type like *consent* or *refuse* will contain two participants. One will refer to the person giving the consent or making the refusal; the other will refer to the 'thing' that is consented to or refused. In many instances this 'thing' will be an action which the person consents or refuses to undertake. The first participant has the semantic role of AGENTIVE, and the second – when it is an action – has the role of EVENTIVE, which occurs as an included proposition.

> [36] The chairman refuses *to forecast future business*
> [A38: 28]
> [37] The buyer declines *to give an indication of the future of the buildings* [A11: 143]
> [38] The British Government has agreed *to give similar 'facilities' to German troops in Britain* [B06: 39]
> [39] They consented *to take a fourteen-week course*
> [D13: 21]

The included proposition with EVENTIVE role is, in each of the examples, in the form of an infinitive clause, i.e. 'to forecast future business' in [36] and so on. You will have noticed that the form of the included proposition varies with the meaning of the situation type: *start/stop* have infinitive or participle clauses, *like/prefer* similarly; *be likely* has a *that*-clause, and *consent/refuse* an infinitive clause. Before we consider these various types of 'embedded' clause, we will look at propositions which function as specifiers of participants.

Propositions as specifiers of participants

We discussed the specification of participants in Chapter 5 in terms of identification, possession, quantity, classification and description, and how these were realised predominantly in the form of words (adjectives, determinatives and the like). We also noted that this specification, at least the classification and description types, could be realised by clauses rather than words, i.e. by propositions. The following are some examples of clauses used as classifiers of participants:

[40] Eleven-year old Nancy O'Brien, the girl *who was missing from her home for four days*, was kept locked in an attic   [A12: 4]
[41] the body *which makes the rules*   [A08: 212]
[42] the agreement *reached in 1945*   [A29: 75]
[43] the crowds *waiting to greet Mrs Kennedy*
                                                                                [A31: 104]
[44] the best way *to rule out such a tragic contingency*
                                                                                [A06: 241]

In each of these examples, the noun participant (*girl*, *body*, etc.) is classified by means of the proposition following it. The proposition is in the form of a relative clause ('who was missing. . .', 'which makes the rules') in [40] and [41], in the form of a past participle clause ('reached in 1945') in [42], in the form of a present participle clause ('waiting to greet. . .') in [43], and in the form of an infinitive clause ('to rule out. . .' in [44].

In the examples at [40] to [44], the specifying propositions all perform a function of classification: they define which noun participant is being talked about, they restrict the reference of the noun participant to a particular instance or subset of possible referents. Non-finite (participle and infinitive) clauses of specification most often have this 'defining' or 'restrictive' function, but relative clauses may on occasions have a descriptive – that is, 'non-defining' or 'non-restrictive' – function, as in the following examples:

[45] Nancy, *who had been missing from her home at Burneside since last Thursday,* was found yesterday in the locked attic of a house. . .   [A12: 11]

[46] the builder, *who still has not made himself known* [A13: 175]

Whereas in [40] the 'girl' is defined by the accompanying relative clause ('who was missing from her home for four days') – we are finding out who Nancy is – in [45] the relative clause accompanying 'Nancy' serves merely to provide further description of her – we know by now who she is and this is just a piece of additional information. Similarly, the 'body' in [40] is defined by the relative clause 'which makes the rules', while the 'builder' in [46] is just further described by 'who still has not. . .'. In writing, non-defining relative clauses are usually distinguished from defining ones by being separated with a comma from the noun participant being specified (compare [45]/[46] with [40]/[41]). In speech, the distinction is made by assigning the non-defining relative clause to a separate tone-unit (intonation pattern) from the noun being specified, whereas a defining clause is usually included in the same tone-unit as the noun.

[*Exercise 1*]

Embedded clauses

In syntax, the included propositions that we have been discussing in this chapter are referred to as 'embedded clauses', since they are embedded within sentences. We have up to now used the term 'sentence' to refer to the syntactic counterpart of a proposition. We will continue to use the term 'sentence' to refer to an independent or main proposition, and we will use the term 'clause' to refer to a proposition which is part of another proposition, either as a participant or as a specifier. A clause which functions as a participant in a sentence, that is, which takes the place of a noun, is termed a **nominal clause**. A clause which functions as the specifier of a noun may be termed an **adjectival clause**.

Clauses are of two main types in terms of their structure: **finite** and **non-finite**. Finite clauses have essentially the same grammatical features as declarative sentences: they contain a finite form of the verb and have a Subject showing agreement in person/number (where relevant) with the verb. That is to say, the verb form of a finite clause shows the present/past tense distinction, and if the tense is present and the Subject is 3rd person singular the verb form has the appropriate –*s* inflection, unless the verb showing tense is a modal auxiliary. Finite clauses include: *that*-clause [47], *wh*-clause [48] and relative clause [49].

[47] They did not know *that he understood English*
[K29: 130]
[48] He wondered *whether she might cry*   [K06: 48]
[49] I could see ahead the house *which must be hers*
[K15: 68]

In the sentence at [47], the *that*-clause ('that he understood English') is functioning as Object; in [48] the *wh*-clause ('whether she might cry') functions as Object in the sentence; and in [49] the relative clause ('which must be hers') modifies the noun *house*.

Non-finite clauses are distinguished from finite clauses by having a non-finite form of the verb and by being able to occur without a Subject. Non-finite verb forms include: the infinitive (*to speak*), the present participle (*speaking*), and the past participle (*spoken*). The infinitive may also occur without *to* as a 'bare' infinitive. Non-finite clauses, therefore, include: inf-clause, either *to*-inf [50] or bare inf [51]; –*ing*-clause [52]; and –*ed*-clause [53].

[50] She wanted *to speak to you rather urgently*
[N22: 98]
[51] She never saw *her husband fire a gun* or *speak of shooting*   [L14: 115]
[52] The Duke, *possibly speaking from experience*, stated: 'Most unskilled jobs are reasonably well-paid and many look attractive'   [B06: 222]
[53] They are reminded of the words *spoken to them earlier*   [D11: 77]

The infinitive clause ('to speak to you rather urgently') in [50] functions as Object in the sentence. In [51] the two bare inf-clauses ('. . . fire a gun', '. . . speak of shooting') have a Subject ('her husband') and they have the syntactic function of Object in the sentence. The participle clauses of [52] ('possibly speaking from experience') and [53] ('spoken to them earlier') have the function of modifier of the nouns *Duke* and *words* respectively.

Before we discuss each of these types of clause in more detail, we present a summary of the embedded clauses we have discussed so far in the form of the following diagram:

[54]

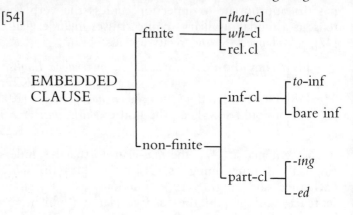

That-clause

We begin our detailed examination of embedded clauses with the finite *that*-clause, which has a nominal function. *That*-clauses are essentially finite sentences introduced by the conjunction *that*. There is a potential for much confusion here, since the word-form *that* functions as a demonstrative (determinative and pronoun), as a relative pronoun (see below), and as a conjunction. As a conjunction it is most likely to be confused with the relative pronoun, since they both introduce embedded clauses. But the relative pronoun *that* can be substituted by one of the other relative pronouns (*who*, *which*), whereas the conjunction *that* may not.

We have noted *that*-clauses already as indirect statements ([9]/[10]), where they function as the syntactic Object of a verb of speaking or thinking. We noted too that the Object function is the most typical of the *that*-clause.

However, we find *that*-clauses with a number of other syntactic functions besides. Consider the following examples.

[55] It is disappointing *that the young directors of the new wave made their best films at the beginning* [C02: 127]

[56] The only surprise is *that she didn't get a letter too*
[C10: 38]

[57] I have heard suggestions *that 'Candid Camera' is 'rigged'* [C17: 191]

[58] There's the advantage *that no one knows what you're writing about* [C06: 42]

[59] I and my husband are so sorry *that we shall not be able to welcome your Majesties to London in July*
[A10: 109]

In the example at [55], the nominal *that*-clause ('that the young . . . beginning'), despite its position in the sentence, has the syntactic function of Subject. The Predicator is the verb *be*, and the sentence also contains the adjective *disappointing*, functioning as a Complement. The Subject does not take up its expected initial position because of a principle operating in the organisation of English sentences known as 'end-weight'. According to this principle, long and weighty elements will tend to take up final position in a sentence. Consequently, in [55], the long *that*-clause Subject is 'extraposed' and its initial position in the sentence is held by the 'dummy' *it*. Subject *that*-clauses regularly undergo extraposition, on the end-weight principle. Object *that*-clauses may also be extraposed if they are followed by another element, e.g. a Complement or Adjunct.

[60] Lawrence makes it clear *that the labour-saving machine is a public benefactor* [C13: 195]

Here the Object is the *that*-clause 'that the . . . benefactor', in a SPOC structure, with *clear* as the Complement. The Object *that*-clause is extraposed (moved to the right of the Complement) and its place taken by the dummy *it*.

In the example at [56] the *that*-clause ('that she . . . too') functions as Complement in a SPC structure. The sentence is 'equative': the Subject and Complement are reversible.

[61] That she didn't get a letter too is the only surprise

The sentences at [57] and [58] contain *that*-clauses with a different function. In both cases they are linked with a noun: in [57] the *that*-clause 'that "Candid Camera" is "rigged"' is linked to the noun *suggestions*; in [58] the clause 'that no one . . . writing about' is linked to the noun *advantage*. Although they are associated with nouns, these clauses are *that*-clauses and not relative clauses: the *that* cannot be substituted by an alternative relative pronoun (*which*); it functions merely as a conjunction and has no other meaning. And yet, like a relative clause, the *that*-clauses in [57] and [58] are elaborating nouns. However, this structure is parallel to the case of nouns 'in apposition', e.g.

[62] Mr Plod, the policeman

Here two nouns have the same reference and would have the same syntactic function in a sentence; one noun (*policeman*) elaborates the other (*Mr Plod*). Similarly, the *that*-clauses in [57] and [58] are in apposition to the nouns *suggestions* and *advantage* respectively. For this reason, such *that*-clauses are known as **appositive** *that*-clauses. They commonly occur with nouns derived from verbs ('deverbal' nouns), where the verb would typically have a *that*-clause as Object, e.g. *suggest* and *suggestion* in [57]. But appositive *that*-clauses are not restricted to deverbal nouns, as *advantage* in [58] illustrates.

Finally, [59] illustrates a *that*-clause ('that we shall . . . in July') functioning as the complement of an adjective (*sorry*). We may regard this function as akin to the Object function with a verb. The *that*-clause is selected by the adjective, just as verbs select their Objects and Complements. That is to say, the range of adjectives that may be complemented by a *that*-clause is limited, in a way that the range of adjectives which may be modified by an adverb like *very* or *so* [59] is not. Consequently, a *that*-clause as adjective complement is seen as having a nominal rather than a modifying function.

We noted earlier the confusion that may arise in identifying *that*-clauses. This confusion may be confounded by a further feature of some *that*-clauses: the introductory *that* may be omitted. For example, [9] could be rewritten as [63] and [56] as [64].

[63] Tarrant thought he had hidden his perturbation
[64] The only surprise is she didn't get a letter too

The conjunction *that* is most frequently omitted from *that*-clauses functioning as Object [63] or as Complement [64]. It may be omitted from Subject *that*-clauses only if the clause has been extraposed. So, [55] could be rewritten as [65].

[65] It is disappointing the young directors of the new wave made their best films at the beginning

Wh-clauses

This second kind of finite clause is of two types. First of all, there is the type introduced by *whether* or *if*, which represents a reported polar interrogative clause (see examples at [14]/[17]). These *wh*-clauses are like *that*-clauses, in that the *wh*-word has merely the role of a conjunction. The clause itself, without the introductory conjunction, is in effect a finite sentence. The conjunction *whether/if* is thus a marker of an indirect polar question, in the same way that *that* marks an indirect statement with appropriate verbs.

The second type of *wh*-clause, which includes indirect *wh*-questions like those in the examples at [15]/[16], is also introduced by a *wh*-word, but in this case the *wh*-word has a function (as Subject, Object, Complement or Adjunct) in the clause. So, not only is the *wh*-word a clause-introducer, it is also an element in the structure of the clause itself. Consider the following examples.

[66] The real question is *what we should put to the Soviet Government as a basis for talks*   [B02: 31]
[67] It says *what is necessary*   [B01: 181]
[68] They have seen *how modern trends in education are helping to prepare the children for the years ahead*   [B25: 71]

The *wh*-clause in the example at [66] is introduced by *what*. The clause functions as Complement in this 'equative' sentence. Within the *wh*-clause, *what* fills the Direct Object slot. The *wh*-clause has the structure: 'someone *put* something *to*-someone *as*-something' (SPOdOiA) – and *what* fills the 'something' slot. Just as in direct *wh*-questions ('What should we put to the Soviet Government as a basis for talks?') the interrogative *wh*-word has a function as an element in the sentence, so too in indirect *wh*-questions, the *wh*-word has a comparable function.

Indirect questions are, however, not the only type of structure to be expressed by *wh*-clauses. The sentences at [67] and [68] illustrate another type of *wh*-clause. In [67] the *wh*-clause ('what is necessary') functions as Object in the sentence, which has SPO structure. Within the *wh*-clause, *what* functions as Subject in a SPC structure. The verb in the main sentence is a verb of stating rather than a verb of questioning, so that the *wh*-clause cannot be construed as an indirect question, equivalent to 'What is necessary?' It is paraphrasable rather by 'the thing which is necessary' or 'that which is necessary', that is, by a 'noun + relative clause'. For this reason, *wh*-clauses of this type are referred to as **nominal relative** clauses.

The *wh*-clause introduced by *how* in [68] is of the same type. Here the *wh*-clause is again Object in the (SPO) sentence; but within the *wh*-clause, *how* functions as Adjunct in a S ('modern trends in education') P ('are helping') O ('to prepare the children for the years ahead') A (*how*) structure. The *how* is paraphrasable by 'the way in which', so making the *wh*-clause a nominal relative. Besides sharing the same structure as *wh*-interrogative clauses, nominal relative clauses are not always clearly distinguishable from them. Consider the following example.

[69] *What should concern us* is *how this policy is to be administered*   [B15: 106]

Both the Subject and Complement slots in this SPC sentence are filled by *wh*-clauses. The Subject *wh*-clause is a clear example of a nominal relative, paraphrasable by 'the thing which. . .' or 'that which. . .' The Complement *wh*-clause, however, could be interpreted either as an interrogative [70] or as a nominal relative [71].

[70] What should concern us is: how is this policy to be administered?

[71] What should concern us is: the way in which this policy is to be administered

This ambiguity, or coalescence, justifies us in treating such clauses as a single type.

Relative clauses

The third and final kind of finite clause we are considering is the relative clause, which is unlike the others so far discussed, because its sole function is as a modifier of nouns: it is an **adjectival** clause, not a nominal clause. Relative clauses are introduced by relative pronouns (listed at [72]), which, like the *wh*-words of *wh*-clauses (except *if/whether*), have a function within the relative clause.

[72] who   whom   whose   which   that

The basic distinction here is between the relative pronouns which relate to nouns referring to persons (*who*, *whom*, *whose*) and the one relating to non-person nouns (*which*). *That* as a relative pronoun may relate to both person and non-person nouns.

[73] Even the Councillors *who had no particular use for the Catholic religion* were impressed   [D16: 140]
[74] It is the stone *which the builders refused*   [D04: 33]
[75] Render to Caesar the things *that are Caesar's*
                                [D16: 170]
[76] And it will be the child *that suffers in health*
                                [B14: 121]

The example at [73] illustrates personal *who*; [74] illustrates non-personal *which*; [75] has *that* relating to a non-person (*things*) and [76] has *that* relating to a person (*child*).

Clearly, then, the form of a relative pronoun is determined to an extent by the nature of the noun that the relative clause is modifying. But it is also determined, at least for the personal relative pronouns, by the syntactic function that the pronoun fulfils within the structure of the relative clause. Consider the following examples.

[77] Cavafy was the first modern Greek poet *who contrived to be patriotic without being romantic*
                                [C12: 72]

[78] Rosa befriends two Poles *whom she meets in a factory* [C11: 119]

[79] He double-crosses the five pals *with whom he lives* [C04: 23]

[80] The lovers, *whose chief scene was cut at the last moment*, had comparatively little to sing [C01: 49]

In the example at [77], the relative clause ('who contrived . . . romantic') is introduced by the relative pronoun *who*, which is the form used when the personal relative pronoun functions as Subject within the relative clause. The relative clause in the example at [78] ('whom she meets in a factory') has the personal relative pronoun *whom*, functioning as Object in the relative clause. This is the form of the personal relative pronoun which is also used when the pronoun functions as complement of a preposition, as in [79]: *with whom*. While the *whom* form of the relative pronoun is still widely used in writing, it is becoming less used especially in speech and is being replaced by *who*. So, [78] may be heard as [81], and [79] as [82].

[81] Rosa befriends two Poles *who she meets in a factory*

[82] He double-crosses the five pals *who he lives with*

The other form of the personal relative pronoun, illustrated in the example at [80], is *whose*, which has the function in a relative clause of possessive (genitive) modifier of another noun. In [80] it is part of the Subject noun phrase 'whose chief scene' and substitutes for 'the lovers'. Interestingly, this relative pronoun, which we have assigned to the 'person' group, appears not to be restricted to association with personal nouns.

[83] This is an able and intelligent book *whose limitations reflect the magnitude of its ambitions* [C09: 128]

[84] When an advertisement contains statements *whose factual truth is doubtful*. . . [B01: 102]

The noun to which *whose* relates in the sentence at [83] is *book*, though a degree of 'personification' seems to be happening in this sentence, since the writer also uses adjectives (*able*, *intelligent*) that are more usually applied to persons. In [84] *whose* relates to *statements*, a clearly non-personal noun. The alternative formulation with *which* [85] is rather cumbersome, which may be the reason why the use of *whose* is extended to non-personal nouns.

> [85] When an advertisement contains statements, the factual truth of which is doubtful. . .

The non-personal relative pronoun, therefore, has the same form (*which*) for all the syntactic functions it might have in a relative clause, e.g. Object ([74] above), Subject [86], Complement [87], prepositional complement [88].

> [86] An exhibition of these works *which is now on view in a Berlin gallery* is most impressive [C02: 21]
> [87] He appears as the pedant, *which for all his good nature he really was* [D09: 146]
> [88] This is a particularly controversial area *in which scientists easily stray beyond their competence* [C14: 52]

Let us turn finally to *that* as a relative pronoun. We have noted that it may relate to both personal and non-personal nouns, but there are certain restrictions on its use. It is used only with restrictive or defining relative clauses (discussed above, p. 178), and it cannot be used directly after a preposition, e.g. to substitute for *whom* in [79] or for *which* in [88], though it may be used with a preposition if the preposition is placed at the end of the clause, as in [82]. We have cited two examples above, containing *that* as a relative pronoun: in [75] *that* functions as Complement in the relative clause, and in [76] as Subject. The example at [89] illustrates *that* as Object in the relative clause, and in [90] *that* is a prepositional complement.

> [89] That was the first point *that Mr Hammarskjold made* [B01: 131]
> [90] It is *to* this course *that your correspondent refers*, presumably [B27: 135]

In [90] the preposition (*to*), which belongs with the verb (*refer to*), has been taken from the relative clause and attached to the noun being modified; the writer presumably wished to avoid a clause-final preposition ('It is this course that your correspondent refers to, presumably').

One concluding point remains to be made about relative pronouns. It concerns the condition under which a relative pronoun may be omitted. A relative pronoun may be omitted if it functions as Object or prepositional complement in a restrictive relative clause. If the relative pronoun as prepositional complement is omitted, the preposition then takes up final position in the relative clause. For example, [78] could be rewritten as [91], [74] as [92], [79] as [93], and [90] as [94].

[91] Rosa befriends two Poles she meets in a factory
[92] It is the stone the builders refused
[93] He double-crosses the five pals he lives with
[94] It is this course your correspondent refers to, presumably

[*Exercise 2*]

Infinitive clauses

An infinitive clause contains a verb in the infinitive form, usually with *to* (e.g. *to sleep*). It also differs from a finite clause or sentence in that it may not, and frequently does not, contain a Subject. Infinitive clauses have no counterparts, therefore, as independent sentences: they function only as embedded clauses, mainly nominal. Consider the following sentences containing infinitive clauses, which illustrate some of the syntactic functions that they may fulfil.

[95] It was hard *to express all she felt*   [M06: 105]
[96] The motive would be *to serve this home of his, in which his heart lay*   [M02: 148]
[97] He decided *to slip down to the canteen for a cup of coffee*   [M02: 12]
[98] I am unwilling *to undertake any adventure without her*   [M03: 154]
[99] Farland reviewed his own decision *to say nothing of what he'd learned during the day*   [L16: 20]

In the sentence at [95] the infinitive clause ('to express all she felt') functions as the Subject of the (SPC) sentence. The same process of extraposition applies to infinitive clauses functioning as Subject as applies to *that*-clauses with this function. The initial position in the sentence is filled by a 'dummy' *it*, and the Subject clause is moved to the end of the sentence. [95] could be rewritten as [100]:

[100] To express all she felt was hard

The infinitive clause in the sentence at [96] ('to serve . . . heart lay') functions as Complement. The sentence has the structure: S ('the motive') P ('would be') C (infinitive clause), where S and C are in an equative relationship. In [97] the infinitive clause ('to slip . . . coffee') functions as Object in the sentence, which has SPO structure. The sentence at [98] has the structure: S (*I*) P (*am*) C ('unwilling to . . . without her'); the infinitive clause is part of the Complement of the sentence and functions as a complement to the adjective *unwilling*. Finally, in this group of sentences, the infinitive clause in [99] functions as an appositive to a noun: the deverbal noun *decision* and the infinitive clause 'to say . . . learned' are in an appositive relationship.

Our examples of infinitive clauses in [95] to [99] are all without a Subject. Who or what the Subject of the clause is intended to be can be deduced from the other elements of the sentence. Often the Subject of the infinitive clause will be the same as that of the sentence, as in [97] and [98]. Or it may be an element within the infinitive clause itself, e.g. *she* in [95], *his* in [96]. When the Subject of the infinitive clause is different from that of the sentence or is not unambiguously recoverable from another element, it may be supplied as an element of the infinitive clause. Consider the following examples.

[101] What do you want *me to do?*   [M04: 65]
[102] I have arranged *for her to have the car*   [N01: 151]
[103] What I want is *for Cousin Hilary to advance me the money Rose left me in her will*   [L05: 107]
[104] It's easy *for you to talk*   [K09: 126]

In [101] the infinitive clause ('me to do') functions as Object in the sentence ('the thing that is wanted'). It has a Subject (*me*), which is different from the Subject of the sentence (*you*). Although *me* has Subject function, it has the object form: *me* and not *I*. This would seem to be explicable from its position in the sentence: after a verb (*want*). Infinitive clauses containing Subjects and which have Object function in sentences regularly have this kind of structure. When infinitive clauses have other sentence functions – and occasionally when they have Object function too – the Subject of the infinitive clause is usually introduced by the preposition *for*, as in [102] to [104]. In [102] the infinitive clause has Object function; *arrange* typically associates with the preposition *for*. In [103] the infinitive clause ('for Cousin Hilary . . . in her will') has Complement function in the (SPC) equative sentence, and in [104] the infinitive clause ('for you to talk') is an extraposed Subject in a SPC structure:

[105] For you to talk is easy

In some dialects of English the Subject of an infinitive clause is always introduced by *for*, even in cases like [101], e.g.

[106] The other one, Diablo, does not like *for me to get on the back*   [N07: 51]

Returning to the example at [101], there is another type of sentence containing an infinitive clause as Object which bears a superficial resemblance to it, but is in fact different. Two examples follow.

[107] Tell Second Officer Pike *to come here at once*
                                                    [M05: 68]
[108] We ask you *to go back there*   [M06: 76]

The verbs in these sentences (*tell, ask*) enter ditransitive structures (e.g. 'tell someone something'); there are therefore two Objects in each of these examples. The infinitive clause represents one Object (direct), and the preceding noun/pronoun ('Second Officer Pike'/*you*) the other Object (indirect). It is always the Indirect Object which is taken to be the Subject of the Direct Object infinitive clause. Indeed, the noun/pronoun in this position is sometimes seen as having a double function. If the Subject of the infinitive clause is to be other than identical with the Indirect Object of the sentence, then it should theoretically be possible to insert one with the *for* introductory preposition: [108] might be rewritten as [109].

[109] We ask you for Lydia to go back there

This sounds rather forced, and it is more usual to use a *that*-clause instead:

[110] We ask you that Lydia might go back there

The unnaturalness of [109] reinforces the view that the noun/pronoun has a double function of sentence Indirect Object and infinitive clause Subject.

There are two further forms of the infinitive clause which occur mainly as Object in a sentence. The first is the *wh*-**infinitive**, a non-finite version of the finite *wh*-clause: the infinitive clause (without Subject) is preceded by a *wh*-word, which has a function in the infinitive clause.

[111] I will decide *what to do with her letter*   [K14: 179]
[112] The magician must know *when to turn the screw*
[K09: 34]
[113] Sonia knew *where to begin*   [K23: 154]

In [111] *what* has Object function in the infinitive clause: 'to do what with her letter'. In [112] *when* has Temporal Adjunct function in the infinitive clause, and in [113] *where* has Locative Adjunct function.

The second additional form of the infinitive clause functioning as Object is the **bare-infinitive**, typically following verbs of perception (*hear*, *see*, *feel*, etc.) and with a Subject.

[114] Andrea heard *her go racing upstairs*   [P09: 177]
[115] She saw *him grasp hold of you*   [P04: 171]

In [114] the Object of the sentence is the bare-infinitive clause 'her go racing upstairs'. Notice that the Subject *her* is, as with Subjects of *to*-infinitive clauses, in the object form, because of its position in the sentence. In [115] the bare-infinitive clause is 'him grasp hold of you', again the Object of the (SPO) sentence.

The infinitive clauses we have considered so far all have a nominal function. Infinitive clauses also have a minor **adjectival** function as specifiers of nouns. We have seen an infinitive clause in apposition to a noun [99], and there is a further example at [116].

[116] John fought back his inherited desire *to snub the man*   [N04: 69]

Here, 'to snub the man' is appositive to the deverbal noun *desire* and replicates the sentence structure 'someone desires to-do'. Adjectival infinitive clauses are not as easy to distinguish from appositive infinitive clauses as appositive *that*-clauses are from relative clauses, since the same test cannot be applied (see p. 182). We are reliant on being able to refer a structure to a sentence replication in the case of an appositive infinitive clause, and to a relative clause replication in the case of an adjectival infinitive clause. Consider the following example.

> [117] I would never have the courage *to use it*   [K16: 7]

Here the infinitive clause ('to use it') has arguably an adjectival function in respect of the noun *courage*, and it could be replaced by an appropriate relative clause:

> [118] I would never have the courage *with which I might use it*

Conversely, the structure in [117] may not be replicated by a sentence structure: there is no 'someone courage to-do' in English. However, it is possible that we are here dealing with a lexical gap, where *desire* (noun) has a counterpart *desire* (verb), but *courage* (noun) does not. In the case of the following example no such uncertainty exists.

> [119] Fred Winter is unquestionably the jockey *to follow*
> [A07: 28]

The noun *jockey* does not replicate as a verb, and this infinitive clause has a clear relation with a relative clause.

> [120] Fred Winter is unquestionably the jockey *that one ought to follow*

The implication of [119] is that Fred Winter is the 'one and only' jockey to follow. It is in this kind of context that adjectival infinitive clauses are typically found, e.g. with *one* as the 'noun' in the phrase 'the one to. . .' [121], or in the structure 'the – superlative adjective – noun – to. . .' [122].

> [121] You may be the one *to feel glad that I didn't promise*
> [K18: 120]
> [122] To stand firm, he declared, was not to invite war, but the surest way *to avert it*   [A05: 125]

The sentence at [122], interestingly, contains three infinitive clauses: 'to stand firm' as Subject (of *was*), 'not to invite war' as Complement (of *was*), and 'to avert it' as modifier to *way* linked with the superlative *surest*.

Participle clauses

Like the infinitive clause, participle clauses contain a non-finite verb form – present or past participle – and do not have a corresponding independent sentence. They are found only as embedded clauses. The present participle (*–ing*) clause has a wider range of functions, both nominal and adjectival, than the past participle (*–ed*) clause, which is restricted to adjectival uses.

–ing-clauses

Present participle or *–ing*-clauses contain the verb in the present participle form. As nominal clauses they have a wide range of functions in sentences and occur both with and without a Subject. The following examples (without Subjects) illustrate the range of functions of *–ing*-clauses.

[123] *Learning to live* is like *learning to skate*
[C08: 202]

[124] He began *selling left-handed teacups to a gullible public* [C17: 213]

[125] Her other interest is *collecting Victoriana*
[C15: 186]

[126] Mr Hibbert denounces our Government *for feebly drifting into so unnecessary a war* [C08: 11]

The sentence at [123] contains two *–ing*-clauses. The first of them, 'learning to live', has Subject function in the (SPC) sentence. Unlike *that*-clauses and *wh*-clauses with Subject function, *–ing*-clauses are not usually extraposed. If they are extraposed, then it is for stylistic effect, and the *–ing*-clause is set off from the rest of the sentence by a comma in writing and a separate tone-unit in speech. With extra-position, [123] would be rephrased as [127].

[127] It is like learning to skate, learning to live

In [124] the *–ing*-clause ('selling . . . public') has the function of Object in the (SPO) sentence. In [125] the *–ing*-

clause ('collecting Victoriana') has Complement function in the equative (SPC) sentence. The sentence at [126] has the structure: 'someone *denounces* someone *for*-something'. The –*ing*-clause ('feebly drifting . . . war') fills the 'something' slot and so has the function of prepositional complement, as does 'learning to skate' in [123].

We turn now to –*ing*-clauses with Subjects, illustrated in the following sentences.

[128] I cannot remember *any other great literary figure doing so* [C01: 146]

[129] She watched *him eating* for a moment [L11: 187]

[130] I felt they couldn't be certain about *my being there* [L02: 156]

[131] Rose would never have consented to *Hilary's borrowing the money he needed* [L05: 207]

The –*ing*-clause in [128] has Object function in the (SPO) sentence. It is 'any other . . . doing so', in which the noun phrase 'any other great literary figure' functions as Subject. In [129] the –*ing*-clause ('him eating') functions as Object of the perception verb *watch*. Note that the Temporal Adjunct 'for a moment' is dependent on *watch*, not on *eat*: it is an element of the sentence, not of the –*ing*-clause. The –*ing*-clause has a pronoun Subject (*him*) in the object form, like the pronoun Subjects with infinitive clauses. This is not, however, the only form in which a pronoun Subject of an –*ing*-clause appears. In [130] the –*ing*-clause 'my being there', which functions as prepositional complement to *about*, the Subject (*my*) has the possessive (or genitive) form. Similarly, in [131] the –*ing*- clause ('Hilary's borrowing . . . needed') has a Subject (*Hilary's*) in the genitive form, though here it is a noun. The genitive form of the Subject with –*ing*-clauses is usually felt to be more formal, and by some speakers/writers to be more 'correct'. It is generally preferred if the –*ing*-clause has Subject function in the sentence.

We have so far considered –*ing*-clauses with a nominal function. Those with an adjectival function occur in two positions: as the modifier of a noun [132], and as the Object Complement of a sentence [133].

[132] It seems aimed in particular at the sixth-former
beginning to specialize [C14: 16]

[133] Mr Hudson and lady love Lollo find themselves
playing chaperon to the girls [C06: 139]

The *–ing*-clause ('beginning to specialize') in [132] modifies
the noun *sixth-former*; and in [133], 'playing chaperon to the
girls' is Complement in the (SPOC) sentence. An *–ing*-
clause which modifies a noun can be rephrased using a
relative clause [134], though modifying *–ing*-clauses cannot
always be directly related in this way to a relative clause,
since stative verbs may also appear in the present participle
form in such clauses, e.g. *resemble* in [135] which must be
rephrased as in [136].

[134] . . . the sixth-former who is beginning to
specialize

[135] The highways *resembling vast arteries* poured the
flood tide of commerce and private pleasure in
four entirely different directions [P03: 10]

[136] The highways which resemble vast arteries. . .

When *–ing*-clauses function as Object Complement, as in
[133], they may also be regarded as having an adjectival
function; they are equivalent to an adjective in that function.

–*ed*-clauses

Past participle or *–ed*-clauses have the verb in the past
participle form. They have only an adjectival function,
either as Object Complement in a sentence, or more
commonly as the modifier of a noun.

[137] He found his mood *reflected in her face*
[K28: 197]

[138] We will continue the conversation *started at the
Doria Palace* [K04: 190]

In the sentence at [137] the *–ed*-clause 'reflected in her face'
functions as Complement in the SPOC structure, and in
[138] the *–ed*-clause 'started at the Doria Palace' modifies the
noun *conversation*. If we relate this *–ed*-clause to a relative
clause we will find that it nearly always corresponds to a
passive in the finite clause.

[139] . . . the conversation which was started at the Doria Palace

In the case of Complement –*ed*-clauses – and the same is true of Complement –*ing*-clauses – when just a participle form of the verb occurs, it is not always possible to determine whether we should analyse it as a verb (and so a clause) or as an adjective, especially if the word is well established as an adjective in other contexts, e.g.

[140] I found all the ways of escape *closed*   [K20: 124]

Closed occurs as an attributive adjective ('a closed door'). If we were to add an Agentive *by*-phrase to *closed* in [140], it would clearly become an –*ed*-clause:

[141] I found all the ways of escape *closed by the police*

By itself, however, *closed* could be replaced by *impassable*, an adjective. Such ambiguity of analysis reinforces the argument for treating Object Complement –*ed*-clauses as adjectival.

We conclude this chapter with a summary diagram of the types of embedded clause in English (compare [54]).

[142]

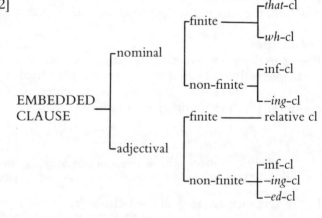

[*Exercise 3*]

Exercises

Exercise 1

Identify the included propositions in the following sentences, and say what type of clause each one is (e.g. *that*-clause, infinitive clause). Suggest what semantic function the included proposition has within the main proposition.

1. He agreed to marry Jimena Diaz   [F30: 57]
2. It is likely that the tour will start in Bucks in late August   [A42: 49]
3. I don't like being called a spy   [N07: 139]
4. The boat had started to fill up with water   [K21: 177]
5. I told you not to come here   [K19: 31]
6. The work, which includes complete modernisation of the entire drainage system, will cost about £50,000
                                                   [A36: 42]
7. I am wishing my whole life away, she thought
                                                   [P25: 28]
8. All members of the Council were animated by the desire to make Huddersfield worthy of its citizens
                                                   [A30: 93]
9. He wondered how his mother would find it   [K27: 88]
10. He promised that Leamington would not hang back
                                                   [A36: 147]

Exercise 2

Identify the finite embedded clauses in the following sentences. Say what type each of them is (*that*-clause, *wh*-clause, relative clause) and what their syntactic function is (Subject, Object, Complement, etc.).

1. Junko goes to live with a young architect whom she respects greatly and who feels sorry for her
                                                  [C16: 129]
2. What is at stake is whether the West recognises Herr Ulbricht or Mr Krushchev as responsible for East Berlin   [B21: 184]
3. It appears to me that the members of the Court of Appeal in the Chappie case were aware that that might be the result of their decision   [H18: 146]

4. The example that has confronted Southern Rhodesia is the Congo [B19: 54]
5. I knew that the garden lay near that part of the estate which included a strip of coastline edged with precipitous cliffs [K12: 49]
6. The truth is that at least a dozen selections could have been made from the same source [C08: 140]
7. There is much prophecy that the new heart-throb of the year will be Warren Beatty [C17: 46]
8. I wonder if other readers are aware of this discrepancy [B24: 189]
9. Kant killed the God whose existence can be proved by reason [D09: 63]
10. It would now seem that Wicki's name must be added to this list [C02: 14]

Exercise 3

Identify the non-finite embedded clauses in the following sentences. Say what type each of them is (inf-cl, –ing-cl, –ed-cl) and what their syntactic function is.

1. The proceedings opened with Colleano's giving me a summary of the case [L24: 42]
2. It'll take long enough to work right through from bow to tail [M05: 108]
3. I wondered what to do next [K15: 89]
4. She conquered the compelling desire to take a quick glance at the picture of Everest [N16: 189]
5. She heard him start up the car [P04: 29]
6. Lee was impressed with the accommodation provided for a planter [K02: 110]
7. I cannot help adding one sample of Wellington's style [C08: 148]
8. She did find painting children particularly interesting [C15: 140]
9. It is the best time to make a change [E37: 39]
10. It must have been no easy task getting it into place [L08: 140]

CHAPTER 8

Propositions as Circumstances: Adverbial clauses

In this chapter we continue our discussion begun in Chapter 7 of included propositions and their grammatical counterparts, embedded clauses. In the previous chapter we considered propositions functioning within other propositions as a participant or as the specifier of a participant. We are now going to consider propositions which function within other propositions as **circumstances**. In grammatical terms, the previous chapter dealt with nominal clauses – those functioning in noun-like positions as Subject, Object, Complement, appositive, prepositional complement – and with adjectival clauses – those functioning in adjective-like positions as noun modifier, Object Complement. This chapter deals with **adverbial clauses** – with adverb-like functions as Adjunct or Disjunct.

[1] They're bound to want pretty solid new evidence
   before they'll agree to reopen the case   [L04: 164]
[2] Cuddy peeled off five notes *before stowing the*
   remainder away   [L10: 107]

In the sentence (proposition) at [1], the adverbial clause (included proposition) 'before they'll agree to open the case' functions as a Temporal Adjunct, providing the circumstantial information 'when' (they're bound to want. . .). The adverbial clause is a finite clause, introduced by a subordinating conjunction, which signals both that it is an embedded adverbial clause and the type that it is (i.e. Temporal). The sentence at [2] also has a *before*-clause as a Temporal Adjunct, though here the adverbial clause is a non-finite –*ing*-clause.

This introduces the types of included propositions and embedded clauses that we are concerned with in this chapter. We will proceed by looking at the various kinds of circumstantial meaning that such clauses may express, such as 'time', 'place', 'condition', 'reason', 'comparison', and so on. We will then review the grammatical forms that adverbial clauses may have. We begin with the meanings relating to time, place and contingency.

Time, place and contingency

In our discussion of circumstances in Chapter 3, we noticed that propositions contain information relating to time and place more frequently than any other kind of circumstance. While place is not often expressed as an included proposition, time is. The **time** at which two events take place relative to each other is clearly an important piece of information when telling a story or giving a report of something that happened. It is not unusual therefore to find a proposition set in a time relation to another proposition, where one of the propositions – marked by a time subordinator – is included within the other (main) proposition.

Two events may be in a successive time relationship, in which one event follows on another, or they may be in a simultaneous time relationship, in which the events occur at the same time or at least overlap in time. In a successive time relationship, the main proposition may be marked by the subordinator introducing the included proposition as either preceding it in time or as following it. There are then three basic temporal relationships between main and included propositions: before [3], while [4], and after [5].

[3] Unfortunately, he saw me *before I spotted him*
[L16: 191]
[4] I'll cover him *while you frisk him*   [L17: 116]
[5] He called for me *soon after I got back to the flat*
[L07: 11]

The main proposition in [1] precedes the included proposition: *before* indicates the time of 'he saw me'. The same time relationship may also be marked by *till* [6] and *until* [7].

[6] She stumbled along the embankment *till she reached*

a point right beside the main Mardsley Road   [L22: 66]

[7] He wasn't even a suspect *until you got that note*
[L18: 189]

In both these examples the event in the main proposition precedes that in the proposition introduced by *till/until*, though they differ from the example with *before* at [3] in having the temporal meaning 'up to the point that' rather than simply 'at a point preceding'.

Returning to the example at [4], the two events represented by the propositions occur at the same time and cover the same span of time. Indeed the two propositions could be reversed:

[8] You frisk him while I cover him

Simultaneity does not always involve an identical span of time; it may involve one event lasting over a period of time (the one represented by the included proposition) and the other (the main proposition) occurring at some point during that period.

[9] This came *while you were upstairs*   [L18: 111]

The coming of 'this' occurs at some point in the period 'while you were upstairs'.

In the example at [5], the main proposition occurs at a time following the event represented by the included proposition introduced by *after*: 'I got back to the flat' and then 'he called for me'. With a similar meaning to *after* are the subordinators *as soon as* [10], *since* [11], *when*.

[10] His resignation would certainly be demanded *as soon as the truth became known*   [L24: 123]

[11] Have you been about at all *since you've been here?*
[L11: 7]

Again, the events of the main propositions follow those of the included propositions.

Clearly, the conjunction of two propositions by means of a subordinator like *before*, *while* or *after* is not the only way in which time relationships between events may be expressed. They may be expressed, for example, with an embedded present participle clause:

[12] *Quickly taking his coat and hat from the vestibule
closet*, he rushed from the house without a word
[M01: 178]

[13] *Having made his choice*, he stayed with it
[K18: 44]

The present participle clause in [12] ('Quickly taking. . .')
implies simultaneity of the events in the two propositions.
In [13] the perfective form of the participle ('Having
made. . .') implies successivity of the events: the one
referred to by the included proposition precedes that in the
main proposition.

Alternatively, the temporal relationship may be shown
in separate propositions. This may be done by the
propositions having different tenses; for example, [3] may
be rephrased as [14].

[14] I *spotted* him. Unfortunately, he *had already seen*
me.

The past perfect tense, *had seen*, sets this proposition at a
time prior to that of the first proposition with *spot* (in the
simple past tense). The relationship may be implicit in the
mere juxtaposition of independent propositions; for
example, [4] may be recast as [15].

[15] You frisk him. I'll cover him.

The contextual implication is one of simultaneity. It may be
made explicit by a conjunctive adverb:

[16] You frisk him. *Meanwhile* I'll cover him.

Or compare [7] with [17]:

[17] He wasn't a suspect. *Then* you got that note.

To consider all the ways in which events may be related to
each other temporally would take us far beyond the scope of
this chapter, which is specifically about included propositions.

So we turn to the expression of **place** by means of
included propositions. This is not a common means of
expressing LOCATIVE circumstances, which are more
frequently found as prepositional phrases. As included

propositions, LOCATIVE circumstances are usually introduced by the subordinator *where*.

[18] They'll stay *where they are*   [K09: 140]
[19] She appeared *just where the sand dividing us from the*
     water was narrowest   [K12: 136]

An alternative subordinator which may introduce an
included place proposition is *wherever* [20], though as we
shall see it may have another function.

[20] There is a thin white line *wherever wave meets rock*
     along the island shores   [E15: 137]

The other function of *wherever* is to introduce an
included proposition expressing **contingency**. Contingency
is related to time and place, but has a more general
reference, equivalent to 'in the circumstances' or 'on the
occasions'. Other subordinators that refer to contingency
are *whenever* and *once*.

[21] *Wherever the issues were put clearly*, sections of the
     movement reaffirmed their original stand
                                                     [B06: 125]
[22] I practise four hours a day *whenever I am able*
                                                     [F44: 183]
[23] *Once they know where she is*, all the fortune-hunters
     in London will be after her like flies after bad meat
                                                     [K19: 160]

The included proposition in each of these examples
expresses a general circumstance, contingent on which the
event of the main proposition will take place.

Condition, concession and contrast

The next group of circumstantial included propositions have
meanings which are usually expressed in propositions rather
than by any other means, and they frequently take up initial
position before the main proposition. A conditional circumstance expresses the condition under which the main
proposition is or may be true or under which it will or may
occur. To put it another way, the main proposition is
contingent on the conditional circumstance [24]. A con-

cessive circumstance implies that the main proposition is unexpected or surprising in view of what is expressed in the concessive [25]. A concessive thus contains an element of contrast, but this is the primary meaning of the third type of circumstance under this heading, where the included proposition is set in contrastive opposition to the main proposition [26].

> [24] And *if he needs spectacles when in hospital*, he gets
> them free [B14: 72]
> [25] I was born in London, so I am also a Southerner,
> *although I have lived in Oldham for more than 30 years*
> [B23: 207]
> [26] Our doctors aim to keep people well, *while it
> pays western doctors to keep them sick* [B21: 124]

The conditional circumstance in [24] is introduced by *if*, the typical subordinator for a condition; in [25] the typical concessive subordinator *although* introduces the included proposition; and in [26] the contrast circumstance is introduced by *while*.

Conditions may be either **open** or **hypothetical**. Open conditions are 'open' because they make no assumption about whether the condition is fulfilled or unfulfilled, or about the truth of the main proposition – they leave the question open. Hypothetical conditions reflect the belief of the speaker that the condition is unfulfilled; they are a way of reflecting on how things might have been, had circumstances been different. Compare the following pair of sentences: the first [27] contains an open condition, the second [28] a hypothetical condition.

> [27] *If you do not do this*, you may have to pay more tax
> than you need [B05: 159]
> [28] It would be pleasanter *if such cruel and feudal
> performances as tiger and rhino hunts were dropped from
> future royal programmes* [B01: 51]

The condition in [27], 'if you do not do this', is indeterminate with respect to its fulfillment: the sentence is a piece of advice and it may or may not be taken. In [28] the writer implies that they do not believe that the condition ('if such cruel . . . royal programme') will be fulfilled; royal programmes will go on including these activities; the writer is merely speculating on how different things might be.

Hypothetical conditions are distinguished from open conditions by having the tense of both the conditional proposition and the main proposition 'backshifted'. If the condition refers to the present or the future, the tense of a hypothetical conditional is backshifted to the past; and if the condition refers to the past, the tense is backshifted to the past perfect. The sentence at [29] contains an open condition; its hypothetical counterpart is given at [30].

[29] *If present trends continue and there is no increase*, the Burmese will disappear one day   [B05: 188]
[30] *If present trends continued and there was no increase*, the Burmese would disappear one day

Notice the backshifting of *continue* to *continued*, *is* to *was*, and *will* to *would*. The hypothetical nature of the condition in [30] may be emphasised by the use of 'subjunctive' *were*.

[31] *If present trends were to continue and there were no increase*, the Burmese would disappear one day

Consider one further example, this time of a past condition. The hypothetical version [32] comes first and then its open counterpart [33].

[32] *If he had obeyed their instructions* the Krupp empire would have been broken up long ago   [B13: 63]
[33] *If he obeyed their instructions* the Krupp empire will have been broken up long ago

The sentence at [33] serves as a prediction, allowing the fulfillment of the condition. Sentence [32] is hypothetical, what might have been: the Krupp empire still exists.

A number of subordinators besides *if* may introduce conditional propositions. The next most common is the negative *unless* [34], and then: *as/so long as, assuming that, on condition that, provided that* [35], etc.

[34] It would take me nearly 97 hours to do it, *unless I did carbon copies*   [B22: 133]
[35] The means of setting talks going are clear enough, *provided that the Soviet Government wishes to talk at all*   [B02: 19]

The proposition at [34] includes a hypothetical condition,

and the one at [35] an open condition.

Concessive circumstances, as we noted earlier [25], are typically introduced by the subordinator *although*, or by its more informal variant *though*, e.g.

> [36] There are grounds for hope, *even though the present constitutional conference in London may achieve little*
> [B19: 68]

This example shows clearly the meaning of the concessive: the main proposition is surprising (that there are grounds for hope) in view of the information contained in the concessive proposition (that the conference may achieve little). Besides *(al)though*, concessive propositions may be introduced by *while* or *whereas*, though their occurrence is more limited with this meaning, and they also introduce circumstantial propositions with other meanings (time, contrast).

> [37] *While the Advisory Council will be concerned mainly with children of average ability*, they are charged also with considering those who fall below average
> [B19: 43]

Here the subordinator *while* could be replaced by *though* or *even though*, and it would be possible to insert *nevertheless* in the sentence of the main proposition: both tests indicate a concessive relationship.

While and *whereas* are the typical subordinators that introduce circumstantial propositions of **contrast**: see [26] and the following examples:

> [38] In all four contests the Liberal vote rose, *while both Tory and Socialist votes slumped*   [B26: 208]
>
> [39] Our exports to Germany will now be a little cheaper for Germans to buy, *while the goods which Germany exports will be made a little dearer*
> [B01: 66]
>
> [40] *Whereas everything in Boccaccio is hard, elegant and general*, in Chaucer it is muted, peculiar, full of objects that are unexpected and yet oddly characteristic   [C07: 196]

In these examples the two propositions are in each case being set beside each other in a relationship of contrast.

Either of the propositions could be introduced by the contrast subordinator, though the emphasis of the message would be changed: compare [36] with [41]:

[41] In all four contests both Tory and Socialist votes slumped badly, while the Liberal vote rose

Sometimes the meaning of contrast is combined with that of concession, so that an interpretation involves reading a proposition as an instance of both, as in the following example with the subordinator *whilst*:

[42] *Whilst the Government can bring forward legislation at Parliamentary level*, the work of ensuring that such services are put into operation depends to a great extent on the local authority [B26: 187]

Reason, purpose and result

These three meanings of included circumstantial propositions are grouped together because they all provide some explanation for the motivation of the main proposition: the cause or reason why something happened or was done [43], the purpose behind an action [44] and the consequences of an action or event [45].

[43] She's there *because the priest meddled in politics*
[D16: 146]

[44] The Saviour took part in flesh and blood *in order that He might be the Kinsman-Redeemer of all the seed*
[D12: 95]

[45] A shell dropped close, shattering a soldier's arm *so that it hung by a thread* [F23: 128]

The included reason proposition in [43] is introduced, typically, by the subordinator *because*. The purpose proposition in [44] is introduced by the compound subordinator *in order that*, and in [45] the included proposition is introduced by *so that* to express result.

Reason propositions in fact represent a number of meaning relationships with the main proposition. In [43] the reason ('because the priest meddled in politics') represents a cause, of which the main proposition ('she's there') is an effect. In [46] the proposition introduced by *because* represents a 'motivation' for the action of the main proposition:

> [46] The matter is mentioned *because the puzzle of Mr Wilson's new novel is to know clearly what he is saying and where he is standing* [C09: 15]

In [47] the reason proposition, introduced by *since*, represents a circumstance – a combination of a reason and a condition – under which the main proposition will take place.

> [47] This represents work and activity that cannot hope to be completed, *since the sea will never be too full* [D03: 35]

As this example illustrates, *because* is not the only subordinator to introduce reason propositions. *Because* and *since* are the most commonly occurring subordinators of reason (further examples at [48] and [49] below); less commonly occurring are *as, for* and *seeing that*.

> [48] The snake kills your uncle, *because he is another man*, and lets your aunt go, *because she is a woman*, and so couldn't become a rival [F12: 92]
> [49] The premises are generally utilized in a strictly practical manner, *since the wholesaler's appeal is to the businessman* [F41: 169]

Besides the two *because* reason propositions in [48], note also the result proposition, introduced by *and so*.

We illustrated a **purpose** proposition at [44] with the *in order that* subordinator. More commonly, a purpose circumstance takes the form of a *to*-infinitive clause, with no subordinator [50]. If the purpose *to*-infinitive clause has its own Subject, then it will be introduced by *for* [51].

> [50] The nursemaid tiptoed into the baby's room *to see that 20-month-old Charles Jun. was sleeping* [C06: 205]
> [51] Britain was providing the cloak *for Germany to build an air force bigger than that of France* [B06: 17]

The purpose proposition in [50] begins with 'to see that. . .'; this opening could be paraphrased by 'in order to see that', as may all *to*-infinitive purpose clauses. Similarly, the purpose proposition in [51] could be introduced by 'in order for Germany to build. . .'. One further commonly occurring subordinator introducing a purpose circumstance is *so that*, which we have noted already (in [45]) as the typical subordinator for result propositions. In [52] the proposition introduced by *so that* is a purpose circumstance, while in [53] *so that* introduces a result proposition.

> [52] At all costs this must be covered up *so that the important conference with the VIP can take place*
> [C15: 62]
> [53] The sanction of the second commandment has also gone, *so that the new Catechism now contains no mention of God's penal wrath against sin*   [D10: 176]

The *so that* for the purpose proposition in [52] could be replaced with *in order that*, while the *so that* for the result proposition in [53] could be replaced by *with the result that*. The two uses of *so that* are thus clearly distinguished.

A **result** proposition is, then, most commonly introduced by the subordinator *so that* (further example at [54] below). Alternatively, a result circumstance may be introduced by *so* or *and so* (see [48], above, and [55]).

> [54] His sister, Alice, a woman of fine, artistic perception, had the deep windows of the keep, with their stone seats, glazed with clear glass *so that the views from each appear like framed pictures*
> [F29: 55]
> [55] He was an officer of the UVW, I was an officer of NUVW *and so our ways were set to meet*   [F16: 219]

Notice how in [54] the *so that* proposition has a result meaning because the verb (*appear*) is in the simple present tense form. If we were to add the modal verb *might*, we would change the meaning to 'purpose' ('so that the views from each might appear like framed pictures'). This perhaps illustrates that, though the meanings are clearly distinguishable, they are nevertheless also related.

Comment and sentence relatives

We turn now to some included propositions which are not circumstantial in the strict sense of that term. They are propositions that are included in a main proposition, often interrupting it, but which function more as a comment on it than as a circumstance of its occurrence.

[56] That, *I think*, calls for no detailed description here
[L24: 112]

[57] She would be the sole beneficiary, in the normal course of events, *which would make her a very rich young woman indeed*
[L05: 8]

In [56] the comment proposition is 'I think', which interrupts the main proposition. In [57] the comment proposition is in the form of a relative clause introduced by *which* ('which would . . . indeed'); it relates to the whole of the preceding main proposition, not to any single item in it, and so is called a 'sentence relative'.

Comments, like 'I think' in [56], represent attitudes of the speaker to the main proposition. 'I think' marks tentativeness on the speaker's part: compare 'I believe' in [58]:

[58] There is, *I believe*, a good deal to be said on humane grounds for at least dropping a hint
[L24: 19]

You will note from both [56] and [58] that the comment proposition is set off from the main proposition by commas in the written form and has a separate tone-unit in speech. Another kind of comment proposition has the function of seeking the hearer's attention and is usually in the 2nd person form.

[59] Otherwise, *you see*, it pulls the pockets of one's trousers out of shape
[K16: 128]

[60] *You know*, this is the greatest opportunity we'll ever have
[K26: 136]

The comment propositions here are 'you see' and 'you know', respectively. Sometimes the comment propositions are more elaborate than these simple 'Subject + Predicator' clauses, e.g.

> [61] *I must tell you*, Prime Minister, we're heading for an ugly crisis – and *I'm obliged to say this* – Melville has a very heavy responsibility in this matter
> [K03: 205]

There are two comments in this example, both similar in type: 'I must tell you' and 'I'm obliged to say this'. They are both used to excuse a speaker saying something to a superior that this person would not want to hear.

Sentence relatives are similarly set off from the main proposition by a comma in writing and a separate tone-unit in speech. They represent a more elaborated comment on the main proposition than those found in the simple comments like 'I believe' and 'you see'. Sentence relatives are normally introduced by *which* ([57], above, and [62]), or occasionally by *in which case* [63].

> [62] He won't be able to work at all with his right hand or arm – perhaps never again, *which is a serious thing for a family man with seven young children* [L23: 37]
> [63] The reason for his escaping from the asylum was presumably to get as far away from confinement as possible, *in which case he would naturally go in the opposite direction* [N21: 29]

Comparison

We come finally to included circumstantial propositions of comparison, which relate one proposition (the included one) to another proposition (the main one) for similarity [64] or comparison [65].

> [64] Loose tongues wag here, *just as they do everywhere else* [P08: 184]
> [65] He sat himself down *as if the whole day was before him* [K19: 180]

The similarity proposition is marked by the subordinator

just as in [64], and in [65] the comparison is signalled by *as if*.

Similarity propositions are typically introduced by *just as* or *as* or *exactly as*. In a more informal style, *just/exactly like* may also be found.

> [66] She saw that everything that had happened in the past twelve hours had happened *just as it had been ordained*   [K14: 72]
>
> [67] His sister Margaret would look beautiful in that dress, he thought wistfully, *just like an angel would look*   [P28: 10]

The similarity between the propositions may be emphasised by the use of *so* as a correlative to introduce the main proposition, e.g.

> [68] *Just as* there are two kinds of lampshade . . . *so* there are certain types of face. . .   [P19: 42]

In many instances, e.g. [64], [66], [67], similarity propositions have the additional meaning of 'manner'. In [64], for instance, as well as drawing the similarity, the *just as*-proposition also describes 'how' the loose tongues wag.

Comparison propositions similarly often combine a manner meaning with the comparison meaning, as in [65], where the *as if*-proposition describes 'how' he sat down. Besides *as if* as a subordinator, comparison propositions may also be introduced by *as though*.

> [69] Then they became embarrassed, *as though this were something not meant for them to see*   [K17: 171]

Comparisons are usually hypothetical, marked in this example unequivocally by the subjunctive *were* with a singular Subject *this*. Comparison propositions introduced by *as if* and *as though* need not be in the form of finite clauses. In fact, all three types of non-finite clause occur with the comparison subordinators: infinitive [70], present participle [71] and past participle [72].

> [70] They grouped themselves around him, smiling and demonstrative *as if to show where their sympathies and loyalties lay*   [K03: 36]

[71] Her eyes were large and dreamy *as if gazing upon some celestial vision* [P14: 80]
[72] Instead he frowned to himself for a moment, *as though lost in thought* [P08: 176]

Summary

We have now reviewed the major types of circumstantial proposition and here is a summary table of the meanings we have discussed, together with the subordinators typically associated with each of them.

[73]

CIRCUMSTANTIAL MEANING	TYPICAL SUBORDINATORS
Time – before	before, until, till
– same	as long as, so long as, while
– after	after, when, since, as soon as
Place	where
Contingency	whenever, wherever
Condition	if, unless, provided that
Concession	(al)though, whereas, while
Contrast	whereas, while
Reason	because, since, as
Purpose	to-inf, in order that, so that
Result	so that, and so
Comment	I believe, think; you know, see
Sentence relative	which, in which case
Similarity	just as, exactly as
Comparison	as if, as though

[*Exercise 1*]

Adverbial clauses

Included circumstantial propositions have their grammatical expression in embedded adverbial clauses. Adverbial clauses function mostly as optional Adjuncts in sentences. Occasionally the Adjunct may be obligatory, e.g. the Place clauses in [18] and [19]; or an adverbial clause may function as a Disjunct, e.g. the comment clauses in [56] to [63]. In the odd instance, just as Temporal and Locative phrases may sometimes take on participant functions as Subject,

Object, etc., so too an adverbial clause may function similarly, e.g.

> [74] It seemed *as if she was being called upon to make a quick decision and was finding the process difficult*
> [P21: 70]

Here there has been obligatory extraposition with the verb *seem*: *it* is a dummy holding the place of the Subject, which is the extraposed *as if*-clause.

Adverbial clauses may be **finite** or **non-finite**, though they most frequently have a finite form. As finite clauses, they are introduced by a subordinating conjunction which, together with the context, indicates the 'meaning' of the adverbial clause; e.g. *because* indicates 'reason', *although* indicates 'concession', and so on. Some subordinators, however, are used with more than one type of adverbial meaning: *since* may indicate 'time (after)' or 'reason'; *so that* may indicate 'purpose' or 'result'; and so on. Besides context and the subordinator, a contribution to the meaning of an adverbial clause may also be made by the tense or modality of the clause. We noted how a change in tense/modality could change a *so that*-clause from a 'result' meaning to a 'purpose' meaning in [54]. Similarly, open and hypothetical conditions are in part distinguished by tense/mood – past or subjunctive for hypothetical conditions (compare [27] and [28]).

Non-finite adverbial clauses also usually occur with a subordinator, though the infinitive clause occurs without one with the meaning of 'purpose' (e.g. in [50]). Time adverbial clauses occur as present participle clauses with a subordinator, e.g. the *before*-clause in the following.

> [75] He studied the photograph for a long time *before throwing aside the book and returning to his study of the racing column*
> [L10: 87]

We have also seen that the whole range of non-finite clauses occurs with the comparison subordinators *as if* and *as though* ([70] to [72]). Other types of subordinator occur only with finite clauses, e.g. those for reason, purpose and result, and those for condition and concession.

Like other Adjuncts, embedded adverbial clauses are relatively mobile elements in a sentence; though, because of their length, they do not usually occupy a medial position. Some adverbial clauses will more naturally take up final position than initial position because of the logical order entailed in the propositions. This is the case, for example, of result clauses, where a result usually follows from some state of affairs expressed by the sentence. But with reason clauses, for example, the reason may be stated first [76] or given afterwards [77].

[76] *Because we were both under 21*, the firm refused to sell to us   [F14: 67]

[77] She has no idea of the cost of things, *because she's never had a home of her own to run*   [F14: 116]

It seems, however, that the more common position for reason clauses is finally, as indeed it is for most, if not all, the adverbial clauses. The exception to this is the conditional clause, where it is frequently the case – perhaps even in the majority of instances – that the condition is stated first before the state-of-affairs that depends on the condition, e.g.

[78] *If the UN forces were thick enough on the ground*, such incidents as that at Matadi would not happen
[B01: 133]

Summarising, embedded adverbial clauses are usually introduced by a subordinator, with the exception of *to*-infinitive purpose clauses and comment clauses (like 'you know'). Mostly they have a finite form, but non-finite clauses occur with some categories of meaning, notably purpose, time and comparison. Adverbial clauses may occur initially or finally in a sentence, though the latter is generally the preferred position.

[*Exercise 2*]

Exercises

Exercise 1

Each of the following propositions contains at least one included circumstantial proposition. Identify the circumstantial propositions and say what meaning each of them has (i.e. Place, Concession, Result, etc.).

1. A nice simple sergeant of the Carabinieri arrives in a strange village at night to investigate some irregularities concerning the town clerk [C03: 143]
2. He sponged off him until he died just after the war [L01: 22]
3. You see, if he really is as bad as he says, the sensitivity of some nerves would be bound to be affected at the finger extremities [L23: 91]
4. To ridicule them only pushes them farther into themselves, so that they become unable to speak about it to anybody [D06: 16]
5 .Whenever I try to bring to mind this detail of the afternoon sensations, it disappears [K23: 126]
6. Although we are a state monopoly our aim is to be as competitive as if we had rivals breathing down our necks [B08: 26]
7. This was not a possibility which Colleano felt able to accept so long as another, and much likelier, explanation of the circumstances remained open to him [L24: 188]
8. This is the more surprising, since certain incidents recounted of Robin Hood in the ballads are also told of border heroes [F27: 121]
9. Poor, darling Papa had underrated him, which was natural, as they were so different from one another [K13: 61]
10. Indeed unless it is faced there is a danger that the UN representation itself will disintegrate as individual countries decide to withdraw their men [B19: 187]

Exercise 2

Provide the subordinator for each of the adverbial clauses in the following sentences. If you think that more than one is possible from the structure and context of the sentence, then say so.

1. Her books should be read at a sitting if possible, . . . the plot and characters are only revealed by the cumulative effect of the dialogue [C09: 141]

2. He has, too, certain advantages, . . . these will not necessarily prove decisive [B17: 130]

3. The herring will spawn . . . the suitable gravelly bottom soil coincides with their final ripeness [E06: 36]

4. The engine of the doctor's car revved loudly in the drive . . . he controlled it clumsily [K06: 56]

5. He laid his first bricks during hostilities and has gone on ever since, . . . he can now recommend all the essential tools and clothes [F09: 177]

6. I'll pad up the wound, and send help . . . I get out [L03: 100]

7. That is the principal reason why he never speaks with notes; he couldn't read them . . . he had them [B08: 125]

8. Parishes have allowed themselves to be bereft of clergy and some of the Sunday congregation . . . a quiet parish weekend might be spent away from the usual routine [D13: 127]

9. They meet each other . . . Keith's job as a collier on shift work will allow them to [F14: 89]

10. An introduction is a social matter; . . . one would not introduce a friend to, say, one's doctor, . . . a visit to or from the doctor is not a social occasion [F08: 92]

CHAPTER 9

Combining Propositions: Co-ordination and conjunction

In the previous two chapters, we have been discussing propositions which are contained as elements within other propositions. We have used the term 'main' proposition for the latter and the term 'included' proposition for the former. In grammatical terms, our discussion has been about 'sentences' that contain 'embedded clauses'. The included proposition or embedded clause was an element in or a constituent of the main proposition or sentence. In this chapter, we are going to consider ways in which independent (main) propositions combine together.

Now, propositions combine together into 'messages' – the topic of our final chapter. In writing, each proposition forming part of a message concludes with a full-stop. There may be no explicit connection made between propositions: a common theme or subject-matter provides the coherence to the message. On the other hand, as we shall see in Chapter 10, there are various devices of 'cohesion' which serve to bond propositions together into a message. Often, though, propositions are combined explicitly by a conjunction word. Sometimes the combined propositions are placed together within the same written unit, bounded by the full-stop. Alternatively, the propositions are assigned separate written units, and the second proposition will include a conjoining word. Compare [1] and [2]:

[1] I am slightly wet, and Buck would be wetter if he had more clothes on   [N03: 169]

[2] I do a lot of things here that I like. And I can ride the mules very well, too   [N07: 49]

In both these examples, the propositions are combined by the co-ordinating conjunction *and*. In [1] the two propositions are separated merely by a comma, whereas in [2] the separation is by means of a full-stop. The choices of punctuation are used by writers to show degrees of connectedness between elements and for stylistic purposes of emphasis, pacing and rhythm.

We shall be concentrating in this chapter, then, on explicit ways of combining propositions, whether the combination occurs within a written unit bounded by a full-stop or whether the combination spans such a boundary. We shall be distinguishing four types of combination: additive, adversative, temporal and causal. (The terms are taken from Halliday & Hasan (1976).)

Additive combination

The simplest form of combination is by means of the 'co-ordinating' conjunction *and*, which has the effect of 'adding on' one proposition to another. *And* is the prototypical conjoiner for the 'additive' meaning.

[3] He held out his hand *and* John could not do otherwise than take it   [N04: 83]

[4] John took the refilled glass *and* looked over the rim at his companion   [N04: 120]

These examples could equally well have been expressed as separate, uncombined propositions: compare [3] with [5] and [4] with [6].

[5] He held out his hand. John could not do otherwise than take it.

[6] John took the refilled glass. He looked over the rim at his companion.

The meaning connection between the propositions in [5] and [6] is now provided largely by the context. In [3]/[5] the second proposition follows on from the first as a kind of result or consequence; in [4]/[6] the second proposition follows as the next event in a temporal sequence. As the conjunction for both these meanings – and many others – *and* clearly has an extensive range of reference.

You will have noticed that in transforming [4] into [6] an AGENTIVE participant (Subject of the sentence) had to be provided for the second proposition. In [4] the process of ellipsis has occurred by which an item in a conjoined proposition may be omitted if it is identical with one in the first proposition. Consider [7], in which there are three propositions in combination:

> [7] He kept away from Service matters, was an excellent host and a splendid raconteur   [N04: 140]

From the second proposition the *he* of the first has been omitted, and from the third the *he* from the first and the *was* from the second have been elipted. Ellipsis – especially of Subjects – is common with the *and* conjoiner.

Other conjoiners that mark a simple additive combination include: *additionally, furthermore* [8], *moreover* [9].

> [8] *Furthermore,* the levelling of the sloping site by the chapel builders had destroyed much of the original surface   [A34: 42]
> [9] *Moreover,* something about the man seemed vaguely familiar   [L11: 61]

These conjoiners are usually found, as in [8] and [9], at the beginning of a proposition which is a separate written unit, and they mark a conjunction with the previous proposition. The co-ordinating conjunction *and* usually joins propositions within a single written unit, while *furthermore, moreover,* etc., usually join propositions in separate written units. Consider, however, the example at [10].

> [10] Two warders (perfectly reputable men) were concerned in the serving of this, *and moreover* they were, as it happened, accompanied on this occasion by one of H.M. Inspectors of Prisons
> [L24: 143]

Not only does *moreover* occur within a single written unit in this example, but it also occurs in combination with *and*, as a kind of reinforcement of the additional information contained in the conjoined proposition.

Another kind of additive meaning is expressed by the co-ordinating conjunction *or*: it has the meaning of 'additional and alternative'.

[11] Coke is temperamental; it can make a good fire, *or*
it can be a most depressing sight   [A36: 168]

There are three propositions in combination in this
example. The second and third are joined to the first by the
semicolon. The second and third form a pair of alternatives,
providing an elaboration of the ATTRIBUTE *temperamental*
in the first proposition. The alternative–additive meaning
may also be signalled by the conjunctive adverb *alternatively*,
either by itself at the beginning of a separately written
proposition (like *moreover* and *furthermore* above) or in
combination with *or*, as in [12]:

[12] Is the Exchequer subsidy distributed to those who
need it, *or alternatively*, is it merely utilised to
bring about a general reduction in rents, regardless
of the income of tenants   [B23: 171]

A third kind of additive meaning combines that of
'additional' with the meaning 'exemplificatory'. The typical
conjoiner is *for example* or *for instance*.

[13] *For example*, from March 1, each item on a
National Health Service prescription is to cost 2s
[B14: 86]
[14] He is, *for instance*, a professional soldier
[B08: 111]

These exemplificatory conjoiners usually introduce the
second proposition as a separate written unit, coming either
in initial position [13] or fairly early in the proposition [14].
However, the two propositions may occasionally be
contained in an undivided written unit [15]; and the
conjoiner may occur late in the proposition, in final position
[16].

[15] These circumstances would seem to point either to
suicide or to murder by trickery – *for example*,
Wynter might previously have been given a
preparation of nicotine under the guise of
medicine   [L24: 157]
[16] I might do, if you give me a lead on something
interesting, *for example*   [L17: 33]

Similar to the exemplificatory meaning of *for example* is the addition as 'reformulation' of *in other words*.

[17] *In other words*, they should carry on as they have been doing for the last 10 years until some bright spark among them can think up something useful
[B24: 223]

Again, this conjoiner usually introduces a combined proposition in a separate written unit. In the following example [18], though, it occurs in the middle of a proposition, because it is reformulating part of the proposition – the included conditional proposition.

[18] If the expenses in question are disallowed by the Inspector of Taxes – *in other words*, they were not 'wholly exclusively and necessarily' incurred – then quite properly they are shown in the accounts under 'Directors' Emoluments' [B10: 8]

Summarising, additive combination of propositions may involve: simple addition (*and*), addition + alternative (*or*), addition + exemplification (*for example*), addition + reformulation (*in other words*).

Adversative combination

Whereas *and* represents the prototypical additive relation between independent propositions, the prototypical marker of the adversative relation is *but*.

[19] Liszt and Tchaikovski were born geniuses *but* they had to learn how to read and write notes [K07: 17]
[20] All right, if that's the way they want it. *But* don't ask me to clean up the mess [K09: 135]

A proposition introduced by *but* adds information to the proposition with which it combines, but the information includes a meaning of 'contrast', 'contradiction' or 'concession'. Like *and*, *but* normally combines two propositions within a single written unit [19]; occasionally the propositions are assigned separate written units, and the sense of contrast is stylistically emphasised [20]. A second proposition introduced by *but* is less likely to have the same Subject participant than one introduced by *and*, but when it does, the same processes of ellipsis may apply, e.g.

[21] He wouldn't be here in Athens already, *but* sitting in some awful little place in South America
[K10: 143]

Here the *but*-proposition has ellipsis of 'he would be' from the first proposition in the combination.

While *but* is the prototypical adversative conjoiner, there are a number of others whose meaning may also be termed 'adversative', including *however* [22], *nevertheless* [23], *yet* [24].

[22] Next morning *however* he was up earlier than usual
[L15: 104]
[23] *Nevertheless* I think autumn planting has much to commend it
[E08: 137]
[24] *Yet* suddenly, with her fifth novel, she has been sifted out by the priests of culture for their own honours list
[C11: 18]

These conjoiners usually introduce the second proposition of a combination as a separate written unit, and they usually occur in initial position (as *nevertheless* in [23] and *yet* in [24]) or as an early item in the proposition (*however* is second item in [22]). Propositions combined by these conjoiners – especially *yet* – may be found on occasions in the same written unit, e.g.

[25] Doc had only judged from what she had told him, *yet* the other side of the story went much deeper
[K18: 62]
[26] Of course everyone knows about hot teapots and really boiling water, *nevertheless* these minutiae are not always properly observed
[E26: 159]

The occurrence of the propositions in the same written unit may also be occasioned by the use of these conjoiners with a co-ordinating conjunction: consider the use of *yet* with *and* in [27], and of *nevertheless* with *but* in [28]. The conjoiners are mutually reinforcing.

[27] They want her to go *and yet* they want her to stay
[C03: 159]

[28] The increase in the physical volume of production
was less marked *but* was *nevertheless* quite significant [E36: 162]

You will note the ellipsis of the Subject participant from the
second proposition in the example at [28].

A further adversative conjoiner is *though*. We discussed
though in Chapter 8 as a concessive subordinator, along with
its more formal counterpart *although*. *Though* – but not
although – is also used as a conjoiner to combine two
propositions where the second has an adversative concession
meaning in relation to the first. A proposition with the
conjoiner *though* is always a separate written unit, and *though*
does not take up initial position. It is often the second item –
or later – and is usually marked off by commas in writing.

[29] By the time he reached the orchard, *though*, it
seemed certain that there was only one intruder
[L16: 161]
[30] I was not far from it, *though*, for there was sea
below me [K12: 49]

In [29] *though* takes up second position after the included
time proposition. In [30] *though* is placed after the main
proposition and before the included reason proposition.

Temporal combination

A third way in which propositions may be combined is
temporally. Temporal combination of propositions may be
a reflection of the reference of the propositions to sequences
of events or actions: as one event follows another in time, so
the propositions referring to those events are linked by
temporal conjoiners to reflect this. *And* is often used in story
telling in this way, especially by children. The simplest
temporal conjoiner is *then* [31], often used in connection
with *and* [32].

[31] He told them in French that it was not necessary
to go to the left and that they would find the
house to the right. He *then* disappeared and they
heard his footsteps retreating [F11: 118]
[32] He unbound her arms *and then* he tried to force the
glass between her lips [P04: 149]

Both these examples are reporting sequences of events which follow one another chronologically. Rather than simply juxtapose them in the reporting, the writers have chosen to make an explicit connection by means of the conjoiner *then*.

Temporal combination of propositions need not be a reflection of chronological sequences of events. It may merely be a reflection of some order in the propositions, as in a procedure [33].

> [33] *Then* the prosecutor sits down and the defence advocate rises to cross-examine you   [F13: 96]

Here the writer is describing some legal proceedings, and the proposition at [33] is shown to be ordered in sequence with respect to the previous proposition by the conjoiner *then*.

Temporal combination as a reflection of succession in time is also expressed by conjoiners such as *thereupon* [34] and *meanwhile* [35].

> [34] The matter was *thereupon* referred to the Court for decision   [H19: 57]
> [35] *Meanwhile* Paris was to pay a war-indemnity of two hundred million francs   [J57: 137]

Thereupon combines a proposition with the preceding proposition with the meaning of 'immediate temporal succession': it is an immediate form of *then*. *Meanwhile* combines a proposition with the previous one in a meaning of 'at the same time as' or 'with the time-span of': it expresses simultaneous occurrence. These two conjoiners normally introduce the second proposition as a separate written unit and occur in initial position or early in the proposition. *Then* as a temporal conjoiner probably occurs most often at the beginning of a second proposition as a separate written unit; but, as [32] illustrates, it may occur in an undivided combination, especially as a compound with *and*.

Temporal combination as a reflection of logical order uses a number of conjoiners which express the various stages in a procedure. These are the enumerative terms, like *firstly*, *secondly*, *finally*, exemplified in [36] to [38]:

[36] *Firstly*, it is a partial view of poetic creation
[J60: 94]

[37] *Secondly*, it stands condemned by the very inadequacy of its presentation [J60: 103]

[38] *Finally*, to complete the picture of food research institutes, mention must be made of the Torry Research Station. . . [H10: 82]

These conjoiners are used, not necessarily in successive propositions, to provide an order for the information in a message and to enable the readers to find their way through the information.

An alternative conjoiner to *finally* is *in conclusion* [39]. A more general term (than *firstly*, *secondly*, etc.) for making temporal combination is *next* [40].

[39] *In conclusion* the Company submitted that they observed the spirit of all Agreements between the Engineering Employers' Federation and the Union
[H19: 138]

[40] I want *next* to tell you of certain appointments consequent upon the reorganisation of the Company into a single trading entity [H27: 20]

While the conjoiners illustrated in [36] to [40] are usually associated with making temporal combinations internal to a message (i.e. in terms of logical order), they may also – apart from *in conclusion* – be used for making time connections in a narrative. They are also usually, as the examples show, positioned initially in a proposition or near to the beginning (*next* in [40]), and the proposition takes up a separate written unit. However, these conjoiners may also be used to combine propositions within a single unit, e.g.

[41] There are two questions here: *first*, is it possible to want or to have a desire for something without wanting to do, and *secondly*, is it possible that one may have what one wants but not want to do anything with it? [J54: 142]

The three propositions in this example could each have been assigned to a separate written unit, but the writer has chosen to show the connection, not only by means of the conjoiners *first* and *secondly* (relating to the *two* of the first proposition), but also by means of the internal punctuation (the colon and commas).

Causal combination

Two propositions are in a causal combination if the second contains a conjoiner which indicates that this proposition follows as the logical result or consequence or deduction from the first proposition. The prototypical causal conjoiner is *therefore*.

> [42] Immigrants starting new jobs totalled 177,500 in 1959, and 236,000 in 1960. Immigration has *therefore* been meeting a real need   [B15: 65]
>
> [43] It has failed to explain to the nation any consistent and practical policy to achieve expansion, and it has *therefore* failed to carry the nation along with it [B12: 31]

Propositions in a causal combination with *therefore* are usually assigned to different written units, as in [42]. If the propositions are contained within a single written unit, as in [43], then the conjunction *and* is usually also present. The conjoiner *therefore* does not often have initial position in the second proposition of the combination, but it does occur in a variety of positions within the proposition. In both [42] and [43], *therefore* interrupts the Predicator phrase, coming after the first auxiliary verb (*has* in both cases). Consider the following examples:

> [44] If, *therefore*, these bags are retained, they should be kept out of the reach of children   [B10: 211]
>
> [45] It is not, *therefore*, possible to lower fares appreciably   [B10: 125]
>
> [46] It is vital *therefore* that, before any form of control is introduced, Britain should consult all her partners   [B15: 110]
>
> [47] It *therefore* comes as no shock to read Dr Lees's conclusion on the drug bill   [B09: 189]

In [44] the conjoiner *therefore* is placed immediately after the subordinator *if* and before the clause proper of the included conditional proposition. The other three examples all have an extraposition structure with a postponed clausal Subject (*to*-inf clause in [45] and [47], and *that*-clause in [46]). But the *therefore* occurs in a different position in each one: after the verb + negative (*is not*) and before the Complement (*possible*) in [45]; interrupting the Complement ('vital that. . .') in [46], i.e. after the adjective and before the adjective-complement *that*-clause; and in [47] directly after the dummy *it* and before the Predicator. *Therefore* is apparently able to interrupt a proposition at almost any point, certainly with greater freedom than other conjoiners.

Other causal conjoiners with a similar meaning to *therefore*, but with more limited privileges of occurrence, include: *so, consequently, as a result*. These conjoiners usually occur as the initial element of a second proposition that is assigned to a separate written unit.

[48] *So* please don't start unloading bundles of old bus tickets at his office [B22: 152]

[49] *Consequently* wages in the public service should be settled by comparison with rates in outside occupations where market forces apply [J45: 21]

[50] *As a result*, Barry and Margaret got married in another church, after a delay of eight days
[A24: 206]

In all these cases, as with *therefore*, this second proposition follows on as a consequence of the previous proposition. Again, like *therefore*, the two propositions may be included in the same written unit, when *and* is also used to connect the propositions.

[51] They are usually students, not trained teachers, *and consequently* their work is most effective when they receive adequate help and guidance from the regular teachers [H03: 26]

A slightly different causal meaning is provided by the conjoiner *for this reason*. The first proposition provides the explanation or 'reason' which justifies or gives rise to the assertion in the second proposition introduced by the conjoiner.

[52] I presume that Mr G. H. Woolveridge's letter (August 23) is written in his official capacity, *and*

it is *for this reason* that I do not think it should be
allowed to pass without comment   [B10: 167]

[53] *For this reason* we find a considerable number
preferring the Disney series of nature films and
asking for more   [J26: 131]

This conjoiner more often occurs as the initial element in a
second proposition as a separate written unit, as in [53],
than as in [52].

A final pair of causal conjoiners have the meaning of
'alternative or different outcome or consequence'. One of
these is *otherwise* [54]/[55], the other is *or* [56] in the sense of
'or else' and thus different from the additive *or*.

[54] It is still important to give the surnames clearly on
the first introduction; *otherwise* circumstances can
easily arise where people never know one
another's surnames   [F08: 139]

[55] *Otherwise* it is hard to explain their refusal to allow
regional differences in prices   [J42: 32]

[56] Shakespeare, he knows, could never have been in
Italy, *or* he would have realised all this
[A18: 131]

As [54] and [55] show, *otherwise* usually occurs initially in
the second proposition, but this may be in the same written
unit as the first proposition [54] or in a separate written unit
[55]. The *or* in [56] is to be interpreted as an 'or else' or
'otherwise': either could be substituted for the *or* in this
example.

This concludes our review of the major ways in which
propositions may be combined as independent elements,
either in a single written unit or assigned to two separate
ones, with the second proposition in either case containing a
conjoiner indicating the 'meaning' of the connection
between the propositions. Example [57] gives a summary of
the meanings and their associated conjoiners.

[57] MEANING   CONJOINERS

Additive	and, additionally, moreover, furthermore; or, alternatively, for example, for instance, in other words

Adversative	but, yet, however, nevertheless, though,
Temporal	then, thereupon, meanwhile, firstly, secondly, finally, next, in conclusion
Causal	therefore, so, consequently, as a result; for this reason, otherwise, or (else)

[*Exercise 1*]

Grammar of combination

We have considered in this chapter ways in which propositions (sentences) combine by means of explicit connecting devices. These devices comprise, on the one hand, **co-ordinating conjunctions** (*and, or, but*), and on the other hand, **conjunctive adverbs** (*moreover, however, finally, therefore,* etc.). As a general rule, co-ordinating conjunctions join sentences within a single written unit, while conjunctive adverbs make a connection between sentences in separate written units. Though this is a general rule, it is not without exception, as we have seen (e.g. [20], [25]). In particular, some conjunctive adverbs may join sentences in a single written unit especially when used together with a co-ordinating conjunction (e.g. [10], [28]).

Let us digress at this point to explain the use of the term 'written unit'. The term is used to refer to a stretch of writing beginning with a capital letter (following a full-stop or beginning a text) and ending with a full-stop. Traditionally, this stretch of writing is referred to as a 'sentence', and that is where the difficulty arises, because in our grammatical description (Chapter 6) we have used the term 'sentence' to designate quite precisely a unit of grammar with a certain structure: a finite verb (Predicator) together with the elements dependent on it (Subject, Object, Complement, Adjunct). It is therefore in order to avoid ambiguity that the term 'written unit' has been used in this chapter to refer to the 'sentence' of writing, since it is in discussing the combination of (grammatical) sentences that the confusion of terms arises.

Co-ordination

We consider first the grammar of the co-ordinating conjunctions: *and*, *or*, *but*. In the examples with these conjunctions earlier in the chapter, they were used to connect sentences. Here is a further example of each.

[58] We're going to drag the boat ashore *and* turn her over [N03: 167]

[59] It will now have to pay more *or* run the obvious risks in upsetting the new American administration [A01: 137]

[60] He wore a thin dressing-gown *but* most of it was under the bedclothes [K06: 81]

As we noted earlier, where co-ordinated sentences share identical elements, or parts of elements, they may be subject to ellipsis in the second sentence. In the example at [60] the sentences do not have any elements in common – e.g. the Subjects (*he* and *most of it*) are different – and so there is no ellipsis. In [59] the words *it will* have been ellipted from the second sentence; that is, the Subject *it*, and the modal auxiliary verb *will* from the Predicator. In [60] also, the Subject (*we*) and part of the Predicator phrase, the future auxiliary *are going to*, have been ellipted from the second sentence.

Consider now the following examples and whether we can invoke ellipsis to account for their structure.

[61] It was large and comfortable and practical [N03: 35]

[62] The wind billowed out and sucked in his baggy black blouse and pantaloons [N03: 129]

We could regard [61] as the combination of three sentences, with *it was* ellipted from the second and third:

[63] It was large. It was comfortable. It was practical

Alternatively, we could regard [61] as a single sentence, with the structure 'SPC', in which the Complement consists of three co-ordinated adjectives. Similarly, we could regard [62] as a combination of four sentences, from which various elements have been ellipted.

> [64] The wind billowed out his baggy black blouse
> [The wind billowed out his] pantaloons
> [The wind] sucked in [his baggy black blouse]
> [The wind sucked in his pantaloons]

The elements not in square brackets combine to give [62]; that is, the elements in square brackets are considered to have been ellipted. Alternatively, we could regard [62] as a single sentence containing a Predicator consisting of co-ordinated verbs and an Object consisting of co-ordinated nouns which share a possessive determinative (*his*). Rather, therefore, than account for cases like [61] and [62] in terms of sentence co-ordination and ellipsis, it would seem more sensible to talk of co-ordination of units smaller than the sentence – clauses [65], phrases [66], words [67].

> [65] No indication has been given of what this increase will be *or* where the troops will be found
> [A20: 12]
> [66] What shall we do with this house – *and* Jill's school? [N04: 20]
> [67] Very correctly, she was handing out the polite *but* casual hospitality due to a new neighbour who had rendered her a small service [K08: 74]

In [65] the *wh*-clauses, appositive to *indication*, are co-ordinated by *or*; in [66] the noun phrases 'this house' and 'Jill's school' are co-ordinated by *and*; and in [67] the words *polite* and *casual* are co-ordinated by *but*. It would be difficult – if not impossible – to account for this last example in terms of sentence co-ordination. With the other two examples it would be possible, but we have to judge which is the more plausible and satisfying descriptive solution.

Returning to the co-ordination of sentences – though the feature to be discussed occurs with the co-ordination of other elements also – we find that sometimes two sentences are connected by a pair of correlative co-ordinating words, one in each sentence. The most commonly occurring pair is '*either . . . or*', e.g.

> [68] He would have to leave the bar and *either* sit in the lounge *or* return to his bedroom [N04: 70]

There are three co-ordinated sentences in this example, with ellipsis in the second and third sentence of Subject *he* and the modal auxiliaries *would* and *have to* from the Predicator phrase. The first sentence is joined to the others by *and*; the second and third present alternative courses of action and are joined by the *'either . . . or'* pair of correlative conjunctions. Two other correlative pairs occur: *'both . . . and'* [69], *'not only . . . but also'* [70].

> [69] Jesus *both* removed men's diseases by his miracles *and* himself suffered their pain on the cross
>
> [D08: 21]
>
> [70] Some local authorities have *not only* carried out a very good business deal for themselves *but also* acquired a beauty spot for their people   [F43: 112]

Notice how the sentences joined by *'both . . . and'* in [69] share the same Subject (*Jesus*), i.e. it has been ellipted from the second sentence; and in [70] the Subject ('some local authorities') and the perfective auxiliary verb *have* are shared by both sentences.

Conjunction

The use of conjunctive adverbs to effect an explicit connection between sentences does not give such a 'tight' connection as do co-ordinating conjunctions. This is reflected in the fact that sentences joined by conjunctive adverbs are generally assigned to separate written units. On the other hand, conjunctive adverbs make a tighter, more explicit, connection than the mere juxtaposition of sentences in a text. They are more commonly used in written styles than in spoken styles of language, to structure texts and signal to the reader how the text is to be interpreted (see further Chapter 10).

Many conjunctive adverbs are single words: *furthermore, though, next, otherwise*. Others have the form of word combinations: *for example, in other words, in conclusion, as a result*. Conjunctive adverbs usually occur at or near the beginning of the conjoined sentence, and with some conjoiners a variety of positions may be taken up, as the following examples with *however* illustrate.

> [71] *However* nothing further happened and I became

curious as to what had apparently fallen   [L15: 28]

[72] Before *however* I had made up my mind as to what I would do with it, the room door unexpectedly opened and Tom entered   [L15: 57]

[73] Next morning *however* he was up earlier than usual   [L15: 104]

[74] He had not been in a hurry, *however*, such grace and slenderness and beauty were all too rare
[L20: 35]

In [71] the conjoiner occurs initially, in [72] after the subordinator in the embedded temporal clause, in [73] after the first (Adjunct) element of the sentence, and in [74] – unusually – in final position in the first sentence. A similar variety of positions can also be taken up by multi-word conjunctive adverbs like *for example* and *for instance*.

[75] *For example*, tea is a commodity of great import-ance to India and Ceylon   [H21: 103]

[76] A very powerful social function, *for example*, is 'sending to Coventry' which cuts the deviant off from social communication with other members of his group   [H12: 62]

[77] None of us could ask for a smarter number, *for instance*, than a black softie calf shoe   [H30: 23]

In [75] the conjoiner occurs initially, in [76] after the first (Subject) element, and in [77] it interrupts the final (Object) element, separating the post-modifying comparative phrase introduced by *than* from its noun *number*.

Conjunctive adverbs have, as we have noted, important functions in the creation and interpretation of messages/texts, and it is to this topic that we turn in our final chapter.

[*Exercise 2*]

Exercises

Exercise 1

For each of the pairs of propositions in the following, suggest which combinatory meaning (additive, adversative, temporal, causal) would most appropriately connect them, and supply a suitable conjoiner, making any necessary ellipsis.

1. I'll write to those agents. I'll try to get a flat in Alverstoke   [N04: 30]
2. The psychologist first looks into his own mind. He interprets other people's minds by what he has found in his own   [F01: 172]
3. Those who said the Congolese could govern themselves will not admit they were wrong. Belgium, bowed down by internal trouble, mourning a terrible air crash, is made their scapegoat   [B04: 16]
4. He has achieved a ripe humour without clowning. He is to sing the Baron with the Hamburg State Opera
                                                              [A39: 68]
5. His father didn't move his head. After a second he turned his eyes   [K06: 85]
6. We must get accustomed to anxiety. We must not let ourselves drift. We must not let ourselves be pushed into panic   [A05: 135]
7. It was good, searching stuff, well presented and well delivered, and showing the stamp of original minds. Somehow I didn't seem up to it   [K26: 152]
8. It must be done very gradually indeed. One must make haste slowly   [A36: 159]
9. Some began to murmur that they should turn back while there was yet time. De Soto was inflexible, refusing to admit that what others found impossible would be impossible for him. There were more immediate dangers to face   [F25: 107]
10. The stock of houses is rising by some 200 thousand a year; the number of households needing separate dwellings over the next twenty years is likely to increase by an average of around 100 thousand a year.

Vacancies are likely to increase by some 100 thousand a year [J47: 38]

Exercise 2

Each of the following examples contains one or more conjoiners (co-ordinating conjunction or conjunctive adverb). Consider how you might rewrite each example, either by using a different conjoiner and/or by varying the position of the conjoiner.

1. Having deposited his baggage and unpacked his overnight-bag he went in search of a drink [N04: 51]
2. He looked at his watch; he would be late for lunch down-town, but perhaps his guests could cool their heels for a little while [K08: 49]
3. They will sooner or later affect the life of every church, and it is therefore essential that on this point the churches learn from each other [B03: 54]
4. The allowance should be claimed within three months of the former husband's death, otherwise some benefit may be lost [H20: 181]
5. Things in themselves are unknowable, but in that case how do I know of their existence? [D09: 50]
6. I think he fills in an important part of the background. Furthermore, dear boy, I think it confirms what we already know of your father's intention to leave the country on the night of October 14th [L04: 128]
7. 'A pity somebody saw us at Brighton,' he said. 'The police, though, can't be sure or they'd have clamped down on you.' [L02: 154]
8. Salisbury, on the 11th, after correspondence with Beaconsfield, telegraphed Horace Walpole to ask Cranbrook urgently for authority to stop Lytton sending the mission until the Russian reply had arrived. Cranbrook, meanwhile, feeling the same way in Scotland, had sent a telegram to Walpole forbidding the departure of the mission until further orders
[J59: 57]

CHAPTER 10

Messages: Texts

We began this book with the question 'What do we talk about?' and in the ensuing chapters we explored many of the kinds of meaning that we communicate by means of language and how these meanings are structured into propositions and expressed grammatically by sentences. We have by and large – apart from in the previous chapter – restricted our consideration to single propositions, but we rarely communicate in single propositions, except for notices ('Passengers must cross the line by the bridge') and brief notes ('Please leave one extra pint today'). Our communication is more usually in sequences of propositions. We will use the term **message** to refer to an act of communication (made up of one or more propositions) and the term **text** as its grammatical correlate.

Variety of messages: sender's choices

When we stop to consider the messages which we receive as hearers or readers and those which we send as speakers or writers in the course of our daily lives, we begin to realise how many and how diverse are the purposes to which we put our facility of communication. We participate in conversations in a variety of contexts – family, work, shopping, leisure; we write and receive letters – personal and transactional; we read newspapers, magazines and books, listen to the radio and television; we consult telephone directories, recipe books, manuals, dictionaries, encyclopaedias; and so on. Any message is the result of a number of choices made by the sender, though it has to be said that these choices are to some extent determined by the context of the message – who the receivers are, what the purpose of the message is.

The first choice that a sender has to make is which medium to use for the message: speech or writing. There are some messages that are normally only in the spoken medium – interaction in the family context; similarly, there are some messages that are normally only in the written medium – a statute or act of Parliament or a legal contract. In some cases the context of the message determines the medium: an advertisement in a newspaper or magazine is necessarily written, but on radio it must be spoken (or at least use the medium of sound), while on television both speech and writing may be used. In wanting to communicate some item of information to another person, however, we may choose either to go and see them face-to-face or telephone them (spoken medium), or we may choose to send a note or letter (written medium). Similarly, we may have views that we wish to make known to a wider audience: we may either call a public meeting and address it (spoken medium) or we may publish a pamphlet or booklet (written medium).

Related to the choice of medium is the choice between dialogue and monologue. We normally associate dialogue with speech and monologue mostly with writing, but also with certain kinds of spoken communication. Dialogue engages two or more communicators who operate as both senders and receivers in the course of the construction of the message; it is the stuff of daily face-to-face interaction. Monologue usually involves one sender and a large number of receivers, either together in one place (e.g. the public meeting) or dispersed, as with a radio audience or the readers of a newspaper or book. Messages in the written medium are normally monologues, usually to dispersed readerships, though we might count an exchange of letters as a kind of dialogue and restricted to two communicators.

A further choice that a sender must make is where to pitch the message on the scale of formality. The choice is determined to a significant extent by who the receiver or receivers of the message are, what the nature of the message is and the social setting in which the communication takes place. Legal statutes, for example, come at the 'very formal' end of the scale, both because they are highly stylised and because they conventionally exhibit complex syntax and specialised vocabulary. At the other end of the scale is spoken dialogue between close friends, which may exhibit colloquial, even slang, vocabulary and generally simple syntax. In some contexts – a public meeting, a letter, a report, a textbook – a sender may choose to be more or less formal, though the range of formality will be subject to constraints, depending on the context. For example, there is a limit to how 'chatty' or 'colloquial' a speaker could become in a public meeting, or a writer in a business report.

Finally, to illustrate the kinds of choices that the sender of a message must make, we consider the selection of 'genre'. By 'genre' we mean, for example, the choice between 'telling a story' and 'making a description'. That choice would need to be made, for instance, if you were telling someone about a house which you had visited. You could either tell it as a 'journey through the house', as if you were telling a story; or you could tell it like an estate agent's 'particulars', a room by room description. One difference between these two genres would be in the tenses of the verbs: the 'journey through the house' account would be in the past tense, while the 'estate agent's particulars' account would be in the present tense. To take another example, suppose that we wanted to make some point of morality or propagate some moral opinion: we could choose to express it in the form of a story, like Aesop's Fables; or we could select a persuasive genre like a sermon or homily, or we could choose to express it as the exposition of a concept. As with the other choices which senders of messages make, the choice of genre may to a greater or lesser extent be determined by the situational context: the report of a road accident, for example, will almost certainly be given in the story genre; a swimming lesson in the genre of instruction, and so on.

Text structure

Messages are realised grammatically as texts. 'Text' is taken to refer to both realisations of spoken and written messages. Texts have structure, just as sentences have structure. Sentences, for example, combine together to form (spoken/

written) paragraphs, and the sentences themselves may be adapted according to their position in a paragraph or text. The sentences in a text relate to each other, tie in with each other, in various ways: texts have cohesion.

Two of the principles which inform the structure of texts are the need to ensure coherence in a text and the need to ensure that the receiver (hearer or reader) knows which is the most important information in a text. Coherence is achieved partly by consistency of subject-matter, partly by the way in which one sentence (or contribution in spoken dialogue) follows on from and relates to the preceding one(s), and partly by the way in which the elements within a sentence (or contribution) are ordered. Generally, the initial element of a sentence both relates back to and creates a link with the sentence or a previous one, and it represents the starting point from which the sentence is structured. A sentence then culminates in the informationally most important element (see the discussion below on 'given' and 'new' information). In speech, intonation normally works to give this final element the chief focus of the intonation pattern. Consider the following sentence.

In the evening, Jerry took Pamela to the bowling alley

As receivers of this part of a message, we would make the following assumptions about the content of this sentence, based on the arrangement of its elements. Under discussion is what Jerry and Pamela did at different times of the day: so the starting point is 'in the evening'. The important information is that it was the bowling alley that he took her to in the evening: so this element takes final, focus position. The intonational resources of speech in fact allow a speaker to vary the information focus in a sentence: in our example, it could fall on *Pamela* or *Jerry*, or even on *evening*. As readers, unless contextual evidence is to the contrary, we usually assign a neutral intonation to a sentence, that is, with 'end focus'. We will be considering later on in the chapter the ways in which texts (specifically written texts) achieve coherence and appropriate information focus.

Examples

To provide illustrative material for the subject-matter of this chapter we shall not be taking examples from the LOB-corpus as before, but from a complete newspaper article, reproduced below. It comes from a regular column written by the Wiltshire farmer and naturalist Ralph Whitlock, published in *The Guardian Weekly*. This article, 'The dew-pond myth' appeared in May 1989. The paragraphs have been lettered A to N, and the sentences within paragraphs have been numbered for easy reference, which means that illustrative examples can be appreciated in their textual context. So, 'F3' refers to the third sentence of paragraph F, and so on.

The dew-pond myth

Ralph Whitlock

A   [1] A downland nature reserve asked me if I could help them with a water supply problem. [2] They wondered whether theirs would be a suitable site for a dew-pond, on which they had heard that I was a bit of an authority.

B   [1] By one of those coincidences which so often occur, within a few days I had received a query from a reader in Alabama on the same subject. [2] He had recently attended a session at which the speaker was asked about dewponds, with fairly negative results. [3] The ponds, he had said, did not collect dew and the word 'dew' was really a corruption of the French 'd'eau', the technique of making them having been introduced to England by mediaeval French monks.

C   [1] The speaker was right on the first count – the ponds are not replenished (to any appreciable extent) by dew – but hopelessly wrong on the second. [2] And thereby hangs an amusing story.

D   [1] But first, the ponds themselves. [2] They are hill-top ponds, features mostly of exposed chalk and limestone hills of southern England, though some are to be found in Derbyshire and other counties. [3] Clumps of tall beeches are adjacent to some though are not essential. [4] They are reputed never to dry up even in the hottest and most prolonged summer, but they are not fed by springs.

E   [1] Some are alleged to be of great antiquity. [2] On a hill overlooking the Vale of Pewsey, in Wiltshire, a pond known as Oxenmere is said to be the pond mentioned in a Saxon survey of A.D. 825. [3] On the principle that a pocket-knife which in the course of time has been fitted with six new blades and three new handles can still be considered the original knife, that assumption may be valid.

F   [1] However, the natural life of a pond in regular use is about twenty or thirty years, after which it will probably need cleaning and patching. [2] After four or five cleanings it will in all likelihood spring a leak and require remaking. [3] The maximum life of a hill-top pond would thus seem to be around 150 years. [4] The ponds were constructed primarily for sheep, whose little hooves tend to consolidate the linings around the edges and so help to prolong their life. [5] The larger hooves of cattle and horses are liable to damage it.

G   [1] Where does the water come from? [2] From dew, said late Victorian savants and wrote learned articles, treatises and even books to prove their point. [3] But they were wrong, as was quickly demonstrated when scientists took the trouble to measure dewfall.

H   [1] The optimum quantity of dew deposited in a single night, under the most favourable conditions of weather and collecting surface, is only 0.0024 inches. [2] If such conditions occurred on most nights, say 300 in a year, the total annual deposit would be only 0.72 inches. [3] As there are only a few nights per year which are that favourable, the actual amount must be very much less. [4] Yet the normal evaporation rate in the regions where most dewponds occur is about 18 inches a year.

[5] So the total annual dewfall could be lost by evaporation in twenty summer days. [6] Clearly dew cannot be the main source of supply.

I   [1] Rainfall is more promising. [2] An inch of rain falling on a surface of 100 square yards deposits 466.5 gallons of water. [3] The average rainfall for typical hill-top sites in England is about 30 inches. [4] The pond would thus receive 13,995 gallons of water a year. [5] Allowing for a loss of 18 inches by evaporation, the water left in the pond would be 13,995 minus 8,397 gallons = 5,598 gallons. [6] Work it out for yourself.

J   [1] That would be adequate to keep the pond from drying up if it were not used by animals, but it could be at risk in a hot, dry summer, when for weeks on end evaporation rate greatly exceeded rainfall. [2] The pond-makers allowed for that by heaping up the material excavated from the pond around the perimeter, creating a rim which more than doubled the catchment area.

K   [1] Supposing our pond 10 yards square is surrounded by a waterproof catchment margin of three yards. [2] The effect is to increase the catchment area from 100 square yards to 256 square yards. [3] With a 30-inch annual rainfall, the quantity of water falling on this area will be 35,827 gallons. [4] Evaporation, however, will occur only from the pond's surface area, which is 100 square yards, and so will be 8,397 gallons as before. [5] The water remaining in the pond will thus be 27,430 gallons. [6] Ample.

L   [1] So why all the nonsense about 'dew-ponds'? [2] Investigating, I found the astonishing fact that 'dew-ponds' are not mentioned in English literature before 1877! [3] It is true that Gilbert White, the naturalist of Selborne, writing towards the end of the eighteenth century, describes the hill-top ponds which he knew, but he does not call them 'dew-ponds'.

M   [1] I came upon the explanation by chance. [2] When

researching for my book *Royal Farmers*, some twelve years ago, I was privileged to have access to the Royal Archives at Windsor, and there I found a letter from King George III to his agent. [3] His Majesty expresses the hope that Mr Dew, the pond-maker, will soon be back at work after his illness, as he wants that pond finished as soon as possible!

N   [1] So there you have it. [2] Mr Dew was an expert pond-maker operating in Hampshire and Surrey. [3] Seventy years later, when he himself had been forgotten, his name was still attached in local tradition to some of the ponds he had made, and certain antiquarians jumped to unwarranted conclusions. [4] A whole pseudo-scientific literature was based on a myth!

Message organisation

Messages of all kinds display organisation, though the degree of organisation varies from the rather loose structures of ordinary conversation through to the highly crafted text of a poem or after-dinner speech. There is a clear difference, however, between spontaneous speech and written messages, including those which are intended to be delivered in the spoken medium, like news broadcasts, drama and other scripted speech. The written medium allows the sender to reflect on, amend and refine the message before it is sent. In speech, on the other hand, the presence of speaker and hearer in the same situational context imposes an organisational constraint on the developing dialogue. In some situations of speech – a school lesson, a committee meeting – the progress of the dialogue is more or less pre-planned, and then directed along its course by the person managing the dialogue – teacher or chairperson. In this section we are going to concentrate on the structure of written messages, as illustrated by the Whitlock article reproduced above.

Given and new information

A written message is sent to a receiver who is remote from the sender. Sometimes the writer knows who the receiver of the written message will be (e.g. in the case of personal letters). Mostly, though, the writer will not know the readers of the message personally, and these may be geographically dispersed. In the case of Ralph Whitlock's article in *The Guardian Weekly*, the readership is internationally dispersed. Writers have to determine how much shared knowledge they can assume in their readers: although Whitlock's readers are dispersed around the world, they are mostly ex-patriates, and he can thus assume a common background knowledge of Britain and British culture.

The question of assumed shared knowledge is important, because writers have no immediate context of situation in which to locate their message. They have to construct their message on the basis of what they think their readers know already and then proceed to unfold their message from that starting point, being sure to be explicit where they think that the information will be new to their readers. Regular readers of Whitlock's column would know what a 'downland nature reserve' is (A1) and could be assumed to understand references to 'counties' (D2), 'Saxon' (E2), 'Victorian' (G1), 'inches' (H1, etc.), 'gallons' (I2, etc.), 'Windsor' (M2), and so on.

Not only must writers proceed from the 'given' information that they assume to be shared between themselves and their readers, they must also organise the monologue message so that there is a progression from 'given' to 'new' information, proposition by proposition and paragraph by paragraph: the 'new' becomes 'given' and forms the starting-point for the next piece of 'new' information. We can see the way in which Ralph Whitlock does this in his article 'The dew-pond myth'. He first of all introduces the concept of the dew-pond and the problem of explaining the name (paragraphs A to C). Then he explains the essential features of these ponds (paragraph D), their life-span (paragraphs E and F), where their water comes from (paragraphs G to K). Finally he returns to the question of the name and provides the unexpected explanation (paragraphs L to N). Similarly, there is a progression from sentence to sentence within paragraphs. Take paragraph F as an example: the first sentence links with the previous paragraph and introduces the topic of this paragraph – 'How long does a pond last?' It proposes the 'new' information that a pond will need cleaning and patching every twenty or thirty years. The second sentence starts with 'cleaning' as the given information and proposes remaking 'after four or five cleanings' as the new information. The third sentence draws the conclusion from the first two sentences with the new information that 150 years is the maximum life of a pond. The fourth and fifth sentences discuss a further aspect of pond life-span. In sentence 4 'the ponds' become the starting-point of given information and the action of small sheep hooves in preserving ponds is new. In sentence 5 the 'hooves' is taken as given from sentence 4, and the new information is the contrasting damage of cattle and horse hooves to the ponds.

The progression from given to new information is a general principle on which messages are organised. But, as with many of these principles of textual organisation, they are not absolute, and they may be exploited, especially for stylistic variation. For example, sentence D3 begins with new information ('clumps of tall beeches'), while the given information ('some', i.e. some ponds) comes in the middle of the sentence. This provides some variety in this paragraph, where all the sentences could have 'the ponds', 'they', 'some', 'they' as the initial given element.

A number of conventions thus inform the organisation of messages. Messages are structured, just as propositions are structured, and receivers have expectations of what a message will be like. These expectations include a general progression from given to new information in the course of a message. They also include expectations arising from the genre of the message: a narrative message will display a progression through time; an argument will propose favoured opinions and adduce evidence in support of those and against contrary opinions; an instructional message will often be organised as a progression of steps in a procedure. Genre therefore imposes a measure of organisation on a message and raises certain expectations in the receiver.

The extent of supposed shared knowledge, the need to create its own context, the demands of the principle of progression from given to new information, the expectations created by different genres – all these influence the ways in which a writer constructs a written monologue and in which a reader processes it.

Text grammar

Texts have grammar, just as sentences have grammar. Just as the grammar of sentences serves to organise and structure the elements in sentences, so the grammar of texts organises and structures the elements of texts. The difference is that the elements of texts are themselves sentences, and the structuring principles of text grammar operate differently from those of sentence grammar. There are three areas of text grammar that we are going to consider: first of all the elements of a text, then the ways in which sentences are adjusted to enable the flow of information in a text, and lastly the ways in which sentences connect in a text and make a text cohesive.

Elements of a text

We have said that a text is made up of sentences. Sentences have the same relationship to texts as words have to sentences: they are the basic building blocks. But when words combine, certain types of word attract other words into their orbit; for example, nouns attract adjectives and determinatives. This structuring principle does not operate in texts: there are not certain types of sentence which attract other sentences into their orbit. Nevertheless, when we see a text written down, it is not usually written as a simple concatenation of sentences: it is divided into paragraphs and perhaps even into chapters – depending on its length. Ralph Whitlock's article above is, for example, divided into fourteen paragraphs. But many early manuscript books did not have paragraph and chapter divisions: this is clear from early manuscripts of the Bible, for instance.

The question we have to ask, therefore, is whether these textual divisions actually represent a principle of grammatical structuring of texts, or whether they are imposed on written text merely to make it more attractive to the eye and more readable. After all, the average size of paragraphs varies from one type of publication to another; newspapers, for example, tend to have shorter paragraphs than textbooks, but then we read newspapers in a different way from which we read textbooks and we need the text broken up more finely.

There is no clear answer to our question. No doubt, paragraphing – among other factors – is important in the kind of visual impact that a text will have, and paragraph divisions may be imposed on a text or altered within a text as an editorial function after the text has been written. On the other hand, there is evidence from the investigation of unwritten languages that in the oral retelling of stories some languages have words or morphemes which signal divisions in the discourse that would correspond to the paragraph divisions of a written text (see Longacre 1983, Grimes 1975). One can also experiment by removing the paragraph divisions of a text and asking a number of people independently to paragraph the text: it is surprising how much agreement there is on where the paragraph divisions should come. This suggests that there is a text-grammatical unit corresponding to the written paragraph, that writers do not make paragraph divisions arbitrarily and haphazardly but as if conforming to a principle of grammatical structuring. At the same time, and working together with the grammatical principle, paragraphing is used in written text as a means of controlling the visual impact that the text is designed to make on the reader.

Let us look at Ralph Whitlock's 'The dew-pond myth' text from this perspective. This text has four clearly identifiable sections, and they are clearly marked. The first section comprises paragraphs A to C and forms the introduction to the article. The second section, marked by a minor (verbless) sentence, the initial conjunction *but* and the conjunctive adverb *first*, comprises paragraphs D to F and gives a general description of dew-ponds with special emphasis on their life-span. The third section, marked by a rhetorical question, comprises paragraphs G to K and discusses the source of the water for dew-ponds. The fourth and last section, also marked by a rhetorical question, comprises paragraphs L to N and provides the explanation for the name 'dew-pond', the question that the text started

with. Anyone making paragraph divisions in this text
would probably recognise this fourfold division: there are
both clear differences of topic and, as we have seen, verbal
markers of the divisions.

   But Whitlock has fourteen paragraphs in his article, not
four. The other divisions, we might argue, arise from the
type of publication it appears in, with its narrow columns
and short lines, and the need to make the print attractive to
the reader. However, they may be seen as being text-
linguistically justifiable, at least in terms of shift of topic,
even if not marked verbally. We might summarise the
topics of the paragraphs as follows:

A   The topic of dew-ponds is introduced
B   An explanation of the name is put forward
C   The explanation is rejected
D   Dew-ponds are described
E   Their supposed great age is doubted
F   A calculation of the maximum life of a pond is made
G   The question of their water source is introduced: not
    dew
H   Calculations show that it could not possibly be dew
I   Calculations show that rainfall could be adequate
J   But not in a hot dry summer: measures to account for
    this
K   Calculation of the effect of making a rim catchment
    area
L   Back to the question of the name: no mention until
    1877
M   The chance discovery of a royal letter provides
    explanation
N   The explanation is summarised and a comment con-
    cludes.

We can see from this that, even where there are more
paragraphs than is strictly necessary for the text-linguistic
structuring of the text, the division into paragraphs is not
arbitrary but motivated by structural considerations of
topic-shift.

Textual adjustment of sentence order

In our discussion of messages earlier in the chapter we noted that generally a progression occurred from 'given' information to 'new' information, within a text and within a sentence. This suggests that the initial element in a sentence normally represents 'given' information, usually taken up from the preceding sentence, and the later elements in a sentence represent the 'new' information. The grammatical terms used for elements in these positions are **theme** or **topic** for the initial position, and **rheme** or **comment** for the final position.

In sentences – the majority – which have a Subject element as topic, it will be the Subject which has the status of 'given' information. For example, in sentence B2 of Whitlock's article, the topic position is taken by *he*: it is given information, referring to the 'reader in Alabama' mentioned in the previous sentence. In the normal course of events we would expect the topic position to be filled by a Subject, in a declarative sentence, and if you look through Whitlock's article you will find that mostly this is the case: it is the textually neutral order of elements in a sentence.

Occasionally, however, an element which is not a Subject is 'fronted'. Look at sentence F2 in Whitlock's article: the initial element is the Temporal Adjunct phrase 'after four or five cleanings', which links with the 'cleaning' of the previous sentence. N3 similarly has a Temporal Adjunct ('seventy years later') as the topic element, serving to mark the time relationships in this part of the text. Adjuncts, especially of time but also of place, may occupy the initial position in a text, particularly when the temporal or spatial orientation is important as a starting-point for information that is about to be given. E2 begins with a quite extensive Locative Adjunct: 'on a hill overlooking the Vale of Pewsey, in Wiltshire'.

Another means by which items may be fronted is the passive construction. The passive in fact produces a Subject in topic position, e.g. in F4, but we take the active form of the sentence as the base form, with the Subject as the AGENTIVE participant, representing our normal perspective on events: people acting on objects or persons. The passive puts in Subject (topic) position an AFFECTED participant. The active form of F4 would be 'They constructed the ponds primarily for sheep'. The topic of the paragraph, indeed of the text, is the ponds themselves, and the constructors receive little mention: the active form does not therefore fit textually. The passive construction thus enables the AFFECTED participant to become topic and provide continuity of information at this point in the text. You will find a similar example of the passive in D4. In both these cases the AGENTIVE participant has been omitted from the sentence; with the passive it would normally be included in a *by*-phrase at the end of the sentence. That may be another reason why a passive construction is used: to bring into final 'most new' position the AGENTIVE. There is no example of the passive being used for this purpose in Whitlock's article, but it may be illustrated by the simple sentence 'The ponds were constructed by Mr Dew', where the new information is the person who did the construction.

Here then an element of the sentence is 'postponed' from its normal position. Postponement brings into 'end-focus' position of new information items that would not normally occur there in the neutral form of a sentence. Sometimes the Subject is postponed, if it is a nominal clause, by means of the process of extraposition (see Chapter 7). L3 is an example in the text. The Subject of this sentence is the *that*-clause 'that Gilbert White . . . which he knew'; its normal position has been taken by the dummy *it*. It is extraposed because it is a long and weighty nominal clause, and the balance of sentences in English requires weightier elements to be placed later. Weighty elements in any case usually represent new information, so that the principles of 'newest last' and 'weightiest last' often coincide. In L3, not only is this principle operative, but there is a good textual reason for the postponement: the *that*-clause in L3 parallels in position and in content the *that*-clause in the preceding sentence, L2.

Branching

One further factor which affects the ordering of elements in a sentence is the relative position of subordinate and main clauses. Essentially, the subordinate clause may occur before the main clause, in which case the sentence is said to be 'left-branching'; or the subordinate clause occurs after the main clause, when the sentence is said to be 'right-branching'. A third, but less common, alternative is 'mid-branching', when the subordinate clause interrupts the main clause. Right-branching is considered to be the more neutral ordering, since the reader does not have to retain subsidiary information in mind before the main information is reached. However, left-branching is not uncommon and often serves both to link sentences and to create a tension in the text by making the reader wait for more significant information. Sentences H2 and H3 in Whitlock's article illustrate left-branching. In H2 the subordinate conditional clause ('if such . . . year') precedes the main clause; it makes a link through 'such conditions' with the preceding sentence, and the really significant information – the paucity of the dewfall – is contained in the main clause. Similarly in H3, the subordinate causal clause links with preceding H2 ('that favourable') and the main clause has the important news – it's even less!

Right-branching can be illustrated by J1 and J2. In both these sentences the main clause comes first, and is followed by subordinate (and co-ordinate in J1) clauses which pile on additional information that extends and modifies the relatively simple statements in the main clause. It is easier for the reader to process, because there is a base (the main clause) onto which to add the extra information. There is no example of mid-branching in Whitlock's text, but we could adapt J1 to illustrate it: 'That would be adequate – though it could be at risk in a hot dry summer – to keep the pond from drying up.' Mid-branching has the effect of stopping the reader short and drawing extra attention to the interruptive item.

Cohesion

We turn now to the third of the topics that we propose to deal with under the heading of 'text grammar'. Cohesion refers to the ways in which the sentences of a text are grammatically and lexically linked. A bond is formed between one sentence and another because the interpretation of a sentence either depends on or is informed by some item in a previous – usually the previous – sentence. Grammatical cohesion may be dealt with under the headings of reference, identification, ellipsis and conjunction; and lexical cohesion includes repetition and collocation. These categories are taken from Halliday & Hasan (1976).

Reference

The cohesive relation of reference involves the use of pro-forms to make the link between one sentence and another. Reference occurs, for instance, with 3rd person pronouns: the *he* which begins B2 is an example. 3rd person pronouns, like other reference items, do not usually refer to things in the world of experience; they refer only within text, to the item that they are standing for. In B2, *he* stands for and refers back to 'a reader in Alabama' in B1; *he* is not interpretable without this reference back to the noun phrase in B1. The fact that such reference back is needed in order to make the interpretation creates a cohesive link between these two sentences and, similarly, for the other 3rd person pronouns in the text – e.g. *they* in D2 and D4, *it* in F2, *they* in G3, and so on. 1st and 2nd person pronouns are not cohesive in this way, since they refer not within the text but outside of it to the writer (*I*, e.g. in A2, L2, M1) or to the reader (*you*, e.g. in I6, N1).

Reference may also be by means of demonstrative pronouns (*this*, *that*). There is an example in each of the two sentences of paragraph J. The *that* in J1 refers to the quantity of water left in the pond after evaporation, discussed in I5. The *that* in J2 has a more extensive reference still, standing for the 'hot dry summer, when for weeks on end evaporation rate greatly exceeded rainfall'. Indeed, demonstrative pronouns – and *it* – may on occasions stand for whole clauses or sentences.

Identification

One of the functions of the definite article *the* (see Chapter 5) is to mark a noun as having been 'already mentioned' in a text. On first mention a noun is often accompanied by the indefinite article *a* or in the plural form by no determinative at all. In paragraph B of Whitlock's article, the noun *dewponds* is introduced in B2 without article, and then it is taken up again – in the abbreviated form *ponds* – in the following sentence B3, when it is now accompanied by a definite article. The definite article marks the noun as the one already mentioned. As with the cohesive relationship of reference, it is this process of looking back in the text to a previous mention which creates a cohesive link. A similar relationship of 'identification' exists between 'a hill-top pond' (F3) and 'the ponds' (F4). Identification may also be indicated by demonstrative determinatives (*this*, *that*) and by possessive determinatives (*her*, *their*, etc.).

Not every occurrence of a definite article or other identifier signals the cohesive relationship of identification. A noun may have definite reference for other reasons, for example because it is expected in the context. The noun *pond-makers* in J2 has a definite article, because it may be safely assumed that ponds must have makers. Or a noun may be definite because of the way in which it is specified: *water* in I5 is definite because it is specified as 'the water left in the pond'.

Ellipsis

The process of ellipsis refers, as we saw in Chapter 9, to the omission of items that are recoverable from a previous sentence or clause. Recovery across a sentence boundary means that the ellipsis is cohesive, since a sentence is interpretable only by reference to earlier text. Ellipsis is most common in spoken dialogue, but it features as a cohesive device in written texts also. In E1, for example, *ponds* is ellipted after *some*, and it has to be recovered in fact from D1. We might also regard K6 as involving extensive ellipsis: '[The water remaining in the pond will thus be] ample.'

Conjunction

We discussed the types of conjunction – additive, adversative, temporal, causal – in Chapter 9. Here, we will merely note how co-ordinating conjunctions and conjunctive adverbs act as cohesive devices in texts. They are cohesive, because they indicate a relationship of conjunction with previous text, usually with the sentence immediately preceding the one containing the conjunctive item. Sentence C2 begins with *and*, making an additive conjunction with C1; D1 begins with *but*, indicating that there is an interruption to what has just been said (in C2), and *but* also features in G3 with a similar function. *However* in F1 links this sentence to the foregoing in a conjunctive relationship of contrast, as does *yet* in H4 and *however* in K4. Causal relationships are indicated by *so* in H5, L1 and N1, and by *thus* in F3 and K5. Temporal connection is indicated by *first* in D1. Conjunction is an important means of making a text cohesive in a very explicit way.

Lexical repetition

Lexical devices of cohesion arise in large part from the content of a text. What the subject–matter is inevitably determines what words occur. How those words are used in successive sentences is a matter of the writer's choice, but the effect may be to create cohesion between sentences. This happens in two ways: when there is the repetition or partial repetition of a lexical item; and when the collocate of a lexical item occurs. Lexical cohesion and semantic coherence are clearly closely related.

The repetition of a word is sufficient to make a cohesive link between two sentences. Throughout Whitlock's article – inevitably – the words *pond*, *dew-pond/dewpond* and *hill-top pond* occur in a large number of sentences; and each occurrence after the first in A2 links those sentences together. Sometimes the repetition is of the simple word *pond*, sometimes the 'partial' repetition of *dew-pond* (in its two spellings!) or of *hill-top pond*. There are other, more restricted, examples of simple repetition: *life* in F1 and F3, *hooves* in F4 and F5, *conditions* in H1 and H2, *night* in H1, H2 and H3, and *favourable* in H2 and H3.

Sometimes the repetition is not of the word-form but of the referent, by means of a synonym. For example, *King George III* (M2) is referred to in the following sentence (M3) as *His Majesty*. The connection may not be even as straightforward as that: *source of supply* (H5) relates back to the question 'where . . . come from?' in (G1), tying those two paragraphs together. Now that is rather a long span of text for cohesion to work over, and we would normally expect the relationship to be between adjacent or nearly adjacent sentences.

Collocation

Collocation is a lexical relationship of mutual expectancy: the presence of a particular lexical item gives rise to the greater than chance likelihood that other lexical items belonging to the same area of meaning will also occur. Because this expectancy – on the part of the reader – exists, collocation has a cohesive function in texts.

In Whitlock's article, the subject-matter of dew-ponds and the lexical item *pond* or *dew-pond* itself makes it likely that a set or a number of sets of other lexical items will occur. They include those concerned with the pond itself and its construction: pond, pond-maker, surface area, collecting area, catchment area, rim, margin, perimeter. Then there are those concerned with the content of the pond: water, dew, rain, dewfall, rainfall, evaporation. There are also those concerned with measuring the contents of the pond: quantity, amount, inches, gallons, total, average. All these lexical items occur in the text, creating semantic coherence, but also providing, admittedly rather loose, cohesion. Grammar again makes its connection with meaning.

Envoi

Language is a fascinating object of study, and what we have managed to consider in this book is only a small part of it. Language is complex, but it has order, organisation, structure: otherwise we would be unable to use it for communicating with each other. I hope that this book has shown you some of the ways in which the aspects of language we call grammar and meaning combine to enable the multitude of communication functions that we call upon language to serve, and I hope that it will stimulate you to go on with the study of language in all its richness and diversity.

References

Dickens, Charles, *A Tale of Two Cities*. Dent 1958

Grimes, J., *The Thread of Discourse*. Mouton 1975

Halliday, M. A. K. & Hasan, R., *Cohesion in English*. Longman 1976

Hockey, S. & Marriott, I., *Oxford Concordance Program*. Oxford University Computing Service 1980

Johansson, S., Leech, G. N. & Goodluck, H., *Lancaster–Oslo/ Bergen Corpus of British English, for use with digital computers*. 1978

Leech, G. N., *Principles of Pragmatics*. Longman 1983

Levinson, S. C., *Pragmatics*. CUP 1983

Longacre, R., *The Grammar of Discourse*. Plenum 1983

McArthur, T., *Longman Lexicon of Contemporary English*. Longman 1981

Proctor, P. *et al.*, *Longman Concise English Dictionary*. Longman 1985

Quirk, R., Greenbaum, S., Leech, G. & Svartvik, J., *A Comprehensive Grammar of the English Language*. Longman 1985

Summers, D. *et al.*, *Longman Dictionary of Contemporary English* (2d edn). Longman 1987

Wilson, Angus, *Anglo-Saxon Attitudes*. Penguin 1958

Key to Exercises

Chapter 1

Exercise 1

1. disappeared (EVENT)
2. sings (ACTION)
3. is (STATE)
4. is (STATE)
5. lies (STATE)
6. reported (ACTION)
7. fall (EVENT)
8. empties (ACTION)
9. reached (ACTION)
10. likes (STATE)

Exercise 2

1. have: TEMPORARY STATE
2. live: STANCE
3. smell: PRIVATE STATE (perception)
4. believe: PRIVATE STATE (intellectual)
5. are: TEMPORARY STATE
6. fear: PRIVATE STATE (emotion)
7. sounds: TEMPORARY STATE
8. ache: PRIVATE STATE (bodily sensation)
9. is: QUALITY
10. think: PRIVATE STATE (intellectual)

Exercise 3

1. are skating: ACTIVITY
2. assume: PRIVATE STATE (intellectual)
3. are getting: PROCESS
4. tapped: MOMENTARY ACT
5. have fallen: TRANSITIONAL EVENT
6. are: TEMPORARY STATE
7. are making: ACCOMPLISHMENT
8. is smoking: GOINGS-ON
9. can feel: PRIVATE STATE (perception)
10. have finished: TRANSITIONAL ACT

Exercise 4

1. shrink: shrinks, shrink, shrank; to shrink, shrinking, shrunk
2. mow: mows, mow, mowed; to mow, mowing, mown/mowed
3. forget: forgets, forget, forgot; to forget, forgetting, forgotten
4. drive: drives, drive, drove; to drive, driving, driven
5. feed: feeds, feed, fed; to feed, feeding, fed
6. talk: talks, talk, talked; to talk, talking, talked
7. shut: shuts, shut, shut; to shut, shutting, shut
8. do: does, do, did; to do, doing, done
9. wear: wears, wear, wore; to wear, wearing, worn
10. burn: burns, burn, burnt/burned; to burn, burning, burnt/burned

Chapter 2

Exercise 1

1. Everybody (RECIPIENT) could see (PRIVATE STATE – perception) the elephant (AFFECTED)
2. This cream (AFFECTED) has gone (PROCESS) sour (ATTRIBUTE)
3. My earrings (AFFECTED) have disappeared (TRANSITIONAL EVENT)
4. Spiders (RECIPIENT) have (QUALITY) eight legs (ATTRIBUTE)

5. My back (AFFECTED) is hurting (PRIVATE STATE – bodily sensation)
6. The bells (AFFECTED) are ringing (GOINGS-ON)
7. These (AFFECTED) are (QUALITY) beech trees (ATTRIBUTE)
8. Our friends (RECIPIENT) don't like (PRIVATE STATE – emotion) the sun (AFFECTED)
9. The children (POSITIONER) are sitting down (STANCE)
10. We (RECIPIENT) think (PRIVATE STATE – attitude) of him (AFFECTED) as a member of the family (ATTRIBUTE)

Exercise 2(a)

1. Your parents (AGENTIVE) are talking (ACTIVITY)
2. My brother (AGENTIVE) has written (ACCOMPLISHMENT) me (RECIPIENT) a long letter (RESULTANT)
3. With these words (INSTRUMENT) he (AGENTIVE) finished (TRANSITIONAL ACT) his speech (AFFECTED)
4. They (AGENTIVE) made (ACCOMPLISHMENT) Stephen (AFFECTED) king (ATTRIBUTE)
5. The floods (EXTERNAL CAUSER) damaged (ACCOMPLISHMENT) a lot of property (AFFECTED)
6. You (AGENTIVE) must fill out (ACCOMPLISHMENT) this form (AFFECTED)

Exercise 2(b)

1. e.g. Charles Babbage invented a computer
2. e.g. The raider shot the security guard with a pistol
3. e.g. The children are swimming
4. e.g. Nathan is wearing new shoes
5. e.g. The company donated a large sum to the charity

Exercise 3

1. We (AGENTIVE) that new video (AFFECTED) tomorrow (TEMPORAL circumstance)
2. She (AGENTIVE) a shower (EVENTIVE)
3. Bob (AFFECTED) in the kitchen (LOCATIVE participant)
4. you (RECIPIENT) the nightingale (AFFECTED) last night (TEMPORAL circumstance)
5. They (AGENTIVE) him (AFFECTED) of theft (EVENTIVE)
6. The artist (AGENTIVE) me (RECIPIENT) his pictures (AFFECTED)
7. you (AGENTIVE) to the concert (LOCATIVE participant/circumstance)
8. The campaign (EVENTIVE) disastrous (ATTRIBUTE)
9. The dentist (AGENTIVE) the filling (AFFECTED) from the tooth (LOCATIVE participant/circumstance)
10. Paddington (AGENTIVE) him (AFFECTED) a hard stare (EVENTIVE)

Exercise 4

1. boys': plural genitive
   boots: plural
   they: 3rd person plural subjective
   football: singular
   Saturday: singular
2. We: 1st person plural subjective
   beds: plural
   meals: plural
   ourselves: 1st person plural reflexive
3. Alfred's: singular genitive
   theory: singular
   everyone: indefinite
   its: 3rd person singular neuter genitive (but often analysed as a 'possessive identifier' rather than a 'possessive pronoun' – see Chapter 5)
   complexity: singular
4. This: singular near demonstrative
   way: singular

you: 2nd person
it: 3rd person singular neuter
5. noise: singular
   you: 2nd person
6. She: 3rd person singular feminine subjective
   crises: plural
7. man: singular
   sweet: singular
   shop: singular
   Lucy: singular
   liquorice: singular
   toffees: plural
   birthday: singular
   present: singular
8. technicians: plural
   your: 2nd person genitive ('possessive identifier')
   computer: singular
   week's: singular genitive
   time: singular
9. company's: singular genitive
   accountant: singular
   something: indefinite
   accounts: plural
10. Who: interrogative
    you: 2nd person
    that: singular distant demonstrative

Chapter 3

Exercise 1

1. out of his kennel: DIRECTION–SOURCE
2. the whole way: DISTANCE
3. back to the little . . . prison: DIRECTION–GOAL
4. on a long bench: POSITION
   in the breakfast nook: POSITION
5. out of the cabin: DIRECTION–SOURCE
   towards the bow: DIRECTION–GOAL
6. outside Santa Maria degli Angeli: POSITION
7. through the crowds: DIRECTION–PATH
   towards the little Frenchman: DIRECTION–GOAL
8. all the way: DISTANCE

from Trento: DIRECTION–SOURCE
9. to it: DIRECTION–GOAL
   along wooded slopes: DIRECTION–PATH
10. to the mouth of the alley: DIRECTION–GOAL
   under a shop awning: POSITION

Exercise 2

1. On a bright unclouded morning: POSITION
   a few days after the visit to the Dona Palace: POSITION
2. until tomorrow: DURATION–FORWARD ORIENTATION
3. once: FREQUENCY
   three times: FREQUENCY
4. Since his last stay there: DURATION–BACKWARD ORIENTATION
5. early one morning: POSITION
   that evening: POSITION
6. for an hour: DURATION–GENERAL
   before lunch: POSITION
7. every morning: FREQUENCY
   tonight: POSITION
   tomorrow: POSITION
8. all evening: DURATION-GENERAL
9. often: FREQUENCY
   several years: DURATION–GENERAL
10. After a long debate: POSITION
   far into the night: DURATION–GENERAL
   till morning: DURATION–FORWARD ORIENTA-TION
   then: POSITION

Exercise 3

1. blankly: PROCESS–MANNER
2. by two young Malay girls: PROCESS–AGENTIVE
3. as far as its final significance is concerned: RESPECT
4. consolingly: PROCESS–MANNER
5. with ball, bats and wicket: PROCESS–INSTRUMENT
6. by a friend: PROCESS–AGENTIVE

7. in this respect: RESPECT
8. actively: PROCESS–MANNER
   by the British Ambassadors: PROCESS–AGENTIVE
9. with a whiff of grapeshot: PROCESS–INSTRUMENT
10. superbly: PROCESS–MANNER
   with his budget: PROCESS–MEANS

Exercise 4

1. despite Villa's seventh-minute lead: CONTINGENCY–CONCESSION
2. because of lack of information about the bidder. . .: CONTINGENCY–REASON
3. if he told me to marry them: CONTINGENCY–CONDITION
4. greatly: DEGREE–AMPLIFICATION
5. so that she would not get upset: CONTINGENCY–PURPOSE
6. so that this year . . . the second course: CONTINGENCY–RESULT
7. because of the irritation: CONTINGENCY–CAUSE
8. slightly: DEGREE–DIMINUTION
   so that it was not . . . rhododendrons: CONTINGENCY–PURPOSE
9. though a little change can mean much: CONTINGENCY–CONCESSION
   much: DEGREE–AMPLIFICATION
10. sufficiently: DEGREE–MEASURE
   to produce the right sort of cry: CONTINGENCY–PURPOSE

Exercise 5

1. to and from Britain and the other . . . states: LOCATIVE prepositional expression
   after 1992: TEMPORAL prepositional
2. again: TEMPORAL adverb
   in Armenia: LOCATIVE prepositional
   over the weekend: TEMPORAL prepositional
3. today: TEMPORAL adverb/noun
   if you want more tax cuts tomorrow: CONDITIONAL clause

tomorrow: TEMPORAL adverb/noun
4. By 1979: TEMPORAL prepositional
   on the Miyazaki test track: LOCATIVE prepositional
   by using superconductors: MEANS prepositional
5. In the morning: TEMPORAL prepositional
   angrily: MANNER adverb
   around its snaking corners: LOCATIVE prepositional
6. by rubber bullets: PROCESS–INSTRUMENT prepositional
   by the police: PROCESS–AGENTIVE prepositional
7. on death row: LOCATIVE prepositional
   in South Africa: LOCATIVE prepositional
   for their alleged involvement in political activities:
   CONTINGENCY–REASON prepositional
8. previously: TEMPORAL adverb
   on a stretch of woodland: LOCATIVE prepositional
   despite injunctions . . . monument: CONTINGENCY–
   CONCESSION prepositional
9. peacefully: MANNER adverb
   to the stones: LOCATIVE prepositional
   at the last moment: TEMPORAL prepositional
   by English Heritage: PROCESS–AGENTIVE prepositional
   last year: TEMPORAL noun phrase
   after police reluctance . . . Cholderton: TEMPORAL
   prepositional
   in on the large . . . Cholderton: LOCATIVE prepositional
   in Cholderton: LOCATIVE prepositional
10. As for the damage . . . here: RESPECT prepositional
    here: LOCATIVE adverb
    by Lord Armstrong: PROCESS–AGENTIVE preposi-
    tional

Chapter 4

Exercise 1

1. present punctual
2. past durative indefinite
3. past punctual definite + past-in-future durative
4. past-in-past indefinite

5. future punctual
6. future-in-past punctual
7. past (state)
8. past (historical present) durative + past punctual
9. future (state) + present punctual
10. past (state) + future-in-past durative

Exercise 2

1. was: past; was setting + nearly: past progressive; awoke + after six: past
2. was about to mount: past; became: past
3. was stopping + continually: past progressive
4. was wondering: past progressive; had been watching: past perfect progressive; talk: bare infinitive
5. had loved + never: past perfect
6. had told: past perfect; was coming: past progressive
7. are going to see: present
8. had been watching: past perfect progressive
9. looked: past; were waving + still: past progressive
10. 've changed: present perfect; 've got: present perfect; said: past

Exercise 3

1. could: ability
2. can + possibly: possibility
3. should: obligation
4. maybe + could: possibility
5. must: certainty
6. be allowed to: permission
7. 'll + probably: prediction–probability
8. might: possibility; be able to: ability
9. would: hypothetical; must: obligation
10. surely: certainty; can: ability

Chapter 5

Exercise 1

1. all: indefinite quantifier; the (twice): definite article
2. a (twice): indefinite article; blackbird's: possessive noun; the: definite article

3. plenty of: indefinite quantifier; those: distant demonstrative

4. some: indefinite quantifier; his: 3rd person possessive

5. those: distant demonstrative; forty: cardinal numeral; the: definite article

6. any: indefinite quantifier; the: definite article

7. that: distant demonstrative; third: ordinal numeral

8. one: cardinal numeral; last: ordinal numeral; his: 3rd person possessive

9. the: definite article; Zechariah's: possessive noun; this: proximate demonstrative; ninth: ordinal numeral

10. all: indefinite quantifier; their: 3rd person possessive; many a: indefinite quantifier; the: definite article

Exercise 2

1. in the road: prepositional phrase; low: adjective; elegant: adjective; little: adjective

2. small: adjective; attractive: adjective; of Joy: prepositional phrase

3. hammering: participle; deep: adjective; slow: adjective

4. sixteen-foot: adjective; strapping: participle; young: adjective; Pomo: noun

5. excellent: adjective; of the finished weave: prepositional phrase; finished: participle

6. other: adjective; important: adjective; of income taxation: prepositional phrase; income: noun

7. monstrous: adjective; which trailed . . . carpet: relative clause

8. of wearing . . . trousers: prepositional participle clause; nice: adjective; red: adjective; old: adjective, blue: adjective

9. blue: adjective; young: adjective; that had been . . . and herbs: relative clause

10. lighted: participle; traffic: noun; that blinked . . . intervals: relative clause; proper: adjective

Exercise 3

[*The abbreviations used are given on p. 168, Chapter 6.*]

1. The (defart) bus (noun.mod) stop (noun)
   a (indefart) deserted (part) island (noun) on an empty street (prep.phr)
   an (indefart) empty (adj) street (noun)
2. McNaught (noun)
   himself (ref.pron)
   the (defart) pilot's (poss.noun) seat (noun)
3. You (pron)
   the (defart) Hungarians (noun)
   the (defart) biggest (adj) eaters (noun) in Europe (prep.phr)
4. A (indefart) belt (noun) of trees (prep.phr)
   the (defart) noise (noun) of the traffic (prep.phr)
5. I (pron.)
   a (indefart) guest (noun.mod) room (noun)
   my (poss) apartment (noun)
6. She (pron)
   two (cardinal num) patches (noun) of red (prep.phr)
   her (poss) cheek (noun.mod) bones (noun)
7. you (pron.)
   these (dem) stitches (noun)
   attractive (adj) articles (noun)
   the (defart) directions (noun) included in this book (non-finite clause)
   this (dem) book (noun)
8. These (dem) young (adj) people (noun)
   a (indefart) healthier (adj) slant (noun) on life (prep.phr)
9. Morris (noun)
   something (indef pron) wicked (adj)
   his (poss) breath (noun)
10. London-born (part) Stokowski (noun)
    a (indefart) reputation (noun) for highly individual interpretations (prep.phr)
    highly individual (adj.phr) interpretations (noun)

Chapter 6

Exercise 1

1. AFFECTED (often accompanied by optional TEMPORAL–FREQUENCY, e.g. 'She sneezed three times')
2. AGENTIVE, AFFECTED, (omissible) LOCATIVE (e.g. 'The thieves abandoned the getaway car in a field')
3. AGENTIVE, AFFECTED, (omissible) SOURCE (e.g. 'The thieves stole the car from a garage/neighbour')
4. AGENTIVE, LOCATIVE–GOAL (e.g. 'The farmer pointed towards the field')
5. AGENTIVE, AFFECTED, (omissible) RECIPIENT (e.g. 'The farmer complained about the car to the police')
6. RECIPIENT, AFFECTED (e.g. 'Can you catch this ball?')

Exercise 2

1. She (S) couldn't scream (P) because of the gag in her mouth (A)
2. What a nice person (C) he (S) must be (P)
3. How many railway employees (S) read (P) books on philosophy? (O)
4. She (S) put (P) the key (O) in the lock (A)
5. His eyes (S) appeared (P) enormous (C)
6. She (S) came (P) home (A) early (A) from the party (A)
7. I (S) called (P) myself (O) a louse (C)
8. Maxwell (S) is (P) a fine chap (C)
9. Members (S) made (P) a path (O) for him (Oi)
10. I (S) have explained (P) this (Od) to him (Oi)
11. They both (S) carried (P) rifles (O) in the crooks of their arms (A)
12. This year (A) the Economic Consultative Council (S) should meet (P) in Accra (A)

Exercise 3

1.

He	was not	on the seat
AFF	TEMP STATE	LOC
Subj	Pred	Adjunct
pron	verb	prep defart noun
3sgmasc	past neg	

2.

Hit	him
MOMACT	AFF
Pred	Obj
verb	pron
imper	3sgmasc

3.

She	put	bread	on the table
AGEN	ACCOMP	AFF	LOC
Subj	Pred	Obj	Adjunct
pron	verb	noun	prep defart noun
3sgfem	past		

4.

The chief in the white coat	was talking	excitedly	with Father Felix
AGEN	ACTIVITY	PROC–MANNER	RECIP
Subj	Pred	Adjunct	Adjunct
defart noun prep.phr (prep defart adj NOUN)	aux.prog verb	adverb	prep noun.mod noun
	past pres.part		

5.

MacCleod	appeared	in the doorway
AFF	MOMEVENT	LOCATIVE
Subj	Pred	Adjunct
noun	verb	prep defart noun
	past	

6.

He	pushed	the case and the lamp	into the boys' hands
AGEN	MOMACT	AFF	LOC–GOAL
Subj	Pred	Obj	Adjunct
pron	verb	defart noun conj defart noun	prep defart poss.noun noun
3sgmasc	past		plural

7.

They	had become	stone quarries
AFF	PROCESS	ATTRIBUTE
Subj	Pred	Comp
pron	aux.perf verb	noun.mod noun
3pl	past past.part	plural

8.

Once	his father	had shown	him	a small automatic pistol from the war
TEMP	AGEN	MOMACT	REC	AFF
Adjun	Subj	Pred	Obj.ind	Obj.dir
adverb	poss noun	aux.perf verb	pron	indefart adj adj noun prep.phr (defart noun)
	3sgmasc	past past.part	3sgmasc	

9. She	was carrying	a big black crocodile bag
POSIT	STANCE	AFF
Subj	Pred	Obj
pron	aux.prog verb	indefart adj adj noun.mod noun
3sgfem	past pres.part	

10. Occasionally	the brothers	dance	round the mother
TEMP-FREQ	AGEN	ACTIVITY	LOCATIVE
Adjunct	Subj	Pred	Adjunct
adverb	defart noun	verb	prep defart noun
	plural	pres	

Chapter 7

Exercise 1

1. to marry Jimena Diaz: *to*-inf clause (AFFECTED)
2. that the tour . . . late August: *that*-clause (AFFECTED)
3. being called a spy: pres.part clause (AFFECTED)
4. to fill up with water: *to*-inf clause (EVENTIVE)
5. not to come here: *to*-inf clause (AFFECTED)
6. which includes . . . system: relative clause (specifier)
7. I'm wishing my whole life away: direct speech clause (AFFECTED)
8. to make Huddersfield worthy of its citizens: *to*-inf clause (appositive)
9. how his mother would find it: *wh*-clause (AFFECTED)
10. that Leamington would not hang back: *that*-clause (AFFECTED)

Exercise 2

1. to live with . . . for her: *to*-inf clause (Adjunct)
   whom she respects greatly: relative clause (modifier)
   who feels sorry for her: relative clause (modifier)
2. What is at stake: *wh*-clause (Subject)
   whether the West . . . East Berlin: *wh*-clause (Complement)

3. that the members . . . their decision: *that*-clause (Subject)
   that that might be the result of their decision: *that*-clause (adjective complement)
4. that has confronted Southern Rhodesia: relative clause (modifier)
5. that the garden . . . cliffs: *that*-clause (Object)
   which included . . . cliffs: relative clause (modifier)
6. that at least . . . same source: *that*-clause (Complement)
7. that the new . . . Warren Beatty: *that*-clause (appositive)
8. if other readers . . . discrepancy: *wh*-clause (Object)
9. whose existence . . . reason: relative clause (modifier)
10. that Wicki's name . . . list: *that*-clause (Subject)

Exercise 3

1. Colleano's giving me . . . case: *–ing*-clause (prepositional complement)
2. to work right through . . . tail: inf-clause (extraposed Subject)
3. what to do next: *wh*-inf-clause (Object)
4. to take a quick glance . . . Everest: inf-clause (appositive)
5. him start up the car: bare-inf-clause (Object)
6. provided for a planter: *–ed*-clause (noun post-modifier)
7. adding one sample . . . style: *–ing*-clause (Object)
8. painting children: *–ing*-clause (Object)
9. to make a change: inf-clause (noun post-modifier in comparative construction)
10. getting it into place: *–ing*-clause (extraposed Subject)

Chapter 8

Exercise 1

1. to investigate some . . . clerk: Purpose
2. until he died just after the war: Time-before
3. You see: Comment
   if he really is as bad as he says: Conditional
4. so that they become unable . . . to anybody: Result
5. Whenever I try to . . . sensations: Contingency

6. Although we are a state monopoly: Concession
   as if we had rivals . . . necks: Comparison
7. so long as another . . . to him: Time-same
8. since certain incidents . . . heroes: Reason
9. which was natural: Sentence Relative
   as they were so different from one another: Reason
10. unless it is faced: Conditional
    as individual countries . . . their men: Time-same

Exercise 2

1. since
2. although
3. wherever
4. as if
5. so that
6. as soon as
7. if
8. in order that
9. whenever
10. therefore/and so; since

Chapter 9

Exercise 1

Following are the sentences as they originally appeared in the corpus:

1. I'll write to those agents and try to get a flat in Alverstoke.
2. The psychologist first looks into his own mind and then interprets other people's minds by what he has found in his own.
3. Those who said the Congolese could govern themselves will not admit they were wrong. So Belgium, bowed down by internal troubles, mourning a terrible air crash, is made their scapegoat.
4. He has achieved a ripe humour without clowning and as a result is to sing the Baron with the Hamburg State Opera.

5. He father didn't move his head, but after a second he turned his eyes.
6. We must get accustomed to anxiety and not let ourselves drift or be pushed into panic.
7. It was good, searching stuff, well presented and well delivered, and showing the stamp of original minds. Yet somehow I didn't seem up to it.
8. It must be done very gradually indeed. In other words, one must make haste slowly.
9. Some began to murmur that they should turn back while there was yet time. But De Soto was inflexible, refusing to admit that what others found impossible would be impossible for him. Meanwhile there were more immediate dangers to face.
10. The stock of houses is rising by some 200 thousand a year; the number of households needing separate dwellings over the next twenty years is likely to increase by an average of around 100 thousand a year. Vacancies are therefore likely to increase by some 100 thousand a year.

Exercise 2

One example of a rewrite of each sentence is given.

1. After he had deposited his baggage and unpacked his overnight-bag he went in search of a drink.
2. Having looked at his watch, he saw that he would be late for lunch down-town. Perhaps his guests could cool their heels for a little while.
3 They will sooner or later affect the life of every church. Consequently, it is essential that on this point the churches learn from each other.
4. Some benefit may be lost if the allowance is not claimed within three months of the former husband's death.
5. If things in themselves are unknowable, how do I know of their existence?
6. I think he fills in an important part of the background, and moreover, dear boy, I think it confirms what we already know of your father's intention to leave the country on the night of October 14th.
7. 'A pity somebody saw us at Brighton,' he said, 'but the

police can't be sure, otherwise they'd have clamped down on you.'

8. While Salisbury, on the 11th, after correspondence with Beaconsfield, had telegraphed Horace Walpole to ask Cranbrook urgently for authority to stop Lytton sending the mission until the Russian reply had arrived, Cranbrook was feeling the same way in Scotland and had sent a telegram to Walpole which forbad the departure of the mission until further orders.

Glossary of terms

	relating to circumstances	6
adverbial clause	a type of embedded clause having an adverbial function, usually as Adjunct	8
adversative combination	a type of combination of sentences, by means of an adversative conjoiner (e.g. 'but')	9
Affected	the participant semantic role of 'passive victim' in a situation	2
agentive	characteristic of actions, which have some human or other instigator, by contrast with events	1
Agentive	the participant semantic role of the person instigating or causing an action	2
Agentive	a type of Process circumstance	3
Amplification	a type of Degree circumstance	3
amplifier	a type of intensifier	
appositive	two juxtaposed elements having the same syntactic function	7
article	a subclass of determinatives: indefinite 'a', definite 'the'	5
aspect	a grammatical category associated with the verb which refers to the distribution of an event in time	4
Attribute	the participant semantic role identifying or characterising another participant	2
auxiliary verb	a small set of verbs, including be, have, do and the modals, which mark tense, aspect and modality	4
branching	the relative position of a subordinate clause to a main clause	10
case	the grammatical category associated with nouns and	

	pronouns which marks their syntactic function	2
causal combination	a type of combination of sentences, by means of a causal conjoiner (e.g. 'therefore')	9
Cause	a type of Contingency circumstance	3
circumstance	an element peripherally involved in a situation type, giving background information	3
clause	a dependent sentence	3
co-ordination	the joining of sentences, clauses, phrases and words by means of a co-ordinating conjunction	9
cohesion	the grammatical and lexical links between sentences in a text	10
collocation	a type of cohesion by means of collocationally associated lexical items	10
command	a functional type of proposition	6
comment	a proposition, like 'I think', which interpolates a comment into another proposition	8
comparative	an inflection of adjectives	5
comparison	a type of included circumstantial proposition relating propositions for similarity or comparison	8
Complement	the functional slot in a sentence filled by an adjective or noun relating to attribution	6
complementation	the elements in a sentence whose presence is determined by the Predicator	6
Concession	a type of Contingency circumstance	3, 8

Condition	a type of Contingency circumstance	3, 8
Conjunct	a type of Adverbial	6
conjunction	a class of words used for joining syntactic elements	9
conjunction	the process of combining sentences by means of conjunctive adverbs	9
conjunction	a type of cohesion by means of conjunctive adverbs	10
conjunctive adverb	a subclass of adverbs, functioning as conjoiners	9
Contingency	the semantic role of circumstance relating to the question 'Why?' or 'Under what conditions?'	3
declarative	the sentence type associated typically with statements	6
definite	definitely specified, e.g. of a noun or of time	4
Degree	the semantic role of circumstance relating to the degree to which something happens or is the case	3
demonstrative	group of words (this/that) which has a 'pointing' function	2, 5
dependent	a relation of compatibility between subordinate (dependent) and a superordinate element	6
determinatives	a class of words which accompany nouns and provide for their identification	5
Diminution	a type of Degree circumstance	3
direct speech	speech quoted as it was said	7
Direction	a type of Locative circumstance	3
Disjunct	a type of Adverbial	6
Distance	a type of Locative circumstance	3
downtoner	a type of intensifier	5
Duration	a type of Temporal circumstance	3

durative	an aspect representing an action or event as taking place over a period of time	4
–ed-clause	a type of embedded clause, with a past participle form of the verb	7
ellipsis	the omission of items, creating a structural gap; a type of cohesion	9, 10
embedded clause	a sentence that functions as an element in another sentence	7
emphasizer	a subclass of adverbs which modify adjectives	5
event	a situation-type where something 'happens'	1
Eventive	the participant semantic role of a happening involved in a situation	2
exclamation	a functional type of proposition	6
exclamative	the sentence type associated typically with exclamations	6
Experiencer	the Recipient of a private state	2
External Causer	the participant semantic role of the inanimate causer of an action	2
finite/non-finite	forms of the verb: finite are tensed forms, non-finite include infinitive and participles	1
Frequency	a type of Temporal circumstance	3
fronting	the bringing of an element into theme position which would not normally occupy it	10
gender	the grammatical category which represents the distinction between masculine, feminine and neuter	2
generic	a type of identification,	

	referring to things as a class	5
genitive	the case associated with possession	2
given information	information that is assumed by the encoder to be shared, or that has been already mentioned in the text	10
Goal	a type of Direction Locative circumstance	3
goings-on	a type of event referring to something happening over a period of time	1
gradable	of adjectives etc., capable of expressing degree and comparison	5
identification	a type of specification of participants, to identify which participant is being referred to	5
identification	a type of cohesion by means of determinatives	10
imperative	the sentence type associated with commands	6
indefinite	not definitely specified, e.g. of a noun or of time	4
indirect speech	speech reported in an embedded clause	7
infinitive clause	a type of embedded clause containing an infinitive verb form	7
inflection	the suffixes on nouns, verbs, etc., which signal grammatical categories	1, 2
–ing-clause	a type of embedded clause, with a present participle form of the verb	7
Instrument	the participant semantic role of the tool by the means of which an action is performed	2
Instrument	a type of Process circumstance	3

intensifier	a subclass of adverbs which modify adjectives for gradability	5
interrogative	word or clause which asks a question	2
interrogative	the sentence type associated typically with questions	6
intransitive	a sentence pattern which does not include an Object	6
iterative	repeated through time	4
left-branching	where a subordinate clause precedes a main clause in a sentence	10
lexical repetition	a type of cohesion by means of the complete or partial repetition of lexical items	10
Locative	the circumstance semantic role of place and direction	2
Manner	a type of Process circumstance	3
Means	a type of Process circumstance	3
Measure	a type of Degree circumstance	3
message	the combination of propositions to form an act of communication	10
mid-branching	where a subordinate clause interrupts a main clause in a sentence	10
minor sentence	a sentence not containing a verb	10
modal verb	a small set of verbs (e.g. can, may, will, must) used to express notions of possibility and certainty	4
modality	a grammatical category concerned with the possibility and necessity of situations	4
modifiers	the class of items accompanying nouns associated with classification and description	5
momentary event/act	a type of event/act which only lasts a moment of time	1

necessity	a type of modality	4
new information	information that the encoder of a text considers to be not-shared by the decoder	10
nominal clause	an embedded clause which functions in typical noun slots in sentence structure	7
nominal relative clause	a type of *wh*-embedded clause, which may be paraphrased by a noun/pronoun + relative clause	7
non-finite	see *finite*	
noun	a class of words whose chief function is to represent participants	2
noun modifiers	members of the word-class of nouns which may function as modifiers of other nouns	5
noun phrase	a noun and its accompanying determinatives and modifiers	3, 5
number	the grammatical category which distinguishes between singular and plural	1, 2
numerals	a subclass of quantifiers referring to definite quantity	5
Object	the functional slot in a sentence in addition to the Subject which is filled typically by a noun	6
orientation	the point in time – present, past or future – from which an event or action is viewed	4
paragraph	a subdivision of a text composed of sentences	10
participant	an element essentially involved in a situation type	2
participle	non-finite forms of the verb, present and past participle,	

	used in forming complete tenses	1, 5
participle clause	a clause whose verb is in the present or past participle form	7
Path	a type of Direction Locative circumstance	3
perfective	an aspect associated with pre-present and past-in-past time	4
person	the grammatical category which distinguishes the speaker (1st), the addressee (2nd) and others (3rd)	1, 2
Position	a type of Locative circumstance and a type of Temporal circumstance	3
possessives	a subclass of determinatives/pronouns, specifying possession	5
possibility	a type of modality	4
post-modifiers	modifiers of nouns which occur after the noun	5
postponement	the transfer of an element to final position in a sentence for the purposes of end-focus or end-weight	10
pre-modifiers	modifiers of nouns which occur before the noun	5
Predicator	the functional slot in a sentence filled by the verb	6
preposition	the class of words which relate nouns to other sentence elements and have circum-stantial meanings	3
private state	a type of state referring to intellectual, emotional, perceptual and bodily states	1
process	a type of event that brings about a change of state	1

Process	the semantic role of circumstance relating to the question 'How?'	3
progressive	see *durative*	4
pronoun	the class of words which function as substitutes for nouns and marked for person, number, case	2
proposition	a complete semantic structure comprising a situation type with dependent participants and circumstances	6
punctual	an aspect representing an action or event as taking place at a moment in time	4
Purpose	a type of Contingency circumstance	3, 8
quality	a permanent type of state	1
quantifiers	a subclass of determinatives, identifying a noun for number or quantity	5
question	a functional type of proposition	6
Reason	a type of Contingency circumstance	3, 8
Recipient	the participant semantic role of the person receiving goods or the locus of emotion or cognition	2
reference	a type of cohesion by means of pro-forms	10
relative	type of pronoun which relates a relative clause to the noun it specifies	2
relative clause	a type of embedded clause, introduced by a relative pronoun, which modifies a noun	7
Respect	the semantic role of circumstance relating to the question 'In respect of what?'	3
Result	a type of Contingency circumstance	3, 8

Resultant	the participant semantic role of the element resulting from a process or action	2
rheme/comment	the final element(s) of a sentence, representing new information	10
right-branching	where a subordinate clause follows a main clause in a sentence	10
sentence	a complete syntactic structure comprising a verb and the elements dependent on it	6
sentence relative	a relative clause which functions as a comment on a whole sentence	8
sentence type	general forms of sentences	6
situation type	the general term to refer to actions, events and states	1
Source	a type of Direction Locative circumstance	3
specific	a type of identification, referring to particular members of a class	5
stance	a type of state referring to the position of someone or something	1
state	a situation-type where someone or something is somewhere or has some characteristic	1
statement	a functional type of proposition	6
subject	the functional slot in a sentence filled by a noun which agrees with the verb	6
Subjunct	a type of Adverbial	6
superlative	an inflection of adjectives	5
Temporal	the circumstance semantic role of time	2
temporal combination	a type of combination of sentences, by means of a temporal conjoiner (e.g. 'then')	9
tense	the grammatical category which distinguishes between present and past	4

text	the combination of sentences in a cohesive and coherent whole	10
that-*clause*	a type of embedded clause, introduced by the conjunction 'that'	7
theme/topic	the initial element in a sentence, usually given information	10
to-*inf-clause*	a type of embedded clause, with an infinitive form of the verb	7
transitional event/act	a type of event/act which refers to a change of state in a moment of time	1
transitive	a sentence pattern which includes an Object	6
verb	a class of words representing situation-types	1
viewpoint adverbs	a subclass of adverbs which may modify adjectives or function independently in sentences	
wh-*clause*	a type of embedded clause, introduced by a *wh*-word	7
wh-*infinitive clause*	an infinitive clause introduced by a *wh*-word	7

Index